Moral Creativity

AAR
AMERICAN ACADEMY OF RELIGION

REFLECTION AND THEORY IN THE STUDY OF RELIGION SERIES
A Publication Series of The American Academy of Religion
and Oxford University Press

SERIES EDITOR
James Wetzel, Colgate University

WORKING EMPTINESS
Toward a Third Reading of Emptiness in
Buddhism and Postmodern Thought

Newman Robert Glass

WITTGENSTEIN AND THE MYSTICAL
Philosophy as an Ascetic Practice

Frederick Sontag

AN ESSAY ON THEOLOGICAL METHOD
Third Edition

Gordon D. Kaufman

BETTER THAN WINE
Love, Poetry, and Prayer in the Thought of
Franz Rosenzweig

Yudit Kornberg Greenberg

HEALING DECONSTRUCTION
Postmodern Thought in Buddhism and
Christianity

Edited by David Loy

ROOTS OF RELATIONAL ETHICS
Responsibility in Origin and Maturity in
H. Richard Niebuhr

Melvin Keiser

HEGEL'S SPECULATIVE GOOD FRIDAY
The Death of God in Philosophical
Perspective

Deland S. Anderson

NEWMAN AND GADAMER
Toward a Hermeneutics of Religious
Knowledge

Thomas K. Carr

GOD, PHILOSOPHY AND ACADEMIC
CULTURE
A Discussion between Scholars in the AAR
and APA

Edited by William J. Wainwright

LIVING WORDS
Studies in Dialogues about Religion

Terence J. Martin

LIKE AND UNLIKE GOD
Religious Imaginations in Modern and
Contemporary Fiction

John Neary

BEYOND THE NECESSARY GOD
Trinitarian Faith and Philosophy in the
Thought of Eberhard Jüngel

Paul DeHart

LESSING'S PHILOSOPHY OF
RELIGION AND THE GERMAN
ENLIGHTENMENT

Toshimasa Yasukata

AMERICAN PRAGMATISM
A Religious Genealogy

M. Gail Hamner

OPTING FOR THE MARGINS
Postmodernity and Liberation in Christian
Theology

Edited by Joerg Rieger

MAKING MAGIC
Religion, Magic, and Science in the Modern
World

Randall Styers

THE METAPHYSICS OF DANTE'S
COMEDY

Christian Moevs

PILGRIMAGE OF LOVE
Moltmann on the Trinity and Christian Life

Joy Ann McDougall

MORAL CREATIVITY
Paul Ricoeur and the Poetics of Possibility

John Wall

AMERICAN ACADEMY OF RELIGION

Moral Creativity

*Paul Ricoeur and the
Poetics of Possibility*

JOHN WALL

UNIVERSITY PRESS

2005

OXFORD
UNIVERSITY PRESS

Oxford University Press, Inc., publishes works that further
Oxford University's objective of excellence
in research, scholarship, and education.

Oxford   New York
Auckland   Cape Town   Dar es Salaam   Hong Kong   Karachi
Kuala Lumpur   Madrid   Melbourne   Mexico City   Nairobi
New Delhi   Shanghai   Taipei   Toronto

With offices in
Argentina   Austria   Brazil   Chile   Czech Republic   France   Greece
Guatemala   Hungary   Italy   Japan   Poland   Portugal   Singapore
South Korea   Switzerland   Thailand   Turkey   Ukraine   Vietnam

Published by Oxford University Press, Inc.
198 Madison Avenue, New York, New York 10016

www.oup.com

Oxford is a registered trademark of Oxford University Press

Library of Congress Cataloging-in-Publication Data
Wall, John, 1965–
Moral creativity : Paul Ricoeur and the poetics of possibility / John Wall.
   p.   cm.—(AAR reflection and theory in the study of religion)
Includes bibliographical references and index.
ISBN-13 978-0-19-518256-9
ISBN 0-19-518256-1
   1. Ricoeur, Paul.   2. Ethics.   I. Title.   II. Reflection and theory in the study of religion.
B2430.R554W35 2005
170'.92—dc22   2004025219

9   8   7   6   5   4   3   2   1
Printed in the United States of America
on acid-free paper

The world stands out on either side
No wider than the heart is wide;
Above the world is stretched the sky,—
No higher than the soul is high.
The heart can push the sea and land
Farther away on either hand;
The soul can split the sky in two,
And let the face of God shine through.
But East and West will pinch the heart
That cannot keep them pushed apart;
And he whose soul is flat—the sky
Will cave in on him by and by.

—Edna St. Vincent Millay, from "Renascence"

Preface

This book argues that moral life is inherently creative. It claims that creativity is element in not just the expression of moral sentiments, the application of moral principles, or the formation of moral cultures, but also the very activity of living morally itself. This argument is made in large part through an examination and critique of the moral thought of the French hermeneutical phenomenologist Paul Ricoeur, especially in relation to his philosophical and religious poetics of the will. But it also enters into a wide range of both historical and contemporary conversations about the relation of ethics to poetics and the possibilities for human moral transformation. In the process, the book draws new connections between ethics and creativity, evil and tragedy, philosophy and religion, and moral thought and mythology. If moral life is creative at its core, this proposition challenges such oppositions and demands a fundamental rethinking of the nature and meaning of moral life itself.

The present work continues a line of inquiry already begun and to be further extended in the future. This book establishes a meta-ethical or justificatory groundwork for conceiving of moral life as creative in the first place. This means that it does *not* propose a complete normative ethics: it does not lay out guidelines for making moral decisions in practice. It is a book about the *kind* of activity that moral practice is, not the activities themselves that might therefore be morally right. Any detailed normative implications of the present inquiry are left to future works. First it is necessary, given a long quarrel in Western thought between the ethicists and the poets, to show what it could mean for moral life to involve a creative capability at all, a capability so much more readily acknowledged in other areas of human thought and practice.

This book's own creation was far from a solitary undertaking, so I would like to thank the many teachers, colleagues, and friends who have contributed toward its long gestation. Foremost among these are Don Browning, who first introduced me to Ricoeur's work and had faith in this project from the beginning, and William Schweiker, who challenged me to go further throughout. Encouragement and insights were also offered along the way by David Tracy, Chris Gamwell, Mark Wallace, Gaëlle Fiasse, David Klemm, Richard Kearney, Derek Jeffries, Linda MacCammon, David Hall, Lisa Boccia, Ian Evison, David Clairmont, Michael Johnson, Kevin Jung, Mathew Condon, Roger Willer, Dan Wall, Rebecca Winterer, and Denise Shephard. I benefited from informal and formal remarks from Paul Ricoeur at a conference in 1999 at the University of Chicago. At Rutgers University, where I have taught since 2000, I have enjoyed remarkable support from colleagues both within and outside my department, including my chairs Stuart Charmé and Charlie Jarrett and my dean Margaret Marsh. I owe deep thanks to Jim Wetzel, editor of the Reflection and Theory in the Study of Religion Series in which this book appears, and to Cynthia Read at Oxford University Press, for seeing this book's possibilities. Finally, words stop short at the gratitude I feel toward my parents, first teachers in creativity, and most of all Clare, my partner in life's poetic journey, and Isabel, its joyful promise.

Contents

Moral Creativity

Creation of Adam, detail of the Sistine ceiling, Michelangelo (1475–1564). Sistine Chapel, Vatican Palace, Vatican State. Photo credit: Scala/Art Resource, New York.

Introduction

The Possibility for Moral Creativity

Images

Michelangelo's painting "The Creation of Adam," on the ceiling of the Sistine Chapel at the Vatican, portrays humanity and God as almost mirror images of one another. God floats through the clouds with a host of angels at his side and stretches out his finger to meet the half-raised finger of a reclined and naked Adam on earth. The two gaze into each other's eyes almost as if at their own shining reflections. Possibly Adam is not fully aware of the gift he is about to receive (or just has?). His face is somewhat empty, and his body is relaxed and unmoving. But God himself (let us return later to the question of gender) is highly anthropomorphic, not only in his appearance and dress but also in his apparent anxiety and desire to bring this divine-human encounter about. Not only is Adam a reflection of his Creator, but the Creator itself is also a reflection in some sense of Adam, so that the two share a certain mirrored likeness.

Michelangelo is of course depicting the line from Genesis 1:27: "God created humankind [*adam*] in his image, in the image of God he created them."[1] This line itself, through its internal repetition, also has a mirrored structure. God appears twice: as the subject who creates humankind, and then as the object in the image of which he does so. At the same time, humanity appears twice: as the generalized *adam* and then as the pluralized "them" (literally: "him") clarified in the next phrase to mean both "male and female." The creation of humankind involves a mirrored imaging in which God makes images of himself which, in turn, serve as God's multiple images on earth.

The term "image" here (Hebrew *tselem*) contrasts sharply with the usual *graven* "images" (using a variety of Hebrew words) of the later prophets and writings. Graven images arise from humanity's *dissimilarity* from God: its inability to picture God, and its turning away from God. However, while human objects might fall short of imagining God, in Genesis 1 humanity itself as a *subject* is claimed, at least primordially, to be something of its own Creator's likeness. This sense is confirmed in Genesis 5:3, where *tselem* goes on to describe Seth as an "image" of his father Adam, explicitly drawing an analogy between the relation of son and father and that of the father (Adam) and God (as Father?). As children are to parents, so also are human beings generally—at least from a mythological point of view—both mirrored in, and themselves mirrors of, their original Creator.

Michelangelo's painting could be said to invite us, finally, to go even one step further. The painting itself is an "image" as well. It is not just a passive reflection of this possible divine-human likeness, as if merely retelling a story; it is also itself gloriously and self-consciously *creative*. It not only depicts (or documents) but also illustrates humanity's—in this case Michelangelo's—capability for creating images of itself in the image of its Creator. The same can be said for the creative work of oral and written culture that originally produced Genesis 1. In both cases, the suggestion can be made that if humanity is created in the image of its own Creator—and, of course, this is a big "if"—then humanity may be defined (at least in part, and in a primordial sense) by its unique capability for creativity of its own: whether in painting, writing, culture, or what have you.

In this case, the painting (and Genesis 1) is not just a single but a double image: an image of human creativity as an image of its original Creator. It is, if you like, a double mirror: a mirror held up to our own humanity that affirms that this humanity is really, ultimately, a mirror of its Creator. Through the mirror of our own creativity we may glimpse also a reflection of the Creator—as if in a glass darkly. A Creator shines through from the other side of the mirror, an invisible image appearing through the visible image of ourselves—and, in the process, revealing to ourselves our own invisible depths. If Michelangelo as the artist, and indeed you and I as his interpreters, can create new images of humanity—of ourselves—then do we not in that very act reflect some kind of primordial and mysterious Creation, so that we are not just passively creat*ed* by God but also, in God's likeness, in some sense actively creat*ive*? Does this not tell us something about the depths of our own very humanity?

Such a notion of human creativity is found broadly in many religious and secular stories and writings around the world. It is not uncommon to define the human being in part by its unique capability to make, invent, and imagine itself and its world in art, technology, and culture. The Genesis 1 mythology itself has been used by Jewish and Christian thought to compare God's creativity to human *pro*creativity: in reproductive fruitfulness and multiplication. The Latin phrase *imago Dei* likewise suggests a certain divine-human creative likeness in the ambiguous meaning of "imago." *Imago* can signify not only reproduction, copy, shadow—as in the more obvious interpretation of Genesis 1—but also imitation, likeness, similitude. In the latter case, humanity's imaging of its Creator can also represent, on a different level, its imaging of its own most primordial possibilities. To "be fruitful and multiply" in the image of a Creator could imply that human beings are ultimately capable, like the gods but in limited and fallen ways, of forming order out of chaos, land amidst the waters, and, as literally in a painting, light out of darkness.

This book argues that some such primordial human capability for creativity is ultimately presupposed in moral life. Moral practice and reflection may seem far removed from creative activity, but in fact, I claim, it is both possible and absolutely necessary that human beings create, on the basis of what has already been created in history, new and hitherto unimagined social relations and worlds. One source of evil in the world is the human propensity to deny its original creative capability by clinging to narrow or fixed historical worldviews from the past, acquiescing in distorted systems of power in the present, or failing to engage with others in the formation of a more genuinely human and inclusive future. Part of our moral responsibility under such fallen conditions is the ever more perfect realization of our own primordially creative possibilities, both in how we act in the world and in how we think about how to act. To be created in the image of a Creator is one way of saying, in part, that we are perpetually responsible for fashioning new moral worlds within the multiplicity, disorder, complexity, and tragedy of human life.

In this I oppose a long separation of the meanings of moral and poetic practice going all the way back at least to Plato. Plato censors the poets in his ideal republic because he thinks they undermine the rationality of the moral order. The poets are morally suspect. They create imaginative fantasies instead of true depictions of reality. They form idiosyncratic "images" of moral truth instead of permanent "ideas" of moral truth itself. Plato's student Aristotle, as we will see, shares such a view in part. Less starkly, he separates practical wisdom (*phronêsis*) as acting well in society from poetics (*poiêsis*) as making objects (such as chairs and buildings) or imitating actions (as in poems and stories). Ethics is about internal human goods like courage and justice; poetics is about external goods like crafts and plays.

This separation was taken up forcefully again in modernity, although along rather different lines. As we will see, Kant's second and third critiques deal with what in his view are the distinct human capacities for moral freedom on the one hand, guided by universal law, and aesthetic freedom on the other, guided by subjective taste. (This separation, however, is not complete.) The Romantics, after Kant, deepen the creative act to the pure expression of subjective genius. This is generally opposed to moral action understood as rigidly objective. And Nietzsche eventually goes perhaps the furthest through his aesthetic transvaluation of values. For him, "every creative deed...issues from one's most authentic, innermost, nethermost regions," which oppose stultifying social mores by moving humankind at last "beyond good and evil."[2] If Nietzsche inverts Plato's prioritization of ethics over poetics, he still accepts Plato's distinction between them.

This long history has given rise to the widespread assumption today, often hardly acknowledged, that human "creativity" may have certain moral consequences—such as those from pornographic art, nuclear weapons, or biotechnology—but in and of itself it is an utterly different kind of practice from that found in morality. The one is subjective, private, and essentially inner; the other is intersubjective, public, and essentially social. It is all very well for the arts and literature, and even the sciences and technology, to invent and discover, but morality somehow stands apart as static, formal, and written in stone like the ten commandments. The task of moral practice and inquiry, on this view, is not to invent moral practices but to recover past virtues or values or to uncover and live by moral standards that are fixed and unmoving. It is not to transform, open up, innovate, or instigate, but to repeat, ground, or bring closure. Moral discourse on these assumptions does not fundamentally create anything new; it is not engaged in social transformation of an essential or necessary kind.

A different tradition with which my account contends is a certain set of assumptions that arise out of the Bible. Western religious thought has a tendency, which is very much alive today, to interpret the biblical notion of "image" in its negative sense, originating in Sinai and the prophets, of *graven images*—that is: idols. As Jean-Luc Marion has said, an idol is something human beings create to represent God in the image of themselves, as opposed to an "icon" that breaks through human images as God's own Wholly Other face.[3] This opposition of morality and idolatry is not restricted to postmodern ethicists like Marion and Emmanuel Levinas. As we will see, it runs as a deep current throughout biblically inspired moral thought both historically and today. It has the powerful historical effect of implying that moral life may be somehow *given* to us whole and pure, without our having also to give it to ourselves by forming its meaning and possibilities.

My claim, in response to this assumption, is that prior to the kind of evil of idolatry to which humanity is indeed all too prone, there nevertheless exists a *still more primordial* human capability for creating our moral worlds as images of our Creator. Such a capability can be affirmed through a kind of moral faith in humanity, yet it is also in a way presupposed in the capability for idolatry itself. Creating idols of the Creator betrays the still more original moral purposes for which human creativity may have been created. The objects we create may become idolic images of God, but we are even more fundamentally subjects capable of creativity as images of God. This is a mythological rather than a merely historical or empirical claim. A "third way" is required between, on the one hand, actual human moral creativity, which indeed proves all too inevitably idolatrous and reductionistic, and, on the other hand, the removal of any likeness between humans and their Creator at all. Such a primordial symbolism may open our imaginations up to moral practice and reflection as capable of creating ever greater, if never complete, love for one another and hope for social renewal.

In contrast with these secular and religious divisions of ethics from poetics, the concept of moral creativity that I develop in this book refashions a number of ideas and suggestions in contemporary moral thought on which it is partly based. These recent developments do not fully describe moral creativity as such, but they do indicate some of its important dimensions and possibilities. They begin to suggest lines along which moral activity may make something new and moral thought may instigate transformation. They also help us reinterpret some ancient indications of the poetics of moral life that have gradually been covered over through the course of Western ethical thought, for both good reasons and bad.

For example, some contemporary Kantians allow for a certain kind of transformative social practice in the formation of shared moral worlds. Kant, after all, demanded that freedom take responsibility for perfecting itself: that it not merely accept goodness from without but *make* itself morally worthy. Others, more inspired by Aristotle and Hegel, have recently claimed an important sense in which human beings develop and re-create their contexts of moral tradition and history. There is a certain kind of creativity involved in the fashioning of the very historical world by which moral practice is oriented. Hegel in particular called this *Bildung*, or cultivation. Still others of a more postmodern persuasion speak of the deconstructive inventiveness of the free play and dissemination of moral "otherness." The "other" calls me to an imaginative self-disruption that creatively undoes, as it were, my own settled moral assumptions and calls me toward the unknown. Yet again, in a more political vein, some liberationists have spoken of the need to oppose historical oppression by radical social transformation, creating new systems of social order ever closer to the kingdom of God. And much excellent work has been done, in addition, at the intersection of ethics and literary studies, to show how important to moral life is the creative moral imagination in educating moral sensibility through metaphors, symbols, and works of fiction.

My argument is that although moral creativity is evident in contemporary moral thought in a variety of practical, historical, deconstructive, and literary ways, it needs to be understood in a more profound sense: as a primordial, original, and absolutely necessary human moral *capability*. Moral creativity needs to be grasped (or re-grasped) as a dimension of our very moral humanity. It is not just a means to larger moral ends, an artistic tool, or even a way of describing moral ends themselves, but part of the very nature and composition of being moral and reflecting on morality in the first place. We members of the contemporary world do not generally have trouble acknowledging a unique and fundamental creative human capability in areas like art, culture, technology, and science. But we do not know how to speak of creativity when it comes to moral life. In this we miss something fundamental about our moral task and our possibilities for moral humanity.

Possibilities

In this introductory chapter, I sketch in broad strokes what such a morally creative capability might look like. And I distinguish it, preliminarily, from some possible alternatives. Most obviously, perhaps, to be morally creative here does not mean simply to express one's own inner subjective feelings in one's practices in the world. Ethical aestheticism does not address the real moral problems of intersubjectivity, otherness, historicity, and power. Neither is moral creativity reduced in the following pages to transforming a present fragmented moral world back toward some traditional Golden Age. The repetition of a historical past, however different from the present, cannot capture the full dignity of the eternal human capability for creating its moral world for itself. Neither is it sufficient to limit moral creativity to the process of applying universal moral principles to particular situations. However original and universal the human creative capability may itself turn out to be, it is something that points, as it were, beyond itself—in excess of itself— to concretely actualized moral worlds that are always yet to be imagined and formed. Nor, finally, does moral creativity consist in a Hegelian march of history toward some eventual historical synthesis or reconciliation. Genuine moral creativity must admit the absolute "alterity" of creative persons in and of themselves and the endless irreducibility of the creation of moral life to any one particular historical expression.

Moral creativity is developed in this book as a primordial human capability that inevitably, at least in part, *fails* in actual human history. I defend this negative side of my thesis on the basis of what Kant calls "radical evil." One of the more unique features of the following chapters is that they seek to throw new bridges between Jerusalem and Athens—between biblical and ancient Greek resources—that differ in part from Augustine's mediations of Paul and Plato and Aquinas's mediations of Christianity and Aristotle. Moral evil from a poetic point of view is best understood as involving a dimension of moral tragedy. As forcefully developed in ancient Greece, and as indicated in part by Aristotle, tragedy is the height of the possibility for poetic moral catharsis. I believe that evil in a biblical sense and tragedy from the Greeks, while quite different, can also be usefully related. A more tragic conception of human evil will allow us to understand moral life in some of its most important poetic dimensions. This means that I join a growing effort in postmodernity—all the way from Friedrich Nietzsche to Gabriel Marcel and Luce Irigaray—to reach more deeply into ancient Greek moral culture than in the more rationalized philosophical orders of Plato and Aristotle, and to discover therein some of moral life's more profoundly tragic mystery.

This does not mean, however, that I simply adopt tragedy as the moral problem itself. This strategy is undertaken in different ways by a number of German idealists of the nineteenth century and some philosophical postmodernists today. This has proven a temptation especially for self-consciously "post-religious" thinkers of the relation of ethics to poetics that in the end, I argue, cannot be sustained. Rather, I use the strange poetic intractability implied in Greek notions of tragedy to *qualify*—in a distinctly poetic way—an essentially Jewish and Christian understanding of "radical evil" as having to do with a fundamental failure of human freedom. A poetics of moral evil is best articulated by marrying a tragic sensibility concerning human finitude with a biblical insistence on human freedom's inscrutable defeat of itself. Western moral thought from Augustine to Kant has long associated moral life with human freedom: an absolutely original and irreducible freedom to choose responsibly or not. I do not defend this broad assumption in this book. Nor do I think it is absent from the ancient Greek tragic worldview. But I argue that moral freedom is itself best understood, at least from a poetic point of view, as deeply conditioned by its relation to the tragically finite historical realities within which it must seek realization.

The poetic moral problem consists, in the end, in the problem of an irreducible *tension* between original freedom and historical finitude. It is not in either pole alone but in their tension with one another that I locate the poetics of radical evil. The term "tension" is one of the central themes of this book. It stands primordially as the created condition for the possibility of moral creativity itself. Creativity is inherently tensional, and tension is to be affirmed as originally good. Both moral practice and ethical reflection must deal in some way with the "tensionality" of human life. However, a productive moral tension is witnessed to and realized, in this world, only by passing through tension in its felt sense of actual moral failure. Pure moral creativity is never itself directly and fully experienced—only its breakdown and our subsequent yearning to bring it about. Moral tension is actually experienced in this world as freedom's inscrutable self-defeat. It lies at the root of moral meaninglessness, violence, and distortion.

This failure or evil is "radical" because, as Kant says, it involves freedom's inexplicable defeat of its own possibilities for freedom, or, in more classical terms, freedom's own self-enslavement. From a poetic point of view, the problem is that human freedom fails to perfect itself in living tension with its world. It fails to render its inherent tension with historical finitude productive and creative of new meaning. This failure can take many forms: hubristic domination over the world, acquiescence in distorted structures of power, violence toward the stranger, acceptance of loss of selfhood, and so on. But in each case the fundamental "poetic" problem is the diminishment of the primordial possibility for creative tension between human freedom and its larger finite world. Human moral freedom is caught up in the worldly trage-dies of fate, passivity, suffering, and destruction, and so itself stands in need of ongoing radical poetic catharsis in order truly to be free—or ever more free—in the world.

The response this book develops to such a moral problem—and hence the positive and central side of its thesis—is that moral creativity is the *still more radical* poetic capability for the human transformation and renewal of its social world. The term "radical"—like other terms I use in this book such as "hyperbole," "excess," and "transcendence"—is meant in this positive way in the sense of transgressing already self-imposed and historically imposed moral limits. It points to a kind of poetic moral freedom that is more mys-terious and primordial than the actual moral freedom each of us in fact realizes in our lives. Moral creativity is still more radical than radical evil. The creative freedom to render human tensions productive of greater human meaning can be affirmed as still more primordial than the freedom to defeat this tension by submitting ourselves to self-enslavement. This affirmation is "religious"—and inherently so—in the sense of witnessing to humanity's own most original, even if paradoxically lost and inexplicable, possibilities for radical self-renewal.

One consequence of this proposal is that I examine the notion of God or gods only insofar as it sheds light on the experience of being human. This does not mean I do not make certain assumptions about God that others may not share: specifically, that it is meaningful to speak of "God" at all, that this God is in part a Creator, and that he or she has a unique (though not exclusive) relation to humanity. When I speak of humanity as a "likeness to" its Creator, it is understood, from a long tradition of religious thought, that this is not the same as speaking of "identity with." To imagine the divine as reflecting the human is not the same as imagining the divine *as* the human. But this book is not a theological treatise. My argument does not start from a conception of the Creator and from there deduce insights into the nature of human morality. Rather, in a more phenomenological way illustrated by the likes of Marcel, Levinas, and Marion, I start from the effort to describe and give meaning to concrete human experience. If this description takes us into our primordial human depths as mirroring Creativity as such, this is only because the human is ultimately and unavoidably mysterious to itself. In particular, the capability for self-creation is something for which no final explanation can be "created" by selves who possess it; it can only be the object of a radically original human affirmation.

The word "radical" in this book is, as a result, not meant in the sense of "radical orthodoxy" but, rather, reflects the different kind of meaning it receives in contemporary Continental phenomenology. Moral creativity neither is nor ever has been—nor ever will be, so far as anyone could tell—completed in human thought or practice. But it can become more or less excessively, hyperbolically, radically realized. It can undo existing horizons of meaning even as it reconstitutes them into new ones. The inner aim or perfection of moral creativity, insofar as we can experience it, lies by its very nature *beyond*. It is excessive of any actually created product—excessive, therefore, of any past, present, or even conceivable future social history. The task of moral creativity involves precisely *transforming* the historical world: making a new world that at once remains this existing world but also, and at the same time, is something more and previously unimagined. It does not lie in the finite historical world alone but, rather, in the ineffable tension by which humanity freely lives in relation to it. This tension is our responsibility. To create history is to exercise a mysterious human capability for exceeding history itself, not just in this particular moment of historical time but in relation to historical time as such.

I describe moral creativity in the following pages with the strange both biblical and postmodern language of "impossible possibility." This, to me, means that moral creativity must be regrasped (*religare*) in its fullest possible paradoxicality and primordial mystery. And this can be done, finally, only in the language of mythology. The following pages are not themselves mythology, but they rely on mythological origins and horizons for generating critical moral meaning. The capability in question is for the transformation of an already inscrutably self-defeated world. It is for a radical new perfection that must appear to us disordered creatures historically and ethically impossible. It recalls us to ourselves as fallen "children of *adam*" nevertheless capable ultimately, even if only in limited ways, of reenacting our own covered-over creative depths. The impossible possibility that we are "fallen" from ourselves is a useful mythology or symbolism precisely for describing humanity's covering over of its own creative potentialities even as they remain nevertheless primordial to humanity itself. An investigation into moral creativity must take on these kinds of poetic human paradoxes.

What, in the end, should moral creativity produce? The answer I develop throughout the following chapters is that human beings are called to produce ever more radically inclusive moral worlds with one another. This language of "inclusivity" does not describe a complete moral norm but, rather, moral life's inner poetic perfection or possibility. It is not meant in the Hegelian sense of historical synthesis, unifying sameness, totality. Rather, it indicates an impossible possibility, or, as one might call it, a transcendental ideal or horizon. From a poetic point of view, inclusivity is never closed but inherently open-ended. What is to be included are not just historical realities but also historical freedoms, and precisely the freedoms of creative selves who are capable of creating history for themselves. Radical inclusivity means inclusion of "the other" in the sense of the singular, the irreducible, the nonsubstitutable—the other as itself also a primordial and mysterious creator. Moral creativity faces the ultimate fact that selves are other both to themselves and to one another. Historical experience is not one of gradually unfolding unity but, rather, one of multiplicity, irreducibility, and open and hidden tension. The possibility for greater social inclusiveness within history is a possibility for ever more radical openness rather than closure, a possibility for the fuller multiplicity of human relations as images of a Creator.

The aim of inclusivity is the aim of rendering the inscrutable moral tensions within ourselves and with one another ever more profoundly productive of moral meaning. A meaningful social inclusivity is itself radical and excessive. It is both incapable of creation by limited selves alone and yet required of all limited selves. Moral creativity could not find its inner perfection in the application of universal principles or the return to a past historical coherency. It aims beyond what any one of us alone could ever actually imagine, beyond to a dark abyss and an always still-unfolding new history or "new creation." Somewhat as in art and science, this history can involve a sense of direction and meaning while still refusing absolute closure. For moral life, perhaps even more radically, the aim consists in the always excessive creation of social meaning that is created simultaneously with one another. Such an aim always exceeds history itself. But it can also provide the tensions of our historical lives with genuine senses of greater transformative promise and direction.

This book does not produce a full or complete ethics. Its purpose is not to lay out normative guidelines for moral decision-making in practice. Rather, it is an exercise in meta-ethics, an inquiry into the nature and meaning of moral life as such. While I investigate a range of normative terms like narrative unity, respect, love, nonviolence, and hope, I do so only to illuminate creativity itself as a primordial human moral capability. I range widely across established distinctions in contemporary moral thought such as between Aristotelians and Kantians, modernists and postmodernists, and philosophers and religionists. The point of ranging so widely is not to produce any sort of grand meta-ethical synthesis. Rather, it is to investigate multiple pathways toward the same underlying possibility: the possibility that moral practice and reflection are somehow, at least in part, creative at their very core.

My argument, then, is that while there is much more to moral life than creativity, nevertheless making, inventing, transforming, and renewing human relations is primordially necessary to it. Living a morally good life involves immersion in the messy discordancies and tragedies of our actual historical present and embracing the task of forming together a radically uncertain future. Pursuing ethical study likewise involves innovative critique, provocation, and transformation. Moral life requires us to render the moral incommensurabilities and violence in which we always already find ourselves into previously unimagined social meaning, to strive for more complex and dynamic forms of moral relationality, and to transform even our conceptions of humanity in the direction of their ever deeper human possibilities. Human beings are primordially capable of responding to the moral tensions of their lives by rendering them productive of ever more radically inclusive moral meaning, even if such a task is endless and fraught with dark alleys and deceptions. It is in our nature to create, perhaps even more radically in moral life than in any other kind of human practice. Moral life may thereby discover that it is called to mirror, in however limited a way, the Creation of humanity itself.

Beginnings

Although it is a certain kind of *beginning* at which I propose eventually to arrive—in human primordial creativity—let me suggest up front the different kind of historical beginnings that orient this endeavor. I use these resources and orientations creatively, illustrating on a hermeneutical level the moral argument itself. That is, I engage quite a wide range of historical and contemporary moral voices, but I do so in a hermeneutically creative way: by listening to them carefully, exploring both their differences and their analogies, and in the end forming them into a new moral picture reducible to none of them alone. In moral reflection as in moral life, we find ourselves always already participants in an ongoing conversation, however much we can and must also actively respond to and transform it. So the question to begin with is precisely in what kind of conversation an investigation into moral creativity might begin?

In the broadest possible sense, moral creativity rests on a humanistic affirmation of moral capabilities. Such an affirmation has deep roots in not just modernity but also what may be called premodernity and even parts of postmodernity. The notion of human beings as endowed with particular moral possibilities (and problems) has taken on a range of secular, religious, aesthetic, ethical, and political manifestations over historical time. This does not mean that rooting moral life in features of the human is not under significant attack today. This is so from many quarters. Some associate humanism with individualism and the undermining of life in community. Others locate the origins of moral life not in the human but in the divine alone. Others attack humanism as a Western tool of colonial oppression. Although it is not my intention to defend the complex and shifting tradition of moral humanism per se, I do respond to these and other critics of originating ethics in the human as my argument unfolds.

This broad starting point means, for me, that moral creativity has to do with profound human capabilities. Just as the arts and sciences appear to be peculiarly human endeavors, or at least to reach specifically human heights, so also moral life can be viewed as realizing distinctively human capabilities for creative transformation. In speaking of moral capabilities I take significant cues from the critical thought of perhaps the most powerful humanistic ethicist ever, Immanuel Kant, even as I question his narrowing of moral thought to formal deontological law, his apparent separation of ethics from aesthetics, and the secondary role he gives in moral life to religion. There are many contemporary post-Kantians who have helped blaze this trail into a more robust and radical formulation of human moral capability, and I consider some of them in the pages that follow.

Even more specifically, I argue that the human creative capability is a religious one. It is ultimately a mystery, a paradox, a primordial origin. It cannot be explained in the same way one would explain empirical facts or even rationally founded metaphysical truths but, rather, lies *behind* thought, explanation, and action as such. Luc Ferry has called such a location of human meaning a "transcendental humanism." As will quickly become clear, this does not mean I adopt a confessional starting point, grounding ethics in a leap of faith peculiar to myself or to a particular traditional framework. In fact, those who believe religious ethics can be performed only once one has signed on to a particular traditional worldview will come under significant criticism in the following pages. As I argue in chapter 1, no merely historical starting point can comprehend the necessity of history's own radical moral transformation. There is no way to speak of historical human moral creativity—as the following pages endeavor to do—without running into humanity's ultimate religious origins and limits. I therefore use admittedly historical symbols and languages to risk speaking, always inadequately, of primordial humanity as such. This is the only language we have for speaking of ourselves in this way. My initial defense for doing so is that, despite their real historical differences, all human beings in some way "create" historical interpretations of their lives.

In ethical terms, the difference between humanity as actually experienced in history and humanity in its primordial possibilities can be named "radical evil." To affirm human moral creative capabilities is to affirm "the human" not in its actual historical appearance but in its still more radical historical possibilities. I develop this approach as something of a middle way between the hermeneutics of Karl Barth and Paul Tillich—similar to mediations proposed by Paul Ricoeur, David Tracy, Richard Kearney, and others—in which humanity itself can be shown to have its own original moral dimensions revealed to it only through religious mythology and symbolism. This does not mean I do not make certain broad assumptions about moral life that arise specifically out of the Western background to which I unavoidably belong. The most basic assumption of my argument, which I presuppose without defending, is the importance and necessity to moral life of human freedom. To be capable of making evil choices—and hence also to be capable of making good ones—is to be capable of acting freely. This assumption has its hermeneutical roots in biblical, Greek, medieval, scholastic, and modern thought, and it is not shared among all possible moral orientations. But my purpose, rather than arguing for moral freedom as such, is to inquire into its specifically poetic and creative meaning.

While I therefore begin, Kant-like, in a kind of a priori reflection, it soon becomes apparent that such reflection returns us to ordinary moral understanding with radicalized religious and symbolic sensibilities. Human moral creativity must constantly appear to us as undermined and distorted by our very own freedom, as indeed Kant himself recognized in his famous antinomies. Yet our very recognition of this problem will suggest, beyond Kant, a more primordial human poetic capability for faith in the freedom to enact genuine moral transformation in our world. Such belongs to human moral life's both mysterious origins and ultimate destiny, however unrealized in history itself and unimaginable in existing historical practice. And it remains the case quite apart from the question of *what* in fact history should be transformed into—a question which, as already noted, is not central to this "meta-ethical" book, even if we find some directions toward it. The point is that we *must* create our moral world, even if we wish we didn't have to.

To connect religious ethics with religious symbolism and mythology will require significant hermeneutical defense. I provide this, in chapter 1, by showing how the phenomenological tradition of the past century in Europe helps us grasp religious moral meaning's own strange and paradoxical voice. The following pages make significant use of religious, and especially biblical, resources. They do not do so as an exercise in biblical studies or biblical exegesis, for which I can claim no special competency. They do so from a strictly philosophical point of view. The point is to listen to what religious myths and symbols may tell us about the meaning of human moral creativity. This indirect approach is compelled by the nature of our object: a human moral capability for making meaning itself. My claims should be judged chiefly on such philosophical and ethical grounds: how these profoundly influential texts in Western culture may help us interpret our own creative human possibilities.

If my argument is correct that there exists a creative human capability akin to that of whatever created it, the myths that could be used to describe it are inherently variable and potentially found in many religious traditions. The theological limitations of this investigation consist primarily in assuming (without defending it) that there is some sense in speaking of the world we experience as being something primordially "created." Of course, we are not speaking of a Creator creating at any specific point in time, for it is historical time itself that is supposed as capable of being created by us in its image. The theological assumption is that only a Creator could have created humankind's radically mysterious creative capability. Certainly, at least, humankind could not have created this itself, for the creative capability would in this case already have existed. What is more, the notion of a human "likeness" to its Creator ("in the image of God") does not imply—as a long tradition of Jewish and Christian theology has made clear—humanity's "identity" with God. But these theological questions are beyond the limitations of this book. Here, we are simply interested in the human phenomenological experience of moral "creativity" itself and its radically mysterious and original nature. The symbolism and mythology of a Creator is approached from this experiential, paradoxical, phenomenological point of view.

This procedure specifically helps us to hear moral hyperbole, to become uncomfortable and disrupted in our settled moral horizons, to be opened further to that which speaks to us at our own very limits, and to experience radical moral tension. This means, among other things, that unlike many today who are using the methods of phenomenology, I view ancient religious texts as holding meaningful possibilities for contemporary moral practice. Religion speaks to us in the rich and multivalent symbolic language of a mystery that is Wholly Other and yet that constantly disrupts and reorients our own moral self-understanding. Religion tells us something about radical self- and world-transformation. We are driven to religious symbolism by ordinary moral thought, but this symbolism in turn speaks back to and changes us. Religious language is not accidental but necessary to our inquiry.

If creativity itself is not fixed but endless—if, at least, its destiny remains for each of us radically unknown—its religious dimensions reveal this endlessness as excessive, unavoidable, irreducible, necessary. Richard Kearney calls this view of religion "the *juste milieu* where a valid sense of selfhood and strangeness may coexist."[4] Religion in this sense is not a classic liberal religion that says the same thing as can be known philosophically but in different words (i.e., "love your enemies" is just another phrasing for the categorical imperative). But neither does it fall into a more recent tribalism in which religious traditions provide their own moral authority (i.e., you should love your enemies because scriptural traditions say so). Rather, religious mythology speaks *at the limits of* ordinary human understanding, pressing it always further toward its own radical inner impossible possibilities. Moral creativity is both human and divine in this sense, calling each of us toward our own ever more primordial humanity.

The thinker on whom the following argument relies the most is the contemporary French hermeneutical phenomenologist Paul Ricoeur. While this book is not a study *in* Ricoeur, it uses Ricoeur's writings extensively both to describe the human moral creative capability and to work out some of its key ethical meanings. Except for the conclusion, Ricoeur's voice figures centrally in each of the following chapters. Chapter 1 explores Ricoeur in the most depth of all, especially his concepts of moral capability, freedom, selfhood, and poetics. Here I argue that Ricoeur's "poetics of the will," in its various philosophical and religious meanings, provides a unique perspective on human creativity that takes us beyond many contemporary distortions (and negations) of moral selfhood. Chapters 2 to 4 use Ricoeur as a mediating figure between a number of traditional understandings of the relation of ethics to poetics—such as in Aristotle, Kant, postmodernism, and contemporary feminism—and my own post-Ricoeurian conclusions. These three chapters begin with larger understandings of the relation of ethics to poetics, interrogate these understandings using perspectives from Ricoeur, and then develop out of this conversation my own constructive proposals concerning the creativity of moral life. In this way, I tie together and critique various strands of Ricoeur's often far-flung writings to advance the specific project of thinking through moral life poetically.

My account of moral creativity may be termed "Ricoeurian" in the limited sense that Ricoeur provides the central philosophical inspiration for it. It is also through Ricoeur's eyes that I read a number of the other thinkers used to advance my argument. (For example, Kant is read from the Ricoeurian point of view—by no means the only point of view possible—of the connection between moral freedom and radical evil.) At the same time, however, Ricoeur himself does not make the argument that moral life is inherently poetic or creative. The "and" in this book's subtitle is to be taken in its strong sense. Ricoeur links morality and creativity, but nowhere does he argue that moral life is creative at its core. Nor does he make this argument in as directly religious-symbolic terms as do I. His writings on ethics and creativity are in fact for the most part quite separate, and he finally still shares in a longstanding Platonic prejudice—which this book seeks to unravel—that ethics remains ultimately a relatively fixed and suprapoetic activity. These assumptions are challenged through a range of dialogues with other ethical thinkers, both ancient and contemporary. What is more, a number of ethicists are employed to criticize aspects of Ricoeur and in the process to open up vistas of moral creativity that Ricoeur's own work closes off. Nevertheless, no other major contemporary thinker, in my view, comes closer than Ricoeur to suggesting how a theory of moral creativity may begin to take shape, and so in many ways it is with Ricoeur that we may fruitfully begin to make inroads into existing moral thought.

Specifically, Ricoeur makes three key contributions to my argument. (1) His vision of phenomenological hermeneutics, even if poetically incomplete, still usefully relates ordinary moral life and religious symbolism. It is Ricoeur who stands in the background—sometimes explicitly, sometimes critiqued—of a range of contemporary efforts in the French- and English-speaking academic worlds to join, without reducing to one another, ordinary philosophical and radical religious discourse. With Levinas, Ricoeur is the chief architect of what is sometimes critically described as phenomenology's late-twentieth-century "theological turn." In the following pages, I make extensive use of Ricoeur's hermeneutical method (even if not always his substantive conclusions) of reading biblical symbolism and mythology to "give rise to thought"—to give rise, that is, through tension and transformation, to greater philosophical understanding. (2) Ricoeur imagines a moral world of large and generous proportions that helps us move beyond some of the hardened divisions today between Anglo-American and Continental ethics, as well as between Kantianism, Aristotelianism, postmodernism, and Judaism/Christianity—divisions under which moral creativity tends, I will argue, to become obscured. Although I agree in several important respects with Ricoeur's ethical critics, I also appreciate and make use of the unparalleled breathing space he opens up for connecting teleology, deontology, and social discourse. (3) But most important, I believe Ricoeur's broad project of a poetics of the will—begun in the 1950s and still very much alive in Ricoeur's most recent work—suggests new grounds upon which ethics and poetics are no longer sharply separable but mutually implied. The possibility that we are morally creative beings, defined by human capability, depends on whether one can defend this kind of poetic moral anthropology. It is through a careful and critical reading of Ricoeur that we will be able to develop the crucial nexus—at the center of this book—of religion, poetics, and ethics.

These beginnings—humanistic, religious-mythological, and Ricoeurian—allow us to form a notion of moral creativity in dialogue with a range of historical and contemporary moral perspectives and as a unique angle on moral life in its own right. My contribution mirrors hermeneutically what I seek to establish ethically: that from within the always already constituted history of languages and meanings of which each of us is a part, we are faced with the demand to create meaning of an ever new and more inclusive kind. I do not pretend somehow to step outside and view from above the humanistic and hermeneutical history to which I belong. But I do wish to refigure this history in significant ways so as to include its deeper poetic moral possibilities. It is paradoxically possible—indeed, required—to press at the limits of one's own received historicity to create a broadened moral world. It is this gesture, both hermeneutical and substantive, whose depths this book seeks to plumb. My argument rests, ultimately, on whether, as in Michelangelo's painting, we can reimagine—however imperfectly—human creativity itself, but now in a moral register.

Tensions

I make this argument by taking several key traditional historical understandings of the relation (or lack thereof) of ethics to poetics and exploring in each case how in fact moral life presupposes a core creative capability. Only in the concluding chapter do I sound the ways in which these various excavations meet up. In this way, the book is organized around four important human moral tensions—each the basis of a new dimension of moral creativity, and each the subject of its own chapter. These four tensions become progressively more complex as the book unfolds, but none is reducible to the others. The history of the separation of ethics from poetics is so entrenched that it must be deconstructed and then refigured from a number of different points of view. One might think of the four following chapters as like different perspectives from which to view a human statue: its mysterious inner beauty revealing itself only as we move around it from many different angles. In our case, however, this statue is alive, and we seek not only to see but also to hear, smell, and touch. In this indirect way, a multidimensional picture of the tensions constituting human moral creativity (including also the tensions *between* these various tensions) may emerge with its appropriate dynamism, energy, and promise.

The four tensions we explore are broadly speaking as follows: (1) between the human self and its moral history, (2) within oneself (as a historical and social being), (3) in relation to the other as irreducibly other, and (4) across systems of social power. These can be described schematically (loosely following distinctions in Ricoeur) as ontological, teleological, deontological, and practical. In order for moral life's creative dimensions to surface fully, these distinctions must ultimately be overcome. No statue is fully appreciated from the single angle of a photograph, even if it cannot be viewed simultaneously from all angles at once. Sticking to any one perspective with too much passion—whether Aristotelian, Kantian, postmodern, or otherwise—only perpetuates ethics and poetics' deep historical separation. Each of these traditional approaches to moral reflection contains within itself, however hidden, its own unique poetic tensions that provide an important perspective on the poetic whole. The general movement *within* each of the following chapters is from (1) a major traditional conception of the difference of ethics from poetics, to (2) a mediating intervention using Ricoeur, to (3) my own conclusions about the radical primordiality of creativity in this particular dimension of moral life. As these inquiries build upon one another, we then are able, in the concluding chapter, to describe in a meaningful and rounded way the underlying dynamics of human moral creativity itself.

Here let me briefly highlight the differences between these four dimensions of moral creativity in order to preclude any misunderstanding of my position as reducible to one dimension over the others. Like Ricoeur and others, I am more interested in transgressing than in defending the boundaries between such perspectives on moral life. I am more interested in using them creatively than in demonstrating one's superiority over the others. Of course, this does not mean I lack basic orientations of my own, as have already been suggested and will unfold more fully in what follows. But the important prize on which I wish to fix our attention is the underlying—and ultimately shared—human capability for moral creativeness itself. All other considerations are strictly secondary, even if still important. What is more, these dimensions should be understood as illustrative rather than exhaustive. One further angle of vision on moral creativity that would be well worth investigation, for example, and which I all too briefly touch upon in the conclusion, is the creative tension between human creativity and "creation" in the sense of the natural environment, perhaps one of the profoundest tensions of freedom and finitude one could imagine.

Chapter 1 explores the "ontological" question of the human "being" (*onto*) as a creative self in history. This chapter relies more extensively than any of the others on the phenomenological hermeneutics of Ricoeur, whose chief contribution to moral thought is widely recognized to consist in his long-developed moral anthropology (description of the moral self). My argument is that, contrary to an array of contemporary proclamations of the death of the moral self, the human being can be reconceptualized—especially beyond the modernist autonomous ego—as existing in the tension between history and innovation, finitude and freedom, passivity and agency: its received social conditions and its capability for their radical transformation. The best place to begin an investigation into moral creativity is the phenomenological overcoming of the Cartesian separation of self and world, but in such a way as still to articulate their fallen human tension.

My argument here is that humanity finds itself simultaneously *created by* an already given history, culture, biology, and set of traditions, communities, and social relations, which, nevertheless, it is also capable of *creating*, in limited ways, into new meaning specifically and singularly for itself. This tension of human passivity and agency lies, as Ricoeur shows, at the very heart of human moral fallibility and evil. It is somehow original and mysterious. Yet it is also the grounds for the uniquely human possibility for self-transformative renewal. The poetic self is ultimately a paradox and mystery to itself. It cannot form an understanding of how it forms understanding as such. Knowledge, explanation, and even skepticism and deconstruction presuppose a prior capability for *making* meaning of one's world—constructive or destructive—a capability that is itself irreducible to any such meaning. For this reason, the following pages are not "theology" in the classic sense of "reasoning about God" (not that such reasoning may not in some ways be presupposed) but, rather, in a more limited and perhaps also more profound way, the interpretation of religious symbols for the sake of regrasping the mysteries of being morally human. It becomes necessary in the end to speak of the poetic self mythologically, in the mode of radically indecipherable origins.

The notion of selfhood as primordial tension is not altogether alien to contemporary moral thought, but it is greatly obscured. One could think, for example, of the Freudian tension of the ego with the id and the superego, tensions within and between cultural forms, or the political tension of oppressed persons and an oppressing class. But generally speaking, many of the battle lines in contemporary moral reflection are drawn around whether one accepts or rejects the free individual of modernity. On the one hand are those who take it as fundamental that human beings are free self-legislators

(Kant), to be protected in their liberty (Mill), or even needing to strive to rise above the herd (Sartre). On the other hand are those who believe moral life is situated instead in a fundamental human passivity: of traditions, of history, of power, of the Wholly Other, or even before alterity. Without necessarily making judgments about these diverse moral projects in themselves, I argue that this contemporary framing of the debate has made it difficult to understand moral life's tensional, creative dimensions. The multiple ways in which moral selves are indeed passively constituted from without does not preclude—indeed, it demands—their capability for creating, on the very basis of these conditions, their own free sense of meaning in the world. At the same time, moral freedom itself lacks meaning altogether apart from its given constituting conditions. It is this poetic tension of freedom and finitude, agency and passivity—and not one pole of it or the other—that I identify as the moral "self" as such, a self indeed mysterious, tragic, paradoxical, and originary.

Chapter 2 then asks the "teleological" question—at our simplest level of specifically moral inquiry—of what it means to create human goods, ends, or purposes (*teloi*). Here I argue that selves are always already constituted by a wide array of possible goods—historical, biological, psychological, social, and so forth—but that these gain teleological meaning only insofar as the self *narrates* them for itself and in relation to others. Narration here is meant in the sense, not just of following moral stories, but more profoundly of creating them. To have a narrative is implicitly—as least for human beings—also to make, form, and refigure it. And this making capability cannot be reduced to any particular narrative as such, but lies at narration's radically primordial origins.

Here I examine the ways in which ethics and poetics are distinguished and related in both Aristotle and contemporary Aristotelianism, critique these by means of Ricoeur's theories of narrative, and then argue for a tensional relation between *being narrated by* one's social conditions and *narrating* them for oneself. A teleological narrative is not just something one incorporates or adopts, but also something one must create and re-create for oneself, as part of one's very identity as a human being. This poetic teleological capability involves the self in the always fallible formation of its own good, a formation that ultimately depends on a paradoxical human "gift" for creative self-narration and renewal. Insofar as goods are human, they are never just carved into nature or history but always also impossibly possible projects of narrative self-formation.

Consider, for example, the situation of a cancer patient whose health insurance does not cover a promising but expensive new treatment. Apart from a host of other moral issues that may be raised, one is a disproportion between the patient's freedom to pursue a range of options and the personal and social conditions within which these options may find expression. Such conditions might include the needs and desires of her family, the economic constraints placed upon her by her health insurance company, the current state of medical technology, the larger availability of health resources in her society, mores and practices within the medical community, and social and cultural attitudes toward illness. To a large extent, such a person faces tragic moral tensions. She may not be able to afford the treatments without economically destroying her family; she may be ready to die but not ready to leave her children; she may face issues of social identity and usefulness and balancing comfort and suffering. Still, she must make some choice. And any choice she makes (including the choice not to choose) will inevitably fall short of resolving all the pressing tensions of her situation. She is forced back, in a particularly dramatic way, upon her own root capability for creating a new narrative of her own life, a narrative that is neither independent of her given social historicity nor utterly determined by it, but instead must be invented to some degree as a radically new way forward.

Such impossible situations face each of us, to one extent or another, in every area of our lives. Any pursuit of teleological goods—from humble day-to-day activities to grand life plans and social projects—is not just a matter of yoking freedom to certain goods over others. Nor can it be divorced from its given situation. The constitution of human aims is on the one hand inherently social, historical, traditional, cultural, and biological, and yet on the other the particular and singular responsibility of each self. The good is always already pre-constituted or pre-created by one's larger situation, and yet each self is called to the unique responsibility of creating this situation anew. Furthermore, ethicists who reflect on goods are called likewise to create new senses of teleological possibility. Goods are at once objective and subjective, exterior and interior, involuntary and voluntary. And it is within this tension, not on one side of it or the other, that the good finds meaning and purpose.

The ultimate creative imperative in this teleological dimension (we have not yet moved to the more complex considerations of otherness and power) is to embrace as far as possible the multiple tensions of one's historical life and create new senses of narrative inclusivity among them. The poetic good can be described as a narrative unity of life, not in the sense of cohesion with an already established tradition of goods, but in the more primordial and radical sense of the self's weaving together the fullest possible dimensions of its existence. In fact, each of us falls short of this human good by anxiously clinging to partial goods, sticking with aims with which we have grown comfortable, glossing over self-alienation and fragmentation, following paths of least resistance, losing touch with situated conditions, and generally failing to include in our narrative identities parts of our historical world that are nevertheless importantly constitutive of it. Creation mythology holds out the impossible possibility of a human capability for coherent self-narration as such, in its affirmation of humankind as having primordially been created in the likeness of an all-inclusive Creator. But for us, such an ideal can serve only as an always excessive horizon—an impossible possibility—in tension with which our own fragmented efforts may find ever more vital renewal.

Chapter 3 raises the stakes by asking about what can be called "deontological" responsibilities and obligations (*deon*) toward others in their irreducible otherness. Here moral creativity becomes more complex. I follow certain strands of contemporary Continental ethics to distinguish "the other" as merely another self following different teleological ends (as, for example, in the Anglo-American deontological ethics of John Rawls) from "the other" in the more radical and genuine sense of irreducibility, alterity, singularity, *différance*, nonsubstitutability. Such an other—the other in its "otherness"—is irreducible to any narrative I may make of it. He or she can appear to me only as exceeding and disrupting any meaning I may give to them as such.

By going back and deconstructing Kant's original deontological reasons for separating ethics from poetics, however, this chapter argues that the demand from others not to be reduced to selfhood does in fact imply a different kind of poetic tension and creativity. The tension is now more complex than that discussed above because it lies not within self-understanding but between self-understanding and the responsibility owed to otherness. Ricoeur can and should be criticized from the point of view of the ethics of alterity, as indeed he is, but he also helps us see that, however other the other may be, the other nevertheless commands a response specifically from the self. This response, I argue, is paradoxically never complete but still required. It can be made only in the mode of open tensionality. This is a different kind of tensionality than that involved in self-narration. It demands from the poetic moral self what I call a "negative" type of creative self-transformation that unravels the self's implicit violence toward otherness. The moral tension here is centrifugal, demanding a creative self-undoing of selfhood and its world in ever more hyperbolic responsiveness to alterity.

Consider what remains perhaps *the* paradigm for the moral problem in Continental moral thought: death camps like Auschwitz. Of the great many ways one may formulate the questions raised by these most horrific of events, one is to follow the Jewish moral thinker Emmanuel Levinas to say that they suggests a violation of the absolute command not to do violence to others *qua* other. What is revealed here is the invisible "face" of the other as absolutely irreducible to any kind of narrative or history whatsoever. My own claim is that here we find a kind of tragic evil: that humanity paradoxically destroys humanity itself. One can identify a profound poetic tension between the demand from (in this case) the Jewish other and the necessity of a response from all selves involved (most of all the Nazis, of course, but also the Allied leaders who had the power to step in, as well as we who live afterward). This tension with alterity is unbreakable, but it is also a call to act, and to act in new and previously unimagined ways. Those who tried to undermine the Nazi program were not simply knocked out of orbit by these others as other; they also made creative human responses to them that were different from the easy lack of responsiveness of those around them. The ordinariness and "banality" of evil, as Hannah Arendt describes it,[5] is met by the extraordinary, the radical, the original, the transformative.

The norm of inclusivity here is of a different kind than the teleological inclusion of historical goods, although, as above, it is also ultimately impossible. It is negative rather than positive. Inclusion of otherness—a paradoxical phrase—means the creative refashioning of one's own world so that the other is *no longer excluded*. Such is ultimately impossible to complete. Nevertheless, creativity is just as much a part of undoing moral meaning as it is of building it up. It is also just as much, if not more, excessive and unending. The tension of other with self requires producing a radically new self. It requires a hyperbolic challenge to accepted understandings and worldviews. This command from the neighbor, the stranger, even the enemy is described in the following pages as a command to love, not in a sentimental or categorical sense, but in the poetic sense of a love for others *qua* other that changes who I am in response to them. This kind of love is eternal, not in being always already present or available, but in calling us to a form of self-renewal that is endless and insatiable. It can be symbolized in the Wholly Other as not only Judge of human violence but also, and even more primordially, Creator of a nonviolent, unalienated world.

Chapter 4 finally takes us to what in my view is the still more complex ethical question of what it means to create social practices in common. Here I explore not individual or relational tensions but social-systemic or ideological tensions between oppressors and oppressed. Here we find some of the most explicit contemporary language of ethical creativity from feminism, discourse ethics, and liberationism, where social marginalization is frequently described as a call for world transformation. Power is such an all-pervasive shaper of our moral lives that it is necessary to imagine transcending social practices and ideals that may offer hope for a better world.

Ricoeur helps us see that this hope for social transformation is fundamentally also a question of the shape and meaning of a society's shared social imagination. Ideology, on Ricoeur's account, is not the raw exercise of power but the inherited horizons of meaning that make society possible in the first place, and as such it requires not overturning so much as constant and radical renewal from the perspectives of alternative possible visions of utopia—"no-places" from which the places we are actually situated may be subject to genuine critical transformation. My own argument is that a more just social order rests at least in part on a new level of human capability for creating its own entrenched world anew. This capability includes both positive and negative (teleological and deontological) elements in the mutual creation of shared life by others with one another. Historical tensions of power may become rendered ever more "inclusive" in the new sense of participated in by absolutely all. As poetic beings, we can hope for the impossible possibility of the "new creation" of our distorted social systems in the direction of human reconciliation of an ever more radical and excessive form.

Take the example of severely poor children, whom we find everywhere from the urban and rural areas of developed countries to vast regions of the southern hemisphere. Thirty-five thousand such children currently die every day from easily preventable diseases and malnutrition. Poor children certainly face teleological issues of narrative self-coherency and deontological problems of being done violence as singular others. But they also suffer from a different kind of tragic breakdown of entire systems of social order, systems precisely on which they cannot help but depend. Child poverty is so widespread in our world today because children cannot compete in the global capitalistic economy, do not generally have a clear voice in political power, are not always treated as fully "human," and are systematically alienated by growing cultures of individualism and rationalism that obscure their special vulnerability. The evil or broken tension here is that this group depends on the very social systems that in fact oppress and marginalize them. Human beings are social animals and yet inevitably develop social systems that exclude genuine participation by all. Children will continue in this state insofar as each of us fails radically to re-create not just ourselves but also the collective social practices and imaginary spaces in which each of us participates.

This dimension of moral creativity is so poetically complex because it involves both a positive and a negative component at once. Positively, a new social order demands endlessly to be formed. There is no way to live in the world without taking part, from birth onward, in systems of shared language, culture, power, and economics, and these systems are shaped between us no matter how "other" from each other we are. Negatively, however, this social world must constantly be deconstructed from the point of view of those groups it subjects to marginalization. There is an endless need for liberation from social oppression. The result is that moral creativity must be practiced, in this case, by oppressors and oppressed alike, but in different ways. Those who wield power need to see how their own primordial humanity calls them to ever more negatively self-disruptive creative inclusion of social participation by others. Those who are marginalized need to find greater poetic empowerment in the affirmation of a positive original capability for social creativity in themselves. Both are called to a poetics of hope, the impossible possibility for the shared creation of a reconciled human world together. Humanity as an "image" of God can be taken up finally into the mythology of a "kingdom" of God that projects before society its own ultimate possibilities and promise.

A complex and truly meaningful phenomenology of moral creativity is developed only insofar as such diverse dimensions have been plumbed one after the other. The concluding chapter takes up the larger thematic resonances between these preceding inquiries by exploring in detail their three most centrally shared components: tension, capability, and inclusivity. These terms collectively describe moral creativity as a primordial human possibility. Through its multiple tensions of moral finitude and freedom, humanity is ultimately capable of creating its own ever more radically inclusive humanity. The impossible possibility of moral life, from a poetic point of view, is that we may live together as images of our own Creator. That human beings must create is absolutely "original." The ancient quarrel of the ethicists and the poets needs to be challenged so that moral practice and reflection may be revealed and imagined as creative at their core. As suggested by Michelangelo's painting, such a poetic possibility can be reflected in the tension and the gap between ourselves and our own imaged origins. Nothing less, in moral life, is demanded of our very humanity.

I

Paul Ricoeur and the Poetic Moral Self

Hamlet comes to the crisis point in Shakespeare's great tragedy when he must decide whether or not to confront his uncle with the crime of regicide, thereby setting himself on a path that risks his own life too. His cry is familiar: "To be, or not to be—that is the question; whether 'tis nobler in the mind to suffer the slings and arrows of outrageous fortune, or to take arms against a sea of troubles, and by opposing end them?" He has a choice: to suffer in silence the fortune he has been dealt by his uncle's apparent crime (and in the bargain to lose his future kingship and become alienated from his mother, now his uncle's wife), or to act and expose himself to an unknown and dangerous outcome. The problem is not just the hand that fate has dealt him. The problem is how to respond to it. What is dramatic and tragic is that Hamlet must decide what is to be his own identity: someone who cowers before the injustice of his "outrageous fortune" or someone who opposes it even at the possibility of death.

This chapter asks what it means for the self to be caught up in a finite, unchosen, and often distorted world—which is true in one way or another for all of us—while at the same time also having the capability, in limited ways, to transform this world creatively into a meaningful world for itself. Such a self must risk "not being" as part of the effort "to be." The embrace of what is yet to be formed—what presently *is not*—is part of gaining the possibility for meaning and identity. This embrace includes even the meaning of one's own death. The self is not just "being" as it already exists or as it is thrown into the world, but also the "not being" of the possibilities it may construct. No one escapes *this* fate, the fate of having to embrace non-being in one's effort to be. To be or not to be is not just a question of particular crises but of the strange fragility, density, and dynamics of being human.

The poetic moral self is defined by a radical capability, at the very onto-logical core of human being, for creatively transforming the meaning of its own already fragmented and given historical identity. Such a self is passive and active at once, utterly finite yet inscrutably free. It is simultaneously lim-ited by the depths of its world conditions and further limits itself by choosing blind self-enslavement to narrow elements within them and failures of mean-ing of its own. But at the same time, to be human involves—paradoxically—the ability to re-create these very same world conditions in innovative ways that invest them with new meaning. Each of us, like Hamlet, is faced with the task of narrating our own already tragically narrated identity, a task that we could not reject even if we tried, not even in suicide.

Such talk of moral selfhood, especially of a creative kind, is controversial in contemporary moral thought from many sides. The very possibility of self-constituting selfhood is thrown into question by our profound embeddedness in history, traditions, structures of power, and biological and psychological forces. It is fashionable in postmodernity to explain all human behavior as reducible to outward and observable mechanisms: class warfare, biological drives, genetic reproduction, cultural expression. The individual is thought to have had its day, a peculiarly modern Enlightenment and Western con-struction that turns out to do violence to difference, to be too thin for moral community, to underwrite world-denying colonialism. Modernity is conceived of as having driven us eventually to an extreme existentialism that values mere freedom in and of itself—stripping moral life in the process of all possible substance and meaning. Or, worse, free selfhood can sound like a Romantic subjectivism in which each of us weaves the meaning of our own lives with purely intuitive abandon.

My claim, in contrast, is that both a creative self and a religiously creative self are successively presupposed within the very notion of a given moral history and society. Neither history, social systems, or traditional narratives, nor moral principles, human rights, or procedures of discourse are free of incommensurabilities, distortions, tragic consequences, or the manipulations of human evil. Passivity alone is never sufficient for moral identity. Rather, there must also be presupposed a moral self—however mysteriously and in-explicably by selves as such—a self that cannot take respite in joining a tra-dition or being a universalized rational ego, but which is unavoidably called to re-make its own thick identity peculiarly for itself. Such a self is not trans-parent to itself but, rather, a primordially lost origin of humanity that is therefore also a destiny and a hope. It is not the empty Cartesian *cogito* that responds to doubt but the embodied and incarnated capability of selves for creating a narrative identity in and through this broken world.

This Mystery Which I Am

Paul Ricoeur's central contribution to both our own investigation and phi-losophical and religious thought generally is his concept of the self. This anthropology has, if anything, been the guiding aim of his complex and productive sixty-year career spanning the entire second half of the twentieth century and beyond. Ricoeur frequently describes his work as taking place at the crossroads of phenomenology, hermeneutics, and reflexive philosophy. This means, in brief, that he seeks to understand how selfhood constitutes self-understanding in relation to its world. If there is a core thesis to Ricoeur's work—and one hesitates to risk such a sweeping assessment, especially when the author is still working—it is that the self is inextricably both passive and active at once. The self is constituted at the intersection of involuntary conditions and voluntary possibilities, historicity and hope, inherited language and its interpretation into meaning, sameness and ipseity—in short, in classical language, finitude and freedom. This view is evident in the titles of many of Ricoeur's two dozen books, from his first major philosophical statement in 1950, *Freedom and Nature: The Voluntary and the Involuntary*, to his reflections on human ambiguity in his 1960 *Fallible Man*, and all the way up to his 1990 masterpiece *Oneself as Another* and his 1998 co-authored work on reflection on revelation, *Thinking Biblically*.[1]

This thread uniting Ricoeur's otherwise highly disparate writings has been picked up by many of his major interpreters. Don Ihde early described Ricoeur's thought as a joining of Husserl's "idealist" phenomenology of objects with Gabriel Marcel and Maurice Merleau-Ponty's "existentialist" phenomenology of the subject.[2] Domenico Jervolino more recently called Ricoeur's a philosophy of "concrete freedom": how the will is realized and given meaning in relation to its larger historical world.[3] Many commentators follow Ricoeur himself in describing his work as a "philosophy of the will," which is not a simple return to the will of Kant and modernity, but a phenomenological hermeneutics aimed at regrasping human intentionality within language, historicity, and society.

My own argument is that this general effort in Ricoeur to think finitude and freedom at once is most precisely, and uniquely, captured by his early phrase "poetics of the will." The ultimate site in Ricoeur in which passivity and agency meet—in other words, in which "the will" comes to realization— is in the creative capability for reconstituting one's already preconstituted world. "Poetics" here clearly does not refer to mere subjective self-expression. Ricoeur rejects both the Romantic will (particularly in German Romanticism) that cries out against social mechanization, and the existential will (so much admired during the first half of his career) that rebels against social conformity. But neither does he reduce meaning and selfhood to its historical conditions, a possibility that is often associated with Hegel's historical Spirit, Marx's historical materialism, or more recently the historicity of culture and language. Ricoeur is deeply conscious of the totalitarianisms that gripped Europe in his early lifetime and affected him personally as a prisoner of the Nazis in World War II. He refuses to reduce human meaning *only* to power, biology, history, or tradition. The poetics of the will, in Ricoeur, is a sustained effort to grasp the possibility for shaping one's own meaning *within* the history and language by which meaning can only be shaped. It is an effort to use the category of the poetic formation of meaning to think beyond the usual dualities of ego and world, *cogito* and *extensio*, bequeathed from modernity and still very much alive today.

To begin to see how this dynamics of passivity and agency might work, we can start with Ricoeur's view of the human body, arguably the place where the dualism most directly breaks down. In *Freedom and Nature*, Ricoeur challenges Descartes's view of the body as divided from the cogito as another object in the world. Building upon the phenomenological analyses of his early teacher and friend Gabriel Marcel[4] (as well as upon Husserl's *Ideen I*, which Ricoeur translated into French), Ricoeur argues that in each and every instance, the body *belongs to* someone. "It is too easy to say that the body appears twice, once as a subject, then as an object, or more exactly the first time as the body of a subject, the second time as an anonymous empirical object."[5] As a phenomenological experience, the body always appears to selves as "someone's body, a subject's body, *my* body, and *your* body."[6] One's own body and others' bodies are neither merely empirical objects nor just tools for one's own (or others') free use, but rather constitutive of the very meaning of being a self. The body gives to the self a complex of "involuntary" needs, desires, energies, dispositions, and goods, but these have *meaning* only insofar as they are also "voluntarily"—meaning freely, reflexively, creatively—taken up into that self's own movements, actions, narratives, and overall efforts to be. This is what it means to call the body a component of "the will." It is not just an object for use but part of the self's own "intentionality": its mode of being itself in the world.[7]

The hard Cartesian lines between subjectivity and objectivity can be replaced with a concept of the "self" as inherently dialectical, not in Hegel's sense of part of an objective dialectics of history, but in the sense of a continuous and dynamic relation of finitude and freedom. Thus, for Ricoeur, "freedom is not a pure act, it is, in each of its moments, activity and receptivity. It constitutes itself in receiving what it does not produce: values, capacities, and sheer nature."[8] Likewise, "if freedom posits itself, it does not possess itself.... Freedom can only attest to itself in the works where it objectifies itself.... Because the causality of freedom does not apprehend itself, it must recover itself by way of the long detour of works and action."[9] As Ricoeur's corpus progresses, one can follow this simple but controversial thesis all the way from his early discussions of the will in terms of emotions, passions, and habits, to his reading of the dynamics of the Freudian "interpretation" of the unconscious, to his theories of how meaning is generated through symbolism, texts, metaphor, and narrative.[10] Ricoeur's is a philosophy that seeks in multiple ways to capture what he calls the self's "only human freedom": a freedom having meaning only in and through its world.[11]

Unlike many contemporary phenomenologists, Ricoeur also claims that this meeting of subject and world—this "being there" or *Dasein*—implies a disproportion within selfhood that must finally be described as a primordial human *fallibility*. The sequel to *Freedom and Nature* is Ricoeur's 1960 duo of books, *Fallible Man* and *The Symbolism of Evil* (paired together in the French original under the title *Philosophy of the Will: Finitude and Culpability*).[12] "Fallibility" means here an ontological "disproportion of the self with itself." This Ricoeur traces through a variety of speculative, practical, and affective levels. In each case, selves are at once conditioned by larger forces in the world and yet responsible for interpreting and appropriating them into meaning for themselves. As in the above-mentioned subtitle of these two works, the passivity of the self's "finitude" cannot be separated from a freedom that implies "culpability." Fallibility refers to the fact that the self is always capable of failing to make meaning for itself in the world. As Ricoeur describes it later in his career, fallibility means that the self's capability for a meaningful life is accompanied by a strange inner *incapability*: the possibility (and in fact at all times in part the reality) that the self will subject itself to meaninglessness. Freedom and world are experienced as standing in opposition through the inevitable violation of their mutually necessary relation. As David Rasmussen has put it, Ricoeur's self is not a settled and fixed entity but everywhere in the process of a fragile self-constitution.[13]

The result of this philosophical anthropology is that the self can reflect on itself, in the end, only as ultimately a mystery to itself. The self finds itself distorted and fragmented and hence not yet fully itself: "To be understood and rediscovered, *this mystery which I am* demands that I become one with it, that I participate in it so that I do not observe it as confronting me at a distance as an object."[14] The mystery is not that the self is really a world-transcending spirit. The mystery is that its own meaning to itself is never fully constituted, is always *on the way* toward becoming. Borrowing language from Marcel, Ricoeur declares selfhood "the Joy of Yes in the sadness of the finite": the possibility for meaning amid meaning's actual ruin and incompleteness.[15] None of us can rest upon either the complacency of history or the assurance of a purely self-legislating freedom. Rather, each of us must constantly reconstitute ourselves. Revising the language of "project" from Husserl, Ricoeur claims that "the person is primarily a project which I represent to myself, which I set before me and entertain, and . . . this project of the person is . . . a 'synthesis' which is effected. This project is what I call *humanity*."[16] Humanity is not a given reality—either in historical appearance or in ahistorical freedom—but a "project" or "possibility" of meaning that each of us constantly undertakes.[17]

I argue later in this chapter—and indeed throughout this book—that Ricoeur more fully appreciates the disproportion between freedom and finitude than he does certain further disproportions that infect finitude itself; or, as I also put it, Ricoeur is more attuned to the relation of agency and passivity than he is to the tragic complexities of (moral) passivity itself. But the value of his notion of the self as ontologically fallible is that it conceives of selfhood as dynamic, open-ended, a project always on the way toward completion. Reducing selfhood to a constituent of its larger world alone makes its identity and meaning already externally determined. This, we will see, is one way that selves can be dehumanized. But reducing selfhood in its essence to freedom alone, to a universal inner human quality, is also problematic. This, too, dehumanizes the human by rendering it overly abstract. True humanity involves constituting oneself as a concrete participant in this world. Our desire "to be" lies in the messy here and now, yet without becoming the here and now as such. To be a self is to be suspended *in media res* between finitude and freedom, to find oneself always in the process of becoming, to be an actuality conditioned by possibility.

The Poetics of the Will

It is this relation of finitude and freedom that brings us to Ricoeur's poetics, which I argue is the most unique and important dimension of his phenomenological hermeneutics of the self. As this "poetics" is also one of the most ambiguous elements of Ricoeur's thought, however, it will take some effort on our part to tease out its meaning and possibilities.

Ricoeur originally proposed the project of a "poetics of the will" in his early *Freedom and Nature*, where it was anticipated to constitute a third stage of his larger "philosophy of the will" begun here. This volume, the first stage, was conceived of as an "eidetics" of the will, meaning (in Husserl's sense) a "bracketing of the [empirical] fact and elaborating the idea or meaning [of the will]."[18] This core "idea," as we have seen, is that the human will is in all areas involuntary and voluntary at once. Such an idea is not observable in the empirical world but rather part of each self's own specifically human mode of being-in-the-world.

Subsequently, the pair *Fallible Man* and *The Symbolism of Evil* were together conceived of as a second stage of this larger project, termed an "empirics" of the will. Empirics is meant here, not in the sense of a positivistic objective description (to which the will is obviously not reducible), but in the phenomenological sense of the self's concrete *experience* of its own will. This experience appears first, for Ricoeur, in the self's experience of evil, where the will becomes reflexively aware of itself through its own breakdown. This strategy of describing the will through its cracks and distortions anticipates Ricoeur's subsequent interest in Freud. Ricoeur claims that this disproportion of the self to itself remains unavailable to a strictly Husserlian eidetics because the pure phenomenological reduction only captures the will in its ideality. The will's breakdown and alienation requires the addition of a new methodology, which Ricoeur eventually (in *The Symbolism of Evil*) comes to describe as hermeneutics. Hermeneutics (to which I return shortly) does not here replace phenomenology but instead elevates phenomenology to a new level where it can symbolize human meaning amid its actual *lack* of meaning. I return to this lack repeatedly in the following chapters under the notion of radical evil.

What, then, is meant by the "poetics of the will"? Ricoeur initially intended for his poetics to occupy still a third level of investigation beyond these first two. However, Ricoeur never completed the intended third volume in which this poetics was to take form. As far as one can tell, this early poetics was meant to describe the possibility for "healing" the wound of evil: the possibility of the will's ultimate reconciliation with itself. Beyond the empirics of the broken will, Ricoeur calls this a "poetics" of the will's "Transcendence."[19] Poetics thus understood would attempt "to grasp willing at its source," to recapture in mythological terms the will as given to itself in "Creation."[20] It would move beyond both eidetics and empirics by recovering the possibility for a transcending affirmation of the human self as ultimately capable of living meaningfully in the world *in spite of* its own evil.

The term "poetics" is used here because the phenomena needing to be described at this third stage are human possibilities that we can only ever begin to imagine. These possibilities point us toward the unknown, the origins of human will before history and its hoped for destiny beyond. As Ricoeur put it originally in 1950:

> The completion of the ontology of the subject demands a change in method, *moving on to a kind of "Poetics"* of the will, suitable to the new realities that need to be discovered. In a basic sense of the word, poetics is the art of conjuring up the world as created. . . . This order of creation can appear to us concretely only as a death and resurrection. It means for us *the death of the Self*, as the illusion of positing of the self by the self, and the *gift of being* which heals the rent of freedom.[21]

This "gift of being" heals the will by resurrecting its own most transcendental possibilities. Only in this way could selves overcome the fallenness and guilt in which they are always already embroiled. In a way, Ricoeur appears here to be moving in the direction of a classic conception of the need for faith in some larger movement of *grace*—which is perhaps not surprising given his Reformed background, but "grace" is a term he in fact rarely invokes (although grace would clearly be understood not as imposed from above but as liberating the will from within).

These early suggestions do, in fact, anticipate many of Ricoeur's later religious hermeneutical concerns with such concepts as "creation" and "gift," as we shall see. And he continues to seek ways of describing what he here calls the will's "uncharacterizable, unobjectifiable, metaproblematic dimension."[22] But in the process of thinking through the concrete symbolism of evil, Ricoeur abandons the notion of what in this early work he had anticipated to be a "leap, in Jaspers' terms, from existence to transcendence."[23] He comes gradually to recognize the ahistoricity of any such transcendental existentialism, as well as the problematic implication of "Transcendence" itself as somehow leaving the world behind. Such a leap, indeed, does not ultimately fit Ricoeur's larger efforts to think freedom within finitude. Healing the disproportion of the self with itself will have to avoid overturning this world by some kind of existential ecstatics, and take its place within a concrete hermeneutics of meaning.

The notion of a "poetics of the will" does not, however, disappear from Ricoeur's thought. Rather, it takes on a range of more situated—both philosophical and religious—dimensions. This more mature poetics becomes evident, in fact, as early as the concluding chapter of *The Symbolism of Evil*, in one of Ricoeur's most well known and enduring phrases: "the symbol gives rise to thought."[24] This claim could serve as a summary (with modifications) of much of Ricoeur's subsequent career. A symbol (at this point Ricoeur is interested in symbols of evil, like stain, defilement, and fall) invites itself upon its interpreter already pregnant with its own preconstituted fullness of meaning. And yet it still demands active and reflective "thought." It still requires some level of interpretation into meaning for the world of a self. Symbols are not complete in themselves but realize their meaning only insofar as they contribute to the project of the will's ongoing formation of its own meaning in the world.

In this way, symbols are poetic forms of language that reveal to us something of our own most primordial humanity. They are the most immediate way to cross the divide between the self's passivity and its agency, the first means by which meaning is received and constituted simultaneously. To symbolize evil in particular is already to begin to overcome evil's radical meaninglessness and disproportionality. According to Ricoeur, symbols involve a "spontaneous hermeneutics":

> I wager that I shall have a better understanding of man and of the bond between the being of man and the being of all beings if I follow the *indication* of symbolic thought. . . . Then there opens up before me the field of philosophical hermeneutics properly so called: no longer an allegorizing interpretation that pretends to a disguised philosophy under the imaginative garments of the myth, but a philosophy that starts from the symbols and endeavors to promote the meaning, to form it, by a creative interpretation.[25]

It is this "creative interpretation" that makes symbols already "poetic." The will is formed neither in the inherited symbolic structures of language, nor in the pure freedom by which these structures may be put to use, but, rather, in their dynamic and ongoing interplay. The will creates meaning by immersing itself in symbolic depths so as thereby to interpret its world that much more profoundly. Symbols are not static objects that arrive fully formed but explosions of possibility by which selves may imagine the meaning of their own world anew.

This specifically hermeneutical poetics of the will is subsequently developed in increasingly nuanced ways in Ricoeur throughout his theories of texts, metaphors, and narratives. Late in his career, Ricoeur claims that over his oeuvre he gradually developed a broad poetics of language:

> *The Symbolism of Evil, The Rule of Metaphor, Time and Narrative* do aspire in several ways to the title of poetics, less in the sense of a meditation on primordial creation than in that of an investigation of the multiple modalities of what I will later call an ordered creation. . . . In this sense, the idea of ordered creation still belongs to a philosophical anthropology in which the relation to biblical faith and theology is held in abeyance.[26]

This larger philosophical poetics of "ordered creation" centers on the unique power of selves to interpret their larger given world into meaning for themselves through language. Metaphors and narratives share with symbols the potentiality for the self's creation of new meaning. Ricoeur's earlier eidetics of the will in fact seems to give way, not so much to a third stage of poetics, as to a recasting of the will itself in poetic, linguistic terms. Both the interrelation and the disproportion of human finitude and freedom are taken up into the plastic and inventive possibilities for meaning that arise out of the interpretation of symbols, metaphors, and stories.

The central capability that emerges in this hermeneutical poetics is the self's ability to use language for "semantic innovation." Semantic innovation refers only secondarily to the ability to make texts (stories, poems, histories, and so on). This ability is only a particularly objectified form of a more fundamental human capability—shared by authors and readers of texts alike, as well as by speakers and listeners—for the creation of meaning in life. Semantic innovation is a way to describe poetically what it means to be human as simultaneously a linguistically constituted and a linguistically self-constituting being.

The self or will's capability for the innovation of language lies at bottom in the poetic capability for what Ricoeur calls "the synthesis of the heterogeneous."[27] A metaphor, for example, draws ordinarily unrelated terms—as in "life is a tale told by idiots" (my example)—into association with one another, so as to innovate or invent a new semantic pertinence for the reader/listener. According to Ricoeur, metaphor is "the most brilliant illustration of the power of language to create meaning by the means of unexpected comparisons."[28] As the French title of his 1975 The Rule of Metaphor—La metaphor vive—suggests, "metaphor is living [vivant] not only to the extent that it vivifies a constituted language. Metaphor is living by virtue of the fact that it introduces the spark of imagination into a 'thinking more' at the conceptual level."[29] Metaphors, like symbols, give rise to thought. The chief difference is that metaphors do so through not just single terms but multiple terms' unexpected comparisons. But in each case the trajectory of their meaning ends not in themselves but in the transformed world of an interpreting self. Ricoeur is speaking here of metaphors not primarily as genres of language but as elements within a philosophical anthropology of what it means to be human.

The most important sense in which the self is poetic for our purposes, however, lies in the self's capability for narration, which, as I discuss in upcoming chapters, plays a central role in Ricoeur's writings on ethics. Both fictional and historical narratives have meaning, Ricoeur contends, not simply in and of themselves as objects in the world (true though this is to a point), but most importantly in their creative synthesis of heterogeneous events, characters, and situations for the world of meaning of their reader. The plot of a narrative is not just the events related in the text itself, but also, and in the final analysis, an imaginative set of possibilities for the self-refiguration of the world of their reader. The true "event" of language is the event of its reader's interpretation. Hamlet's dilemma has "meaning" only insofar as it changes in some way the self-understanding of the play's audience.

This Ricoeurian insistence that meaning is completed only in the inter-preting self resists a broad, though not exclusive, assumption in Western hermeneutics that meaning is complete within texts and speech. This as-sumption views meaning as an object. As we will see, both Aristotelian and Kantian poetics locate poetic innovation in the realms, not of reader, but of author and text. At its extreme, the Romantics locate meaning in the "genius" of the author *behind* the text. But Ricoeur insists that poetics finds its cul-mination instead in the presently existing selfhood of the reader "in front of" the text. Language lacks meaning altogether apart from a "reader" or "in-terpreter" who is capable of exerting a creative power of synthesizing het-erogeneous linguistic elements into an evolving world of meaning for itself. A reader does not just import stories into his own mind, or attempt to glimpse the mind of the author, but also, and more profoundly, actively and willfully refigures them. A novel like Virginia Woolf's *Mrs. Dalloway*, to use Ricoeur's own example, tells the story of a day in the life of a well-to-do Londoner, not just so that Mrs. Dalloway herself may be understood, but ultimately so that each reader may understand something better of themselves, something perhaps about loss, love, and hope in their own lives.

"Poetics" in this hermeneutical perspective relies on the human capability for creatively mediating its finitude and its freedom. Language is neither an objective fact outside selves nor a mere tool for selves to use for subjective expression. More profoundly, it is the medium within which selves may con-stitute and transform their own meaning in the world. As Ricoeur declares, "metaphorical and narrative statements, taken in hand by reading, aim at re-figuring reality, in the twofold sense of *uncovering* the concealed dimensions of human experience and of *transforming* our vision of the world."[30] This passive-active uncovering and transforming of human meaning is further from En-lightenment and Romantic poetics—focused as they are upon the subjective expressiveness of the artist—than it is the poetics of Aristotle. For Ricoeur, Aristotle shows that "the *poiêsis* of language arises out of the connection between *muthos* and *mimesis*"—the connection, that is, between an already given his-torical depths of language (*muthos*) and the possibility for its ordered meaning (*mimesis*).[31] But for Ricoeur this ordered meaning is not contained within lan-guage itself. Rather, language "gives rise" to the possibility for selves' own worlds of meaning for themselves, their own creative new thought.

Hence Ricoeur's poetics of *the will*: a poetics that finds its center of gravity in the involuntary-voluntary practice of forming an already constituted lan-guage into new innovations of meaning for oneself. As Richard Kearney, always an astute reader of Ricoeur, puts it: "Ricoeur's ultimate wager remains a hermeneutics of the creative imagination [so that] replacing the visual model of the image [as in Husserl, Sartre, and Merleau-Ponty] with the verbal, Ri-coeur affirms the more *poetical* role of imagining—that is, its ability to say one thing in terms of another, or to say several things at the same time, thereby creating something new."[32] Imagination does not lie in images or texts as such, but in the possibilities they open up for selves to create new meaning of their worlds. Poetics is not primarily a matter of receiving images from without, but of reconstituting meaning for oneself. Or, as Ricoeur himself says, "despite appearances, my single problem since beginning my reflections has been creativity"—"creativity," that is, of human being-in-the-world.[33]

Narrating Identity

The culmination of this poetics of the will is to be found in Ricoeur's late theory of the self as a "narrative identity."[34] Here, starting in the mid-1980s, Ricoeur finally gets around to describing in depth not just how selves create meaning in their world but also what kind of *self* they thereby create. As Ricoeur says, "narrative identity is the poetic resolution of the hermeneutical circle."[35] It is precisely in creating *one's own story in the world* that understanding and interpretation through language reach their poetic destination. The ultimate trajectory of interpreting the world for oneself is the interpretation of oneself in the world. Narrative identity is not just one area to which human creativity is applied. Neither is it a fixed or merely historical collection of traits. Nor, finally, is it something selves can create independently of their own given historical conditions. Rather, narrative identity is the final site within which the self may respond to its own inner disproportion of finitude and freedom. It constitutes the self's ongoing, evolving, and dynamic interpretation of its own meaning and purpose in the world.

The involuntary or finite dimension of narrative identity is described by Ricoeur with the term "character" (originally used in *Fallible Man* but developed significantly further in *Time and Narrative, Volume 3*, and *Oneself as Another*), by which he means the self's own already given history. "Character" is sometimes mistaken by narrative ethicists as the whole of the narrative person. For Ricoeur, however, it is nothing more than "the set of distinctive marks that permit the reidentification of a human individual as being the same [*la même*]," "the set of lasting dispositions *by which* a person is recognized."[36] It constitutes the self insofar as it is an object. Included in "character" so understood is anything about the self that is experienced by the self at the present moment passively, such as genetic makeup, bodily needs and desires, interests, personality, social roles, historical situatedness, and outlooks on life. Such constitute the self insofar as it is psychologically, socially, and historically observable, by itself and by others.

But character does not exhaust what it means to be a narrative self. Selfhood also involves the voluntary pole of the self's own ongoing narrative self-formation. A narrative identity is always and in every instant *my* narrative or *your* narrative, just as above we saw with respect to the body. This kind of poetic freedom Ricoeur calls "ipseity," or the self's ability, in narrative terms, to project its own life plans, to stick to projects over historical vicissitudes, to uphold promises to others, and in general to participate in the projection and formation of its own narrative identity *for itself*.[37] Ipseity, in short, refers to the reflexive experience "of mineness, of ownness."[38] It is the growing ability, as one commentator on Ricoeur puts it, for the "formation of the moral self."[39] The story of illness is the story of *my* body; that of living in community *my* community; that of belonging to certain societies and times *my* history. All narrative identity is in part, in addition to being received as character, one's own interpretive responsibility.[40]

From this angle, narrative identity includes an element of free self-creativity that is analogous to how selves are responsible for interpreting narrative texts into meaning for themselves. Narrative identity is not only what others can observe as constant over time but also the self-interpretation of a self that remains inherently innovative and self-transformative.[41] As Ricoeur puts it: "Narrative identity is not a stable and seamless identity. Just as it is possible to compose several plots on the subject of the same incidents . . . , so also it is always possible to weave different, even opposed, plots about our lives. . . . In this sense, narrative identity continues to make and unmake itself."[42] This making and unmaking of oneself is reminiscent of Greek *poiêsis* as making, forming, crafting, creating—but now applied to the self's own very person. The self understands and invents itself "both as a reader and the writer of its own life."[43] The various passively given elements of one's ongoing historicity are not merely absorbed into one's identity from without, but also creatively drawn up into the unfolding story one tells and retells of oneself. This distinguishes the narratives the self tells of itself from any narrative that could be told of it by others—its unique element of own-ness. The self creates narratives of itself in order to render productive its own disproportion of finite constitutedness *by* the world and free constitution *of* it.

"Narrative identity" is in the end irreducible to either character or ipseity, but instead mediates these involuntary and voluntary poles of the self in the ongoing story the self weaves and develops of its own meaning over time in the world. Such a story remains more or less fragmented; it can become more or less meaningfully developed and worked out. Furthermore, it can and must be woven in many different ways in relation to the narrative identities of others, so that, as we will see, narrative identity is ethical and moral inherently. But hermeneutically speaking, it is only through its own narrative identity, in the end, that the self may gain and form for itself a certain measure of meaningful ongoing self-constancy. As Ricoeur puts it, "self-constancy refers to a self instructed by the works of a culture that it has applied to itself."[44] The self overcomes its own historical fragmentation, not by adopting a constant historicity, but only to the extent that it develops a coherent and meaningful story of its own. Its historical conditions are not set aside or overridden but, rather, taken up into a "thinking more" at the level of the self's own developing life. Narrative identity is the meeting point of being narrated by history and narrating history for oneself, a meeting point of necessarily ongoing self-formation.

It turns out, in a way, although Ricoeur himself does not exactly say as much, that Ricoeur's theory of narrative identity constitutes a kind of "poetics of the will" after all. I have not yet spoken, of course, of selfhood in any radical or religious sense. But in terms of philosophical anthropology, the will now appears in its full capability for freely forming its own finite being in the world. If human life is filled with an indescribable *lack* of meaning—a sense that we are not who we could be, that we are only fragmented and partial beings—it is also open to the *possibility* for meaning, a possibility which it is each of our responsibilities to poetically make and remake for ourselves. It is not just that we *could* create meaningful narratives of our lives if we so chose. It is that self-creation is part of what it means to be a human being in the world. Even naming one's life as lacking meaning is a way of beginning again to create a narrative of it. Human being and not-being are inextricably related in dynamic self-formation. Their disproportion is overcome only insofar as the self narrates its own concrete identity over time. My own story in the world is neither something handed to me already complete nor something made up however I wish it. It is fashioned through the rich symbols and languages of my world in a process of ongoing narrative self-making.

The Meaning of Tradition

Before examining the religious implications of such a poetics of the will, let me first narrow the discussion to the more specifically ethical question of the meaning of tradition. Such an exploration brings us, in a way, into the heart of the contemporary debate about the meaning of selfhood in relation to history. For it was precisely in part a reliance on tradition that founders of modernist ethics like Hume, Kant, and Mill sought to overcome—in each case (albeit in different ways) claiming the primacy instead of human freedom. From the Enlightenment's point of view, tradition, if left to itself, leads to gross injustices like religious persecution, unresolvable violence like Europe's brutal and devastating Thirty Years War, and all manner of social oppression, irrationality, and inequality.

And yet today it is precisely this abstracted human freedom, removed from its traditional, historical, and social contexts, that so often comes under ethical attack. The modernist autonomous moral self stands accused of empty individualism, cynicism, nihilism, and relativism, and can also be blamed for marginalizing, oppressing, and colonizing the other. Hans-Georg Gadamer argues that "the fundamental prejudice of the Enlightenment is the prejudice against prejudice itself which denies tradition of its power."[45] Alasdair MacIntyre insists that "there is no standing ground, no place for enquiry, no way to engage in the practices of advancing, evaluating, accepting, and rejecting reasoned argument apart from that which is provided by some particular tradition or other."[46] What is common to these disavowals of modernist freedom, despite coming from diverse points of view, is the insistence that moral life has to do in the first place with passivity more than agency, finitude more than freedom, traditionality more than individuality.

Ricoeur's poetics of the will offers a third way. With regard to the question of tradition in particular, it suggests that freedom versus traditionality is a false alternative. The more fundamental ethical problem when it comes to human historicity consists instead precisely in finitude and freedom's creative narrative mediation. On the one hand, just because the self can critique historical traditions does not make traditions morally relative. On the other hand, just because traditions provide languages and histories that pre-constitute moral thought does not mean selves must not also interpret traditions' meaning freely for themselves. Insofar as traditions are *human* phenomena, their ethical meaning must lie somewhere in between.

Ricoeur's implication, which will sound odd to modernists and anti-modernists alike, is in fact that moral traditions ultimately *are* selves. Traditions may effect consciousness before consciousness effects itself, and they may be transmitted only by a larger history of texts. But their meaning, value, and significance are completed only in their interpretation into selves' own unfolding narrative identities. Selves can only be constituted *by* traditions insofar as they are also constitutive *of* them. Likewise, selves can only constitute traditions *into* meaning for themselves insofar as they open themselves to constitution *from* them. A tradition, like a body, is in each and every instance my tradition, your tradition, someone's tradition. Tradition does not merely precede, but more fundamentally is an element *within* the human self's ontological project of meaningful self-formation. In other words, tradition should be understood as an element of the poetics of the will: the self's ongoing effort to create a meaningful identity within the world.

This rather unique view of tradition (moral and otherwise) places Ricoeur in tension not only with the rather flat historicist notions of tradition shared by modernists and antimodernists alike, but also with closer phenomeno-logical notions as well. Ricoeur claims to synthesize on the one hand Husserlian phenomenology with on the other Gadamerian hermeneutics, ending up reducible to neither. Don Ihde claims that Ricoeur's blending of phenomenology and hermeneutics begins as early as Ricoeur's French publication in 1960 of *The Symbolism of Evil*, which would make it the same year as Gadamer's German publication of *Truth and Method*. In subsequent work, Ricoeur critically refashions a great deal from Gadamer into his own reflexive anthropology. Ricoeur is not finally a Gadamerian, however. For one thing, as we see in chapter 4, Ricoeur largely shares Jürgen Habermas's serious objections to Gadamer's *moral* neglect of the realities of traditions' systematic distortions. But, even hermeneutically, Ricoeur's poetics of the will refuses to separate self-reflexivity from hermeneutical historicity, and it is this relation that interests us here.

What Ricoeur takes from Gadamer is the notion that tradition means "historically effected consciousness" (*wirkungsgeschichtliches Bewußtsein*).[47] Gadamer shows that human understanding (*Verstehen*) as such is always already preconstituted by a larger history of language: "Understanding is to be thought of [in hermeneutical theory] less as a subjective act than as participating in an event of tradition, a process of transmission in which past and present are constantly mediated."[48] According to Ricoeur, in Gadamer "the rehabilitation of prejudice, authority and tradition will thus be directed against the reign of subjectivity and interiority. . . . [I]t attests to the resurgence of the historical dimension over the moment of reflection."[49] Beyond earlier hermeneutical thinkers like Friedrich Schleiermacher and Wilhelm Dilthey, Gadamer saw that traditional texts are not just *objects* of reflection, to which hermeneutical processes may be applied in order to divine the intentions of their author. Rather, they carry within them the transmission of the very languages and culture that constitute us as *subjects*. Traditions are not primarily things we apply ourselves to, but depictions of our very understanding's point of departure. It is by reflecting on traditional texts that, for Gadamer, we truly reflect on ourselves: "To be situated within a tradition does not limit the freedom of knowledge but makes it possible."[50]

What Ricoeur questions in Gadamer, however, is his notion of the "distance" between traditional texts and selves. In Gadamer, this distance is one of time: the distance through which history is transmitted from the past into the present. This distance is covered by texts in their capacity to fund the languages by which selves may subsequently interpret themselves. For Ricoeur, however, the distance is more profoundly one of the status of texts in human meaning. Texts belong as much to the present as to the past, opening selves up to new worlds of meaning that challenge existing self-understanding from a new point of view. "Consciousness of being exposed to the effects of history . . . is not reducible [as in Gadamer] to the properly lingual aspects of the transmission of the past. . . . The interplay of distance and proximity, constitutive of the historical connection, is what comes to language [in texts] rather than what language produces."[51] Traditional texts have their origins in the past, but they project before selves *alternative* worlds of meaning for the present, worlds that stand in some contrast to the worlds of meaning those selves already inhabit.

Tradition on this view is therefore not only "historically effected consciousness." Its interpretation is not just a matter of what Gadamer calls "the fusion of horizons" in which tradition uncovers understanding (*Verstehen*). Rather, traditional texts and self-understanding stand in necessary tension with one another. The meaning of a tradition lies not within its texts themselves but in the transformed narrative identity of the self that is formed "in front of" traditional texts. Texts do not "effect" meaning directly but provide indirect opportunities for innovating it. The effect of traditions is not the same thing as self-understanding. Rather, traditional texts challenge self-understanding to become something it is *not yet*. Here, in a way, we find in Ricoeur the partial influence of French structuralism, for as Claude Lévi-Strauss argues, traditions exhibit their own independent linguistic structures. Traditions are not just expressions of our own historical "thrownness" (perhaps here Gadamer is too influenced by Heidegger), but textualized worlds of meaning that stand at a creative distance from the worlds of meaning of those who choose to participate in and interpret them.

It is in this way that Ricoeur begins to include within tradition-oriented hermeneutics what he calls a "hermeneutics of suspicion." This often misunderstood term actually comes from Ricoeur's early work on Marx,

Nietzsche, and Freud. Ricoeur never reduces hermeneutics to suspicion as such, as many influenced by these thinkers have done. Tradition is never simply the enemy, whether economically, historically, or psychologically. Rather, the hermeneutics of suspicion is first used by Ricoeur (prior to further ethical uses that I explore in chapter 4) to insist that historical consciousness is always to be subject to the test of its present meaning *for the self*. Gadamer's "experience of belonging" to traditions is to be balanced against what Habermas calls the human being's "interest in emancipation." While in Ricoeur (as we will also see) this interest does not establish procedural norms to be *applied to* traditions, it does locate the meaning of moral tradition not just in history itself but in its present meaning for actual persons. According to Ricoeur, in an explicit effort to mediate Gadamer and Habermas on this particular point, the meaning of tradition lies in a "dialectic of the recollection of tradition and the anticipation of freedom."[52] The need for suspicion of and emancipation from tradition does not arise, first of all, from traditions' potential for distortion but from the fact that traditions lack meaning altogether apart from the freedom of selves to interpret them.

The best way to understand this development beyond Gadamer is to see how Ricoeur blends Gadamer with Husserl. From Husserl, Ricoeur retains (like many postwar French intellectuals) the notion of meaning as constituted *intentionally*. That is, in phenomenological terms, consciousness is not just received from the past but always also a consciousness *of* something. Meaning is constituted in relation to its present and existing world. This makes self-understanding, at least in part, an ongoing "project" or "task" to be accomplished. "That consciousness is outside of itself, that it is *toward meaning* before meaning is for it and, above all, before consciousness is *for itself*, is this not what the central discovery of phenomenology implies?"[53] Husserl, despite not taking up tradition as a central category himself, helps Ricoeur build a case that traditional texts are not just representations of an already given historicity, but also phenomenological "objects" that draw selves out into a larger world. Any fusion of horizons must at the same time consist in a self's intentional projection of meaning. This notion of intentionality lies in the background of Ricoeur's poetics of the will insofar as the latter involves "willing" as such: not just the reconstitution of history but also the *constitution* of historical meaning as singularly one's own. Traditions ultimately belong to meaning, and not the other way around.

Ricoeur, however, rejects what he views as Husserl's "idealism."[54] After the hermeneutical turn of Heidegger and Gadamer, it is no longer possible to reduce consciousness to perception, as Husserl does. Consciousness constitutes itself only through the indirect mediation of language. Critiquing Husserl, Ricoeur claims that "all interpretation places the interpreter *in media res* and never at the beginning or the end [of understanding]. We suddenly arrive, as it were, in the middle of a conversation which has already begun and in which we try to orient ourselves in order to be able to contribute to it."[55] No projection of meaning onto the world can take place without making use of (even if forming as one's own) existing symbols, metaphors, and narratives.

Indeed, Ricoeur claims, "the phenomenology which arose with the discovery of the universal character of intentionality has not remained faithful to its own discovery, namely that the meaning of consciousness lies outside of itself."[56] It is in texts, Ricoeur claims, that one can make good on Husserl's own ambition to describe consciousness *in relation to* its world, for texts provide the reflexive means for self-consciousness to escape its own enclosed subjectivity.

This dual sense of hermeneutical constitutedness and phenomenological self-constitution is brought together in Ricoeur's distinctive theory of a "hermeneutical arc" of the self's capability for the constitution of its own meaning. In *Time and Narrative, Volume 3* (part of a later set of explicitly poetic writings on narrative), Ricoeur provides his most sophisticated explanation of how tradition plays a role in selves' innovation of self-understanding. This hermeneutical arc is one continuous movement of the self's poetic formation of meaning. But it can be broken down into three simultaneously operating dimensions of "traditionality," "traditions" (plural), and "tradition per se."[57] This "movement" (in a logical rather than temporal sense) parallels Ricoeur's early philosophy of the will. It traces the way in which tradition involves at once a *passive* Gadamerian reception of the past and an *active* Husserlian projection of meaning, which are mediated by the self's production of its own concrete narrative identity. We might call this movement a hermeneutical poetics, since it is still another form of semantic innovation, but now in the fullness of the historicity of the self. It helps us see how tradition functions as a complex phenomenon that belongs ultimately to selves' efforts to create meaning in their world.

The first moment of "traditionality" is closely allied to Gadamer's "history of effects," but even here Ricoeur finds an inchoate sense in which it is actively formed into meaning. According to Ricoeur, "what is at stake in the hermeneutics of historical consciousness is the tension between the horizon of the past and that of the present.... [T]he temporal distance separating us from the past is not a dead interval but a transmission that is *generative of meaning*."[58] This process of a tradition's historical "sedimentation" (a term adapted from Husserl) is more passive than active, but it still involves an element of the self's deliberate taking upon itself of its available linguistic horizons:[59]

> The past is revealed to us through the projection of a historical ho-
> rizon that is both detached from the horizon of the present and taken
> up into and fused with it. This idea of a temporal horizon as some-
> thing that is both projected and separate, distinguished and included,
> brings about the dialectizing of the idea of traditionality.... Effective-
> history, we might say, is what takes place without us. The fusion
> of horizons is what we attempt to bring about.[60]

The subtle difference from Gadamer here is that, while selves *belong to* an effective history, the meaning of their world is not reducible to it. Selves also actively *constitute* their past horizons because they remain ultimately creatures of the present. A good way to think of this relation to one's past is through Ricoeur's above-mentioned notion of symbols. The "spontaneous hermeneutics" evoked by symbols involves not just receptivity to their already given richness but also one's own "thought" given rise to by them.[61]

But the voluntary dimensions of the interpretation of tradition only come to full realization on the second level of "traditions" (plural). The plural is presumably used here because we are no longer speaking of the vast unstructured sea of language that constitutes the "traditionality" into which we are already born, but, rather, discrete objectifications of language in actual texts. Traditional texts can be separated and labeled as, for example, Aristotelian, Buddhist, American, folk, and so on. It may seem odd to see "texts" as introducing into interpretation a greater level of voluntariness, but Ricoeur's point is that their greater distance from the self as objects in the world opens the self up to more active modes of self-interpretation. Texts stand before us as not just expressions of our own given historicity but also expressions in their own right. They are not amorphous sedimentations but relatively distinct and structured linguistic "innovations" of their own, forms of language that someone at some point in time deliberately fashioned into a particular shape and structure.[62] While texts still need to be formed by their reader into meaning, there is a sense in which they have also already been formed as meaningful by someone else (even, incidentally, if that someone else is the same person who later goes back and reads them).

Unfortunately, despite its being one of the most important elements of his hermeneutics, exactly what Ricoeur means by "texts" is not always clear. David Pellauer suggests, and I agree, that Ricoeur means to use the term quite broadly for "any group of signs which may be characterized as a work—i.e. as constituted by a composition, a genre, a style."[63] Ricoeur himself offers up the "written" text as a paradigm because the written text is the form of configured language which is most evidently "fixed" as an exterior phenomenon in the world.[64] But he also ascribes text-like functions to other forms of language like dreams, discourse, and even "meaningful actions."[65] Presumably, on this score, textual "traditions" (plural) could in principle (although Ricoeur does not say so) include oral narratives passed down through the generations, rituals, works of art, and even inherited practices that are repeated over time. One could argue that Ricoeur's emphasis on *written* texts, while understandable given his desire to show how traditions objectify themselves, risks suggesting that cultures that rely on nonwritten forms of language are somehow less critically capable of meaning. If so, we should insist, by contrast, that *any* configured structure of language constitutes a "text" insofar as it appears before the self as an object capable of explication in itself.

What is useful about Ricoeur's notion of "text," however, is that it captures the sense in which, beyond traditionality, language gains a certain "distanciation" or "intentional exteriorization" in and of itself.[66] It is his novel theory of textual distanciation that Ricoeur himself claims is his major contribution to hermeneutical theory. "Distanciation" has in Ricoeur a range of related possible meanings: the emancipation of texts from their original historical situation by lasting over time; their transcendence of the original intentions of their author by becoming fixed in structures; their freedom from the context of their original audience by being able to be read in principle by anyone; and their independent intentionality with respect to their reader— that is, their forming an independent "world of the text" that speaks for itself and is not reducible to any one interpretation of it.[67]

All these meanings of textual distanciation together indicate that, unlike for Gadamer, for Ricoeur a traditional text (like any text) does not simply transmit the past. It also, and even more importantly, stands as an objectivized structure of meaning that must be read and confronted in its own right.

> The moment of distanciation is implied by fixation in writing and
> by all comparable phenomena in the sphere of discourse. Writing is
> not simply a matter of the material fixation of discourse; for fixation
> is the condition of a much more fundamental phenomenon, that of
> the autonomy of the text. . . . What the text signifies no longer coin-
> cides with what the author meant.[68]

This distanciated "autonomy" of texts means they are "proposals of meaning" whose "reference is the truth value of the proposition, its claim to reach reality."[69] As Jean Ladriere has described this element in Ricoeur, texts raise merely inherited language (that is, traditionality) to a hermeneutically "critical" level through their intentionally structured composition.[70] This does not mean that all texts are true—only that they all (in one sense or another) *claim* to be true. Simply by being fixed in writing, a text claims to transcend the particular and the time-bound to say something of larger significance in the world. In contrast with the hermeneutics of Schleiermacher and the Romantics, which view reading as the divination of the "genius" of the author *behind* the text, for Ricoeur reading must enter into the structured intentionality of the "world of the text" itself. Texts are not just expressions of the past but stand as their own distinctively structured phenomena challenging the world of the present.[71]

Traditional (and other) texts ultimately, for Ricoeur, have an emancipatory function. It is true that texts can be used to oppress, but unlike the mass of language into which each of us is unconsciously born, they can also reveal new worlds of meaning to a reader by which the reader may gain new perspectives on their own given historicity. Because they structure language, texts provide the occasion for a self-critical or reflexive distance from language as it is already inherited. The "hermeneutics of suspicion" itself relies on textuality: new manifestos against ideology, poems of the coming Zarathustra, interpretations of dreams and transferences, novels that expose us to new experiences, myths that stretch our imaginations to their limits. Language is not just a sedimentary but also an innovative force, opening up the world of the self as much as enclosing it. As we will see, this distanciated phenomenology of language distinguishes Ricoeur, among other things, from any kind of final Hegelian totalization of history. History is not the expression of an evolving historical Spirit, but an open-ended and partially free and reflexive narrative. "It is the very project of totalization that indicates the break between Hegel's philosophy of history and every model of understanding, however distantly akin, to the idea of narration and emplotment . . . [so that] the leaving behind of Hegelianism signifies renouncing the attempt to decipher the *supreme* plot."[72] Through the interpretative distance opened up by texts, traditional meaning remains infinitely free to renewal, in an ongoing historical story that no past could possibly ever predict.

The culminating moment in Ricoeur's theory of tradition, however, lies not in texts themselves, but in the event of interpretation "in front of the text" in which the self-understanding of a reader is transformed. This "event" of reading separates Ricoeur's view of language from that of a great deal of French structuralism and poststructuralism, to which he is otherwise quite close. The culmination of language for Ricoeur is not textuality per se. Meaning is not caught up finally within textual structures or textual difference. The meaning of texts lies within each particular interpreter of them. Of course, this meaning is constituted in language. But, as Ricoeur insists, it is also constituted ultimately in the expression of the freedom, and the self-constituting poetics, of a self. We return again to a kind of poetics of the will.

The interpreting self is ultimately required, for Ricoeur, because there is an otherwise unbridgeable gap between traditionality on the one hand (language as preconstituted historicity) and textuality on the other (language as configured structure). It is only in bridging this gap or tension that language rises to the level of "meaning" per se. More specifically, the meaning of tradition lies neither in inherited historicity nor in the texts by which history is transmitted, but in history's passive-active interpretation into new self-understanding. As David Klemm succinctly puts it, this third moment in Ricoeur "completes the hermeneutical process because at this stage the meaning of the text is brought out of alienation into familiarity."[73] Simply put, a text itself is just a collection of signs and words, marks on a page; it can have meaning only insofar as it is deliberately refigured into the changed world of an interpreter.

For this reason, Ricoeur calls this culminating third moment of interpretation "tradition per se." Ricoeur's provocative axiom is this: "the process of composition [of a text] . . . is not completed in the text but in the reader."[74] It is here that Ricoeur's unique synthesis of hermeneutics (Gadamer) and phenomenology (Husserl) becomes most clear. Tradition per se is a "claim to truth" in the reader's life—a claim not limited to the structures of the text itself, but constituted by the possibilities for restructuring the being-in-the-world of its interpreter.[75] Hermeneutical interpretation is completed in the way that a self's already *pre*figured historicity, by means of the *con*figurations opened up by texts, is *re*figured into meaning. Texts are ultimately "detours" of language that subject already inherited linguistic forms to new critical reflection, detours that open up possibilities for greater linguistic self-consciousness and self-understanding. Our preconstituted horizons of understanding can also be constituted structurally through textual interpretation. Ultimately, "in hermeneutical reflection—or in reflective hermeneutics—the constitution of the *self* is contemporaneous with the constitution of *meaning*."[76] Tradition per se is nothing other than this event of the self's passive-active intepretation of the meaning of its own historical being-in-the-world.

What is "poetic" here, and the reason I think Ricoeur's hermeneutics is ultimately the expression of a poetics of the will, is that tradition is an event or process of self-transformation. Tradition per se is neither purely preconstituted from the past nor entirely open to free use, but rather a living and ongoing refiguration of linguistic meaning in the self. Like symbols, metaphors, and narratives, traditions are forms of language in which subjectivity gains a concrete reflective purchase on itself. The full dimensions of the interpretation of tradition involve the self's reconstruction of the meaning of its own world. In this, Ricoeur says, tradition is like reading a piece of music:

> Bringing a text to language is always something other than hearing
> someone and listening to his speech. Reading resembles instead
> the performance of a musical piece regulated by the written nota-
> tion of the score. For the text is an autonomous space of meaning
> which is no longer animated by the intention of its author; the au-
> tonomy of the text, deprived of this essential support, hands writing
> over to the sole interpretation of the reader.[77]

Traditional texts are the historical scores by which we may express and deepen present self-understanding. As Ricoeur claims elsewhere, this kind of "mediation by the text is the model of a distanciation which would not be simply alienating...but which would be genuinely creative."[78] What is "creative" here? It is that nothing is simply already given, neither our historicity nor the meaning of texts. What is given is only that human selves are the kinds of beings who can creatively refigure themselves through language, whose traditions are part of their efforts, ultimately, to narrate the meaning of their lives. As Theodore Marius Van Leeuwen has well put it, Ricoeur sees in language "the surplus of meaning"—a surplus of the meaning of historicity, I would add, that it is each self's responsibility to create.[79]

I believe Ricoeur's view of tradition lays to rest the heart of the debate between modernists and antimodernists over the relative moral primacy of traditions or selves. This debate turns on a false dichotomy. Selves can have meaning for themselves only on the linguistic basis of inherited traditions, and traditions can have meaning only for freely self-interpreting selves. The opposition of self and tradition really goes back to Descartes's separation of subjectivity from objectivity, the *res cogitans* from the *res extensio*, a separation which of course is challenged by Husserlian phenomenology and Gadamerian hermeneutics alike. Ricoeur shows that traditions belong to selves under the larger rubric of the poetics of the will. Traditions are not just fixed inheritances from the past, whether through historicity or through texts, but always also, and at the same time, elements within selves' intentional efforts to narrate and transform their own world of meaning. Tradition lies in the dynamic tension between historical passivity and interpretive agency in which language gives rise to thought. Hermeneutics is poetic because this tension is

never the mere repetition of the past but always the past's creative refiguration. Tradition is a peculiarly human phenomenon, contributing to each self's
ongoing formation of a meaningful narrative identity in its world.

I do not want to leave Ricoeur's poetic view of tradition without indicating
one criticism of it that is relevant to our moral investigations in the following
chapters. While Ricoeur well describes the tensions between tradition's finitude and freedom, I do not think he does as good a job of noting the possible
tensions within traditional finitude itself. That is, to put it simply, traditional
histories and texts do in fact frequently oppose the emancipation of self-
understanding and, instead, reinforce existing meaninglessness, violence, and
oppression. Ricoeur's hermeneutics of suspicion allows us to use texts to
critique historicity, but what of the need to critique the uses of those texts
themselves, as well as their historical complicity? On some level, the story of
Adam and Eve might open up ways in which to imagine our own primordially
creative possibilities. At the same time, however, historically this story has had
quite the opposite effect: whether in condemning humankind of unalterable
sin, condoning violence toward non-Christians, or justifying the oppression
of women. There is also the further, and related, problem of the historicity of
traditional texts themselves: that is, the need to critique the situations of
patriarchy and power by which they were composed and transmitted in the
first place. Such conditions should restrict our optimism about the potential use of traditional texts for emancipating our own meaningful self-
understanding, even if they need not destroy it.

I argue in the following chapters that, while Ricoeur rightly relates historicity and freedom around the poetics of self-narration, historicity itself should
add to self-narration a greater sense of moral tragedy. Without abandoning the
poetic tension of freedom and finitude in Ricoeur's hermeneutics, finitude itself
will need to be deepened to include its more disordered and violent dimensions.
Traditions could be called "tragic" in the sense that they easily, perhaps inevitably, underwrite the very moral disenfranchisement they can be used to critique. However much textuality provides a means for the distanciated suspicion
of historicity, history itself should teach us to suspect our use of texts. Ricoeur is
not without resources for suggesting such a moral suspicion of traditions, for
ultimately he is interested in the freedom to transform meaning for oneself. But
without a greater sense for the distortion of language over time—indeed, as I will
argue, without connecting self-narration to human radical evil—he cannot describe the poetics of self-interpretation in its truly fundamental depths. There are
a number of postmodern, feminist, and even contemporary Aristotelian perspectives on moral tragedy that will help us complicate, in this way, our developing poetics of moral meaning.

Creativity Before God

What might this poetics of the will—in all its symbolic, narrative, and traditional dimensions—have to do with religion? Ricoeur has long separated his

religious writings from his philosophical ones, all the way back, in fact, to his abandoned early project of a poetics of the will. This separation is made chiefly for the pragmatic reason of being able to speak to diverse intellectual audiences, many of which are deeply skeptical of religion in any form. In the introduction to *Oneself as Another*, Ricoeur justifies leaving out two of the original Gifford Lectures (on which this book is based) on the self before God, by saying he wishes to avoid the charge of "cryptotheology," or writing from a hidden theological agenda. This is a charge to which he is in fact subject, particularly in the secular academy in France. I return to this separation of discourses shortly. The fact remains, however, that Ricoeur is among only a small minority of twentieth-century phenomenologists to devote significant attention to religious themes, especially religious ethics, and while he distinguishes religion from philosophy repeatedly, he also does not hesitate to point out their connections. Even at the very end of *Oneself as Another*, for example, he characteristically avers that "perhaps the philosopher as philosopher has to admit that one does not know and cannot say whether this Other, the source of the [ethical] injunction, is another person . . . or God—living God, absent God—or an empty place. With this aporia of the Other, philosophical discourse comes to an end."[80]

My argument is that the creation of meaning in the world rests on inherent and necessary, even if able to be bracketed, religious presuppositions. Ricoeur's original project of a poetics of the will related to Creation itself should be taken up again—even if not in the Jasperian existential terms in which Ricoeur originally planned it, and even if Ricoeur himself does not complete it. The human capability for the creation of meaning is ultimately a mystery that cannot be reduced to any humanly created meaning per se. The poetic moral self is a paradox to itself, understandable only in the end in primordial and mythological terms. The creative capability must ultimately be *affirmed*, even if it cannot be seen, as lying at the radical origins of humanity itself. It is called for as a response to the question of why it is possible, despite failure, for human beings to create a meaningful sense for the very capability for creating meaning at all. Religion finds a new kind of significance for ethics, beyond its suspicion from modernity, in a radical hermeneutical poetics.

Ricoeur's own religious hermeneutics has had a significantly greater influence in the English-speaking world than in Europe. David Tracy, for example, uses Ricoeur to argue that religious traditions are "correlated" with the world's present situation, not just in Paul Tillich's sense of answering present questions, but also in the more radically transforming sense of, in turn, questioning the present from a revelatory point of view.[81] Sallie McFague appropriates Ricoeur into feminist theology to speak of what she calls a "reforming, transforming" religious hermeneutics based on "the *tension* which is at the heart of metaphor" (I come back to McFague in chapter 4).[82] Richard Kearney takes up Ricoeur's poetics of symbol and myth to speak of the paradoxical human capability for "narrating" "those frontiers that mark the passage between same and other, real and imaginary, known and unknown" and for approaching "the God who may be."[83] This is not to say that Ricoeur has not influenced the new Continental thinkers about religion such as Jean-Louis Chrétien, Michel Henry, and, most especially, Jean-Luc Marion. But here, the influence is for the most part less explicitly or fully developed.

Commentators on Ricoeur's religious hermeneutics of the self generally agree that it stands somewhere in between two of the great rival religious hermeneutics of the twentieth century: Karl Barth's renewed appreciation for the strangeness and autonomy of the world of the Bible, and Paul Tillich's correlational approach to the meaning of the religious kerygma for the self's contemporary situation.[84] What is less agreed upon is where along this Barth-Tillich polarity Ricoeur's third way should finally be located. Since in large part the issue between Barth and Tillich is the relation of sacred texts to selves—or, the freedom of God to our freedom to interpret God—Ricoeur's mediating position will be an outgrowth of his poetics of the meaning of tradition above. The best way to understand what is poetic about religion in Ricoeur, however, is to see how he incorporates a Barthian imperative of listening to sacred texts in their own disorienting right with a Tillichian insistence that sacred texts have meaning for the reorientation of contemporary culture. The result is what I would call a *poetics of religion* that radicalizes Tillich by way of Barth. Such a view points toward the possibility for a postmodern theology of culture—in other words, a post-Barthian Tillichianism.

Ricoeur's deep sympathy with Barth, shared by a great deal of contemporary Continental religious thought, lies in a desire to preserve sacred texts' originality and force as speaking to human beings in the voice of the Wholly Other. Ricoeur takes up what he calls Barth's "broken dialectic" of textual interpretation, which he contrasts to the conciliatory and conclusive dialectic of Hegel: "[Whereas] for Hegel the dialectic is that of the Spirit that makes the difference between God and the human mind irrelevant, for Barth the dialectic deepens the gap between the Wholly Other and the world of creatures."[85] Hegel's crypto-philosophical view of God is a form of idolism, and "the idols must die so that the [sacred] symbols may live."[86] Like Jean-Luc Marion (who inherited Ricoeur's chair at the University of Chicago Divinity School, a chair first held by Tillich), who is also close to Barth in many ways, Ricoeur insists on a distinction between ordinary and religious meaning so as to refuse the reduction of God to being-in-the-world or even to Being itself. Ricoeur would find nothing strange in Marion's distinction between the idol, which "displaces the limits of our visibility to the measure of its own," and the icon, which "unbalances human sight in order to engulf it in infinite depth."[87] But Ricoeur speaks more broadly of the disorienting intrusion of God into the world through multiple symbolic, mythological, and poetic languages.

This Barthian side of Ricoeur is most evident in Ricoeur's concept of religious "limit-expressions." These function as aporetic forms of language that "bring about the rupturing of ordinary speech" and "burst" or "explode" our all too human structures of self-understanding.[88] The language of "limits" is of course Kantian, and for this reason is suspect among postmodernists. But Ricoeur radicalizes it to indicate, not just the limits of human reason (as in "religion within the limits of reason alone"), but the limits of all human language and meaning. For instance, in God's command to Abraham to sacrifice his son Isaac, despite God having promised Isaac as Abraham's long-awaited heir, the reader finds a disorienting proposal of meaning that exceeds all that can in fact be comprehended. Such hyperbolic, "scandalous" texts do not provide *reasons* for action—Abraham's intentions are, in ordinary moral terms, a ghastly crime—but, rather, press the self-understanding of readers to their extreme imaginative limits. The "limit" here is not a boundary but a disruption. In this way, the self may be exposed to the Wholly Other God who defies exposure by the self.

Such limits are not merely abstract. Rather, Ricoeur attributes their function of disorienting rupture to their very linguistic concreteness, such as in the Bible's creation stories, psalms, prophesies, sayings, parables, and visions of the end of time. For example:

> The extraordinary within the ordinary, such is the logic of meaning in the parables. Consider, for example, the extravagance of the land-lord in the parable of the evil tenants. After having sent his servants, he sends his son. What Palestinian landowner would act in such a foolish way? And what of the host in the parable of the great banquet who searches in the streets for guests to replace those who had been invited? Or the father in the parable of the prodigal son? Does he not exceed all the boundaries of complacency?[89]

Indeed, according to Ricoeur, "there is no parable that does not introduce into the very structure of the plot an implausible characteristic, something inso-lent, disproportionate; that is, something scandalous. Thus it is the contrast between the realism of the story and the extravagance of the denouement that gives rise to the kind of drift by means of which the plot and its point are suddenly carried off toward the Wholly Other."[90] While Ricoeur largely limits himself to examples from the Bible, for which he may justifiably be criticized, his larger argument is that religion's unique function overall (for better or for worse) is to press meaning to its farthest possible limits. Only in this self-disrupting way can it open us to what is hidden at the origins of the world as we can know and understand it.

While it would be tempting on this reading to reject religious symbolism as therefore irrational and unusable for understanding the human self, Ri-coeur claims that this disorienting function of religious language is finally necessary if selves are to regrasp their own primordial humanity. Limit-expressions have exactly the opposite function of what Jean-Francois Lyotard calls "grand narratives," for they question and subvert all totalities of mean-ing, indeed the very project of totality itself. Ricoeur reads Barth, in fact, as having shown decisively that the Bible does not present us with a coherent religious narrative at all. This contrasts with certain North American com-munitarian readings of Barth, following Stanley Hauerwas, as interested in the Bible as a given narrative after which to pattern our lives. For Ricoeur, the function of naming God in the Bible is precisely to "dissuade hearers in some way from forming a coherent project of their lives and from making their existence into a continuous whole."[91] Religious texts bring us up against a Wholly Other who cannot ultimately be narrated, a God beyond Being who radically precedes history as we can ever actually know or tell it, indeed the very origin of the possibility for narrative meaning at all.

Beyond Barth, however, Ricoeur is interested in how this kind of hyperbolic disorientation through religious texts may function as the occasion in the end for radical self-transformation. As we saw above, the reading of texts can be for Ricoeur no more than a moment of distanciation within the larger hermeneutical arc of the self's formation of the meaning of its own world. This is just as true for sacred, disruptive, limit-expression texts as for any other. Disorientation, as Ricoeur puts it, cannot mean anything except insofar as it gives rise to some *reorientation* of self-understanding.[92] This does not mean that religious texts are finally reducible to human meaning. It means that, phenomenologically speaking, they are disruptive only insofar as they are disruptive *of someone.* Even sacred traditions and scriptures are ultimately *my* or *your* scriptures. However disorienting and inexplicable, religious meaning still belongs ultimately to a self, in its ongoing effort to interpret, however impossibly, the meaning of its life.

As Mark Wallace has described it, Ricoeur's biblical hermeneutics therefore involves a "wager"—a wager that "the God who is named in the Bible [can] be experienced again in contemporary communities of interpretation."[93] This wager, Wallace claims, goes beyond merely deconstructing the text or pointing out its strangeness, to include also "project[ing] a world of unimagined possibilities for the believer-reader."[94] This means, in our terms, that religious texts are self-transformative, except now, unlike other kinds of texts, by means of the disorienting rupture of the Wholly Other. The command in Luke 6:27 to "love your enemies," for example (a command to which I return in chapter 3), may be impossible actually to imagine or practice; it may even be scandalous as an actual social norm. But it can nevertheless function to "give rise to thought" by radically reorienting a person's understanding of the meaning of moral love.

It is in this respect that Ricoeur finally embeds Barthian radicalism *within* a larger movement of Tillichian correlation. According to Ricoeur, religious language decenters self-understanding only by opening up new self-interpretation. For Tillich, sacred texts have meaning insofar as they are correlated with the ultimate concerns of the historical situation into which they are interpreted.[95] Tillich's "theology of culture" is an exercise in appropriating scriptural revelation as a response to the questions of contemporary thought and practice (influencing a generation of neo-orthodox, liberationist, and feminist hermeneutics).[96] Ricoeur states his ultimate preference for such correlationism over Barth's heady other-worldliness explicitly: "I would not say that [Barth's] christological turn as such constitutes a breach of the pledge no longer to return to the conciliatory mood of pre-Kantian and post-Kantian theodicies, although I would feel more comfortable with the method of correlation applied to both Christian symbols *and* human experience by Paul Tillich, Langdon Gilkey, and David Tracy."[97] It is this final

Kantian necessity of returning to the world of the self, however more dis-
orientingly than in either Kant or even Tillich, that ultimately makes Ricoeur's
religious hermeneutics poetically self-transformative.

This religious poetics is summarized in Ricoeur's paradoxical notion of
"naming God." Naming God is at once already done by sacred texts as such
and yet also completed in a sacred text's human reader or interpreter. On the
one hand, "naming God, before being an act of which I am capable, is what
the texts of my predilection do when they . . . poetically manifest and thereby
reveal a world we may inhabit."[98] Naming God is initially multiple, poly-
phonic, and "as diverse as narratives, prophesies, laws, proverbs, prayers,
hymns, liturgical formulas, and wisdom writings."[99] But, on the other hand,
to name God is also "to understand oneself in front of the text," "to 're-make'
the world following the essential intention of the poem."[100] Naming God can
only disorient the self insofar as the self can be affirmed as capable of its own
reorientation by the text. Receiving God is not just a passive intrusion of
Wholly Otherness but also an active interpretation of its meaning for oneself.
God is not named if the naming self is not thereby self-transformed—whether
in understanding or in practice, and however far it falls short of God Godself.

What makes naming God different from the interpretation of any other
kind of text, for Ricoeur, is not whether a poetic self-transformation is required, but this transformation's nature and radicality. Naming God names
that which ultimately cannot be named. Naming God is "hyperbolic," in the
sense of exceeding all possible human understanding. God is not reducible to
meaning because God is the origin of the human possibility for meaning as
such. This means, Ricoeur claims, that naming God is always dependent on
God's own prior "summons":

> In receiving the name of God, the self also finds itself *summoned* to
> God. Here the self is constituted and defined by its position as res-
> pondent to propositions of meaning issuing from the symbolic net-
> work [of the Bible and its historical traditions]. Before any explication
> or interpretation, this phrase ["the summoned self"] diametrically
> opposes itself to the philosophical hubris of a self that absolutely
> names itself. However, it does not substitute itself for this philo-
> sophical ideal inasmuch as a self that responds is a self in relation,
> without being an absolute self.[101]

This "self in relation" is a self summoned to radically greater meaning by its
own Creator. "Religion . . . exceeds our ability to measure; it consists in an
excess of tale-telling."[102] More primordial than the capability for creating
one's own meaning in the world is a God who made this capability possible in
the first place, a God thereby "named" only paradoxically through its own
disorienting revelation.

If Ricoeur's religious hermeneutics meets something of his early ambition of a poetics of the will, it does so, not through a wholly distinct existential
poetics of Transcendence (as originally anticipated in 1950), but by radical-
izing his subsequently developed "philosophical" hermeneutics. What is

distinct in "naming God" is not that it escapes the above-described herme-neutical arc of the formation of meaning in the self. What is distinct is that the required self-transformation could not possibly be completed in the terms of this world. It is what Ricoeur and others have called an "impossible possi-bility." The ordinary making of a meaningful narrative identity may be end-less in the sense of continuing over time, but *religious* meaning making is endless in the sense of placing one's narrative identity in relation to time's very limits—limits such as Creation, destiny, and eternity. The latter places the self into the ever-excessive hermeneutical circle of interpreting the meaning of the possibility for narrating this world at all. Ultimate questions of these kinds place the self in poetic tension with what cannot humanly be narrated. Yet such questions can receive meaningful responses insofar as the self can be affirmed as capable, paradoxically, of "naming the whirlwind" to which it belongs (as Langdon Gilkey puts it),[103] of hearing primordiality in new depths of meaning that reveal time and the world's very limits, even though in temporal and worldly terms.

In the next chapter I argue that such a position helps us respond to a profound "antinomy"—as Kant calls it—within the human possibility for moral freedom. If human freedom fails to realize itself in actual worldly goodness, then humanity would seem, paradoxically, to defeat itself and to abandon its own very humanity as free. This inscrutable possibility cannot be reversed by relying on human freedom itself, for it has already enslaved itself to failure (its "radical evil"). The capability for naming God, however, will turn out to include the capability for naming a *still more primordial* human freedom than that actually experienced in the world: an origin of goodness as creativity that its own self-defeat cannot ultimately abolish. The Wholly Other is a name, in part, for a mythological ground of human perfection that is prior to all actual human imperfection, an *excess* of human original goodness always still more radical than human evil. If it is possible to "create" meaningful interpretations of human original goodness, then it may also be possible to affirm the pri-mordial goodness of the self's "only human" freedom.

Creativity in the Image of God

The question remains in the end, however, whether we may finally affirm the human self as not only capable of poetically "naming God" but also capable of a primordial creativity "in the image of God"—in the image, that is, of its own very Creator. If, philosophically, the hermeneutical arc culminates in the self's formation of its own narrative identity, however imperfectly, we may further ask in what, ultimately, the naming of God finally culminates in terms of the radically poetic self. This is the same as asking what kind of hermeneutical self is primordially capable of creating its own narrative identity in the first place.

Ricoeur himself never presses his religious hermeneutics to any conclu-sions about the self as creative in the image of its Creator. He does, to be fair, in one early sentence written in 1960, claim that something like a radical human creativity may have been indicated by the early church fathers: "What should happen if [like these fathers] we should invert the metaphor, if we should see the image of God not as an imposed mark but as the striking power of human creativity?"[104] But Ricoeur goes on to discuss, along the lines of the above, only the sense in which this implies an original kind of human "freedom" (which, like the church fathers, he likens here to that of an adult rather than a child) to interrupt history by imagining its mythological, utopian ideal. Nowhere else in his corpus does Ricoeur again take up the tantalizing religious possibility that a *poetics* of the will (in the sense of describing the will's Createdness) may imply also a poetics *of the will* (the will's own capability for Creator-like Creativity). Indeed, Ricoeur remains significantly truer to his earlier declaration in 1948, in the very last line of *Freedom and Nature*, which reads, "To will is not to create"—meaning the will may find its mythological limits in the divine, but it is "a freedom which is human and *not* divine."[105]

The larger problem here, as readers of Ricoeur well know, is that after his very early ambitions of uniting his new philosophy with religion, Ricoeur quickly separates these realms of his work. Ricoeur's stated reasons for this separation are generally pragmatic, as noted above, having to do with the deep mistrust of theology in the academy, especially in France. Explaining why he omitted the two Gifford Lectures on religion from the final text of *Oneself as Another*, Ricoeur writes that it "has to do with my concern to pursue, to the very last line, an autonomous, philosophical discourse," which he describes as an "asceticism of the argument . . . which marks, I believe, all my philosophical work."[106] The two realms of thought are in fact claimed here to be mutually exclusive: "If I defend my philosophical writings against the accusation of cryptotheology, I also refrain, with equal vigilance, from assigning to biblical faith a cryptophilosophical function."[107]

By making this kind of separation—even if the connections of the two realms of thought are also frequently noted—Ricoeur ultimately prevents himself from pursuing the radical anthropological possibility that the ordinary creation of meaning in the world may rest on a radical creative capability that is ultimately a mystery and a paradox. Ricoeur's stated pragmatic reasons for this separation cover over, I believe, an underlying conceptual problem: how to understand the relation of freedom to history in a sufficiently original way for freedom to appear at once *within* history and yet *transformative of* it. The creative freedom that is in fact self-defeated in history can be grounded finally only by its connection to a still more primordial creative freedom that is still able to be affirmed. Only through such a connection will we be able to reach, both with and beyond Ricoeur, into the very most primordial depths of the poetics of the will.

If the self lies in a tension between freedom and finitude, the voluntary and the involuntary, then its ability to form this tension into its own narrative identity is indeed a profound mystery. This poetic capability would not itself be knowable as part of any narrative identity as such; it would radically precede it. Poetics would precede, in conceptual terms, even the ontological disproportion involved in human fallibility. The symbolism of human creativity must be still more profound than the symbolism of evil. The question is why humankind is primordially capable of making its own world meaningful in the first place, as opposed to remaining lost in meaninglessness or lacking the ability to narrate itself anew. Religious symbols and mythology promise not only to reorient the self's narrative identity in relation to God but also, and even more radically, to speak to the origins and limits of the human possibility for constructing a narrative identity at all.

We can speak of this primordial dimension of moral selfhood only symbolically and mythologically. It is an object of witness and faith, not historical explanation. It can be revealed to us only against our own constricted images of human possibility—glimpsed, as it were, in a glass darkly. Although it is true that the symbolism of humankind in the image of its Creator belongs to specific historical traditions, and although these traditions have in fact been used to dampen as much as to enliven human freedom, in the end the symbolism can also be interpreted to point to an unnamable mystery that exceeds even traditional texts as the very origin of the human possibility for forming them into meaning. The human capability for self-creativity is not reducible to a historical narrative because then it could not provide a response to the question of the human possibility for historical narration as such. Radical self-creativity is a presupposition, not of a metaphysical or a traditional kind, but of a disorienting, hyperbolic, and mythological one. It points to something that cannot ultimately be known. It shares with Kantian presuppositions the fact that it grounds a human possibility; but it names also what must appear, to us, historically impossible. We can justify ourselves as made in the image of our Creator no more than we justify the Creator itself; in this we can only have faith.

The notion of a human likeness to the creativity of its Creator may seem scandalous—indeed, it certainly should—but it is not without symbolic precedent. One of the most direct ways in which this suggestion is posited is in the mythology of Genesis 1:26–28 (which, I reiterate, I am not analyzing exegetically, but listening to for philosophical indications of meaning):

> Then God said, "Let us make humankind in our image [*tselem*], according to our likeness; and let them have dominion over the fish of the sea, and over the birds of the air, and over the cattle, and over all the wild animals of the earth, and over every creeping thing that creeps upon the earth." So God created humankind in his image [*tselem*], in the image [*tselem*] of God he created them; male and female he created them. God blessed them, and God said to them, "Be fruitful and multiply, and fill the earth and subdue it; and have dominion over the fish of the sea and over the birds of the air and over every living thing that moves upon the earth."

Much controversy has long surrounded the meaning of "dominion" in this passage—especially whether it implies lordship or stewardship—and we cannot resolve it here. But prior to dominion is the very first command to humankind in the Bible: "Be fruitful and multiply." This, too, can have many meanings. But is it implausible to suggest some link between this human fruitfulness and multiplication and God's just having been fruitful and multiplied in God's very creation of the world? Indeed, what God has most specifically "multiplied" is himself: in human beings as made in his image. The passage at least opens up the strange possibility that humankind may be commanded to imitate its Creator by creating also (in however limited a way) its own human being in the world for itself.

The poetic phenomenologist Richard Kearney has suggested that this passage is about the human capability for power. He argues that "to be made in God's image is ... paradoxically, to be powerless, but with the possibility of receiving power from God to overcome powerlessness."[108] In this case, human creativity in the image of the Creativity of God implies an impossible human possibility for overcoming all manner of self-limitation, whether from oneself or from the world. This power or capability may be everywhere distorted and misdirected. But from this mythological point of view, it is not thereby destroyed altogether and could ultimately exceed even the self's own incapability. Human power may ultimately consist in being able poetically to make one's own world anew, however fallen it is in reality. To recall the earlier language used here: to be in the world may consist in overcoming non-being through a still more primordial power to be.

In a different way, the theologian of science Philip Hefner has suggested that the symbolism of the image of God indicates that human beings are "God's created co-creators." Humanity is mysteriously (mythologically) endowed with the freedom to make meaning of and in its world. "The image of God should be interpreted ... from the perspective of how [human] nature may be said to be analogous to God. I suggest that the core of this analogy today is the character of *Homo sapiens* as free creator of meanings, one who takes action based on those meanings and is also responsible for those meanings and actions."[109] In my view, Hefner does not plumb the paradoxical symbolic depths of such a freedom as overcoming freedom's own self-enslavement in radical evil, nor does he develop a correspondingly rich picture of morality. But he does show that creativity is evident in humanity's ability to supersede even the determinism of its natural environment and turn this environment to its own culturally constructed purposes, purposes which, in the end for Hefner, belong to "the creation's movement toward fulfillment according to God's purposes."[110]

But more than this, the complex symbolism of Genesis suggests a kind of primordial human creativity in the notion of "image" itself. The most important and final thing that God is said to create is precisely an "image" of itself—namely, humanity. The Creator itself creates, in part, by making its own self-images. Such a suggestion was made in our reading at the beginning of this book of Michelangelo's painting. It is strengthened further by the term "image" (*tselem*) subsequently referring in Genesis 5:3 to Adam's son Seth as created in Adam's "own image." *To image* lies at the very roots of what it means to be human. It predates the human fall but also lives on in broken ways in such things as procreation, mythologizing, painting, and interpreting

and projecting meaning in our world. Perhaps, after the fall, the bodily reproduction of new generations is the closest anyone comes to the primordial
creativity humanity was meant to have. But all meaningful action and thought
takes part in some small way in this paradoxically created and creative, imaged
and imaging, human capability.

Humanity is indeed evidently capable of creating "images" of itself as an
image of its Creator, as in this very Genesis mythology itself, not to mention
the many "images" of God created by religious mythologies, paintings, poems, and rituals around the world. Mythologizing itself—forming language
into meaning—expresses a distinctively human capability for making "images" in the image of a Primordial Image-Maker. I am not speaking here yet
of images in the sense of idols; I'll come to that distorted capability in the
following chapters. I am speaking, rather, of the peculiar power in human
nature to create images at all. Turning Genesis around on itself—holding it
up to its own mirror—we may discover that each of us as human beings is
primordially capable, in the likeness of the image of God, of in some sense
creating our own very humanity.

What is more, the manner in which the Creator creates, in this particular
myth, is precisely through language and time, which are two of the central
components of narration. "Then God said, 'Let there be light'; and there was
light." Do we imagine God using language because we are merely projecting
ourselves upon God—or is there the more profound possibility that God's
using language reveals something also of our own mysterious capability for
using language to create our own narrative world? If we imagine the Creator
creating us through speech, then it is through speech that we may imagine
ourselves primordially also to create ourselves.

Further evidence for this hermeneutical reading is found in Adam's first
act in the Garden of Eden, which is precisely to name the animals and birds
given to him. He receives them passively from God, yet he also actively interprets their meaning. "The Lord God formed every animal of the field and
every bird of the air, and brought them to the man to see what he would call
them; and whatever the man called every living creature, that was its name"
(Genesis 2:19). If this myth names God, it specifically names God as having
given humanity the capability *to name*. What is more, the Garden of Eden
itself, in which this naming takes place, exists in time—not in a timeless
heaven. It belongs to an originary narrative. Within this narrative, humanity is
imagined, not just as one creature among others, but also as the creature who
creates each creature's name and story. Humanity is the naming creature, the
creature who creates names. It is also the only creature who names and tells
stories about God. We human beings are capable of creating a name for
ourselves—as creatures capable of creating in the image of Creation.

Similar suggestions can be found in other parts of the Bible and the
Western tradition. A certain creative call can be heard, for example, in
Abraham's and Moses' injunctions to form a great nation under the sign of
the covenant. A covenant is something that one "makes." Indeed, the cove-
nants here are linguistic creations in which the Israelites are drawn into not

only greater dependency upon God but also a certain greater likeness, since human beings now gradually move from being punished *by* God through Adam's fall to striking something of a bilateral agreement *with* God. The Song of Songs makes a further comparison between human procreation among lovers and reclaiming the original Garden of Eden where Adam and Eve enjoyed fruitful creativity without estrangement. Sexuality and procreation are again obvious symbols for the mysterious human ability to create its own society. The prophets, too, stand in a certain creative tension with their way-ward communities, representing "images" or "faces" of God in their own persons and speech. They speak for God by calling for radical social trans-formation, often against the merely false "images" that have hardened around God instead.

The New Testament contains several images of human creative possibil-ities that I pursue especially in chapter 4. Jesus is affirmed in the gospels as the "Son of God," his disciples as "children of God." The disciples can become (often despite themselves) at least lesser likenesses of the "Son" whom the Father has symbolically "procreated." As "children" of God, human beings may imagine themselves as not only God's offspring but also, like real chil-dren, capable of coming to create "offspring" in turn for themselves—whether that is understood biologically, socially, ethically, or spiritually. The ambiguity of Jesus as both God and Son of God points to a similar possibility in human beings as God's both spirit and image in the world. One particularly appro-priate metaphor for such creativity is Jesus as God's vine: "I am the vine, you are the branches. Those who abide in me and I in them bear much fruit" (John 15:5). Jesus, we might say, is here creating an image of himself as a creative source for the further creative fruitfulness "in" him of his disciples. Another image, of course, is the resurrection—about which I speak further in chapter 4—which symbolizes, if nothing else, the possibility for world transformation, for non-being leading to greater being, of a particularly radical kind.

We can also look to Greek mythology for images of humanity in the likeness of the gods. Homer's heroes are typically marked by their particularly "god-like" (*antitheôi*) character. Odysseus, for example, is a god-like "man of many devices" who plies his creative inventiveness even against the gods themselves.[111] Penelope presents us with the immortal image of her weaving and unweaving Laertes' burial shroud in a divinely inspired cunning decep-tion of her suitors.[112] Sophocles—whose tragic poetics I explore in several later chapters—has his chorus in the *Antigone* praise human inventiveness in its famous choral song: "Many are the wonders [*deina*], none is more won-derful [*deinon*] that what is man. . . . He it is again who wears away the Earth, oldest of gods, immortal, unwearied. . . . He has a way against everything, and he faces nothing that is to come without contrivance."[113] Human creativity, making, and self-inventiveness are well known to the ancient Greeks as something by which humanity shares in divinity.

Finally, several ancient Jewish writers and church fathers speak of the "image of God" as suggesting a call to the human *imitation* of God. Judaism has long spoken of the Sabbath as the time when persons should imitate their

Creator's day of rest—an *imitatio dei*. This tradition continues all the way up to the twentieth-century Jewish ethicist Martin Buber, who in addition speaks of following the righteous example of Abraham as a form of the "imitation of God."[114] The early Christian author Mathetes similarly links imitation to righteousness: "Do not wonder that a man may become an imitator of God. He can...[who] takes upon himself the burden of his neighbor...[and] who, whatever things he has received from God, by distributing these to the needy, becomes a god to those who receive [them]."[115] Clement of Alexandria claims that "He is the [true] Gnostic, who is after the image and likeness of God, who imitates God as far as possible, deficient in none of the things which contribute to the likeness as far as compatible, practicing self-restraint and endurance, living righteously, reigning over the passions, bestowing of what he has as far as possible, and doing good both by word and deed."[116] Origen links imitation of God to comtemplation: "Every one who imitates Him according to his ability, does by this very endeavor raise a statue according to the image of the Creator for in the contemplation of God with a pure heart they become imitators of Him."[117] The Pseudo-Clementine literature links imitation of God to worship: "Warn and exhort the worshippers, that by good deeds they imitate Him whom they worship, and hasten to return to His image and likeness."[118] And later the Jewish Aristotelian Maimonides argues for an *imitatio dei* as humanity's highest moral perfection: "He will then be determined always to seek loving-kindness, judgment, and righteousness, and thus to imitate the ways of God."[119]

Such examples will be multiplied and deepened in the chapters that follow as we work out what a poetics of human primordial creativity might mean specifically for moral practice.[120] For now I simply want to suggest that biblical, Greek, and other symbolisms can sometimes open up a strange and mysterious, even paradoxical, human capability for the creation of its own world. Such primordial creativity could not be reduced to a mere explanation, for explanations are themselves expressions of the human creative ability. Rather, we must touch on something primordial and god-like. Despite its rather mysterious nature, anyone who denies such a self-creative capability is engaged in what may be called a performative self-contradiction, for in doing so they are themselves already creating meaning.

Our creative capability is, in this fundamental sense, not just possible but necessary. Through mythology, we can say that this poetic capability is at once *ours* and yet somehow also primordially *given to us*. It represents the ultimate limits of our simultaneous agency and passivity. Our experience of the loss of self-creativity—in our various inabilities to render productive the tensions of our lives—presupposes the still more original possibility for its greater renewal. It should not be surprising that this ultimately unnamable mystery is not symbolized universally in the same way. What would be surprising would be if human language and culture had not found ways to mythologize its own creative depths at all. From this angle, mythology can be used as a means for reflecting on the human capability, in the face of disorientation and meaninglessness, for language and meaning as such.

In this way, Ricoeur's original ambition to construct a religious poetics of the will may become realized around the primordiality of Creation after all. Now, however, Creation symbolizes not just the origin of humanity but also, in a more radically reflexive sense, the origin of humanity's capability for self-origination. We have, in effect, synthesized Ricoeur's philosophical poetics of the capability for creating one's own narrative identity with his religious poetics of the strange power of symbolism and myth. The human ability for creativity is thereby deepened into its own most primordial and scandalous dimensions. It calls us to a kind of excess: excess of existing narrative identity in the quest for an ever more radical realization of narrative meaning. Such self-creativity is impossible for our own merely human freedom, and this freedom itself destroys itself. But more primordially still remains the possibility that we are images of a primordial Creativity. At the heart of all human meaning and narration—at the very origins of human history itself—is a paradoxical human capability for re-creating our already created being-in-the-world.

When Hamlet asks "To be, or not to be," he is exposed to the brute necessity of re-creating his own sad and meaningless story. Its sharp fragmentation and his inability to know what to do deepen the problem to the point of tragic crisis where its primordial depths may be revealed. The purpose of religion, at least in part, is to draw out such impossibly possible origins of human meaning and identity so that we may recognize and experience our own deepest transformative capabilities. Nowhere is our story complete, not even in the most self-coherent tradition or community, nor in nihilism or death. But nowhere either, at least in this world, is it is finally beyond us to retell our own narrative identity anew. Kearney has described the God of *posse*, of possibility and transfiguration, as "the God who may be," a God who "neither is nor is not but may be."[121] Might we not say that in the image of such a God we too address the paradox of being and not-being with our own mysterious "possibility" for what we may become? Non-being, for us, is not simply death, for death is part of the human story. Non-being is the loss of capability for creating meaning in one's life, a loss which each of us constantly experiences. But non-being is also integral to becoming and transforming, to creating new depths of meaning in our world. That we never perfect this primordial poetic capability does not mean we can avoid its demand, for it is a call to our own very humanity. Our Ariadne's thread, as we now enter the labyrinth of moral discourse itself, is this radical and paradoxical possibility for human self-creativity within our actual histories of incompleteness, narrowness, violence, and oppression.

2

Radical Evil and the Narration of Goods

The simplest and most immediate way in which creativity plays a role in moral life is in the self's formation of the good. By "the good" I mean moral teleology: the aims, ends, and purposes persons seek to fulfill both for themselves and with others in their lives. These aims are not written in stone. Nor, however, are they purely subjective or relative. Rather, they are complex, multiple, ambiguous, changing, and bound up with relationships, society, and politics. They range from more immediate ends like having children, pursuing a career, and keeping healthy to more social ends like developing a sense of community, deepening cultural meaning, and furthering global peace. All of these can generally be included, as Aristotle says, under what constitutes human fulfillment or "happiness" broadly understood. My argument in this chapter is that such fulfillment of the good involves a task of ongoing radical self-formation, not only in its means but also in the meaning and possibilities of its end.

As already discussed, the good can be distinguished, at least for heuristic reasons, from both the deontological right (duties, obligations, and responsibilities to which selves are necessarily bound) and systemic social practices (participation in structures of power).[1] The deontological and social systemic dimensions of moral creativity are the subjects of chapters 3 and 4, respectively. Here, however, it must first be established in what sense persons' teleological aims and purposes in life may be described in part as the kinds of things that human beings make and form, and in what sense this poetic dimension of the good is in the end not just incidental but primordial.

We investigate the good first, not because it is somehow more fundamental than other angles on moral life, but because it is the least complex problem faced by persons as they seek to create meaning in relation to their social and historical worlds. The good does not belong to the self alone, but to the self in community. As Charles Taylor says, "One is a self only among other selves. A self can never be described without reference to those who surround it."[2] The difference between the good and the other dimensions of moral life that I examine is *not* a question of concern for self versus concern for others. It is a question, rather, of the nature or quality of the self-other relation. When it comes to goods, selves are fragmented and incomplete, yet they remain responsible as creative beings for forming meaningful and coherent narrative purposes in their lives alongside others. The narration of goods is necessary for moral life, but it is not sufficient. Questions of the other's absolute otherness from the self and of the distortion of human relations through power—questions that partially relativize the good—are left to future chapters. Goods involve what I have been calling an initial "positive" moral creativity, but they are ultimately to be qualified by "negative" and mixed dimensions of moral creativity as well.

This chapter moves from traditional distinctions between ethics and poetics in the moral thought of Aristotle and contemporary Aristotelianism, to Ricoeur's conception of the good within his philosophical and religious poetics of the will, to my own constructive theory of radical teleological creativity. In the first part, I show that despite separating ethics and poetics, Aristotelianism can ultimately also suggest a connection in the important dynamics of moral tragedy. From Ricoeur we then learn that moral tragedy is nevertheless relative to the self's free capability for active moral narration, along with freedom's paradoxical self-defeat as "radically evil." Putting these Aristotelian and Ricoeurian perspectives together, I then argue that the freedom to narrate goods for oneself stands in a radical creative tension with the self's tragic narrative finitude—in all its familial, communal, economic, societal, bodily, and natural complexities and fragmentation. Moral creativity is the human capability, nevertheless, for forming within this fallen historical situation excessive new possibilities for narrative meaning and purpose.

More specifically, the poetics of the good claims that whatever else may be said about human teleological aims (and of course a great deal more can), they are at least in part to be created by selves into their own ever more radically coherent narrative unity of life. The demand for teleological creativity arises out of the need to disrupt easy life syntheses and to integrate diverse social conditions into one's own meaningful sense of one's world's direction and purpose. "Narrative" well describes this capability because through narratives, divergent events and characters may be formed over time into an ever richer and more fully unified story. And yet, paradoxically, a narrative unity of life is not in fact possible for us socially fragmented and freely self-defeating human selves. As Augustine says, we enslave ourselves to our own sinful self-destruction. A narrative unity of life can be thought only as an impossible possibility, a mythological ideal, a primordial perfection. Against a number of contemporary Aristotelian definitions of "narrative unity," I argue that it is not only not historically achievable, but, because of radical evil, it is also an image of human perfection that always exceeds history's limits. It is not a proximate but rather a hyperbolic end. It cannot be definitively enclosed but rather opens, challenges, and transforms. To create the good is endless and unforeseeable, leading toward a mystery which no one could enshrine or predict.

Ultimately, we can affirm ourselves as capable of narrative unity only insofar as we realize, beyond radical evil, our *still more primordial* creativity as human beings made in the image of our (mythically) unified Creator. Our very humanity calls us toward this excessive ideal, even if everywhere humanity in fact defeats it and hence dehumanizes itself. Such a perfection of the poetic will must be imagined, insofar as we are able, as wholly *inclusive* of every dimension of the self's historical existence that the self, however, in fact *excludes* through its own narrowing and tragic self-fragmentation. The inner poetic aim of inclusivity means something different here than it will mean in future chapters. It refers to the positive hyperbolic ideal, imperfectable but calling us forward nonetheless, of narrating one's social and historical life into a whole.

The possible objections to such a poetics of the good are many. Postmodernity has convinced some that narrative unity is not only impossible—with which I agree—but therefore also universally oppressive and fit only for deconstruction. The lasting power of modernity, in contrast, frequently relegates goods to merely subjective preferences: at best secondary to, at worst destructive of, genuine moral aims of protecting rights and tolerating pluralism. Even those today who accept an important role for goods in moral life typically reduce them to their observable *finite* dimensions: sociobiological purposes, psychological needs, social interests, or traditional and cultural expressions—explicitly opposing these in many cases to any illusion of self-creative freedom. Finally, of course, speaking of the good in terms of religious myths of origins can sound like theological hegemony, an effort to take over the field of moral discourse on irrational and idiosyncratic grounds. Each of these potential critiques will be taken up in this chapter and the argument made instead for a primordial human capability for creating narrative meaning in the world.

Moral Poetics in Aristotelianism

In Book VI of his *Nicomachean Ethics*, Aristotle distinguishes *phronêsis* (practical or ethical wisdom) from *poiêsis* (art or production) in the following way. While *phronêsis* and *poiêsis* have in common that, in contrast with theoretical wisdom, they both deal with "things which admit of being other than they are" ("the realm of coming-to-be"), *phronêsis* "is itself an end," namely "good action," whereas *poiêsis* "has an end other than itself," namely a work of art or a product.[3] This in essence means that *phronêsis* has to do with action in its own right, *poiêsis* with action as a means to something else (a play, a painting, a building). The result is that the one belongs to the realm of ethics, or goods *internal* to action, the other the realm of production, or goods *external* to, or imitative of, action.

It has long been noted by scholars of Aristotle that his *Nicomachean Ethics* has two closely related but in some ways distinct definitions of phronesis.[4] The first definition points to the human capacity to deliberate about the human good as an *end in itself*. Thus, Aristotle defines phronesis as "the capacity of deliberating well about what is good and advantageous for oneself," and this not just "in a partial sense" but regarding "what sort of thing contributes to the good life in general."[5] The *phronimos* (or practically wise person), in this case, is good at grasping the nature of the good. The second definition points instead to the capacity for deliberating well about the *means* to the good rather than the good end itself: "[Moral] virtue makes us aim at the right target, and practical wisdom [*phronêsis*] makes us use the right means."[6] This second definition is made in response to the question of why the intellectual virtue of phronesis would be necessary if one were already directed to the good by moral virtue itself (for example, if one were already courageous by habit, why would one need to deliberate well about courage?). The answer is that true moral virtue involves hitting the right target not just accidentally or for some other reason but *for the right reasons*—that is, by deliberating well concerning the "right means."

However one chooses to blend or prioritize these two aspects of phronesis, the point in Aristotle is that phronesis introduces into moral life a capability for pursuing the good deliberately and by reason, it being the "intellectual virtue" concerned specifically with moral activity. This does not mean that phronesis governs the moral virtues independently—as if virtue came from reason itself, as in Kantian ethics—only that exercising or striving to exercise moral virtue *itself* requires, for human beings as rational creatures, a certain practical wisdom. As Aristotle says, "it is impossible to be good in the full sense of the word without practical wisdom or to be a man of practical wisdom without moral excellence or virtue."[7] As thinking and free beings, we cannot be virtuous by indoctrination or education alone but must be good moral deliberators, too.

It is largely for this reason, however, that phronesis for Aristotle is not *poiêsis*. Phronesis does not produce something new. Rather, it perceives the good that has already been determined by human potentiality and personal habit, and deliberates either about its own true nature or about how to reach it. It understands and pursues a good—happiness or *eudaimonia*—that is already written into the fabric of human nature and society. *Poiêsis*, in contrast, does produce imaginative new "goods" like plays and stories, so that while it may sometimes be a useful instrument for moral life, it is not a specifically moral activity in itself. As Aristotle puts it in his *Poetics*, *poiêsis* merely "imitates" moral action: "The poet... is a poet by virtue of the imitative element in his work, and it is actions that he imitates."[8] The poet may produce a certain cathartic moral effect—indeed, the best poets, the tragedians, do this the most—but this effect only returns us to what was right to do all along. Or, as Aristotle says in the *Nicomachean Ethics*, where *poiêsis* (as in Greek culture at large) is given the wider meaning of "making" or "fabricating" in general (not just stories but also crafts and technologies), poetics is excellent or virtuous according to the quality of its *product*, not according to the moral character of the creative act itself. Echoing Plato's *Republic*, but in a milder way, Aristotle is suggesting, in part, that being a good poet doesn't necessarily qualify one for being or knowing how to be a good person.

One of the most extensive discussions of Aristotelian phronesis today is made by Joseph Dunne, who sees the distinction of phronesis from poetics as central to its meaning and value as a moral term. This distinction is compared by Dunne to Hannah Arendt's division between "action" and "making" and to Habermas's separation of "lifeworld" and "system." On the one hand, phronesis is a genuinely moral activity because it enables us to act and live in common with one another. It is, as Dunne puts it, "the kind of reasonableness fitted to our finite mode of being."[9] On the other hand, *poiêsis* is a species of *technê* or technical skill in making a product, which unrestrained by phronesis threatens to undermine the *polis* and to colonize the moral lifeworld. Poetics is associated with a "deconstructive" tendency in postmodernity toward "self-generating and self-justifying inventiveness to produce for each moment something better—or, nihilistically, just to *produce*."[10] Mere production itself would—and today in large part does—reduce ethical life to the utilitarianism of the marketplace.

Dunne therefore reads Aristotelian phronesis, as do others who find in Aristotle an antidote to modernity, as a needed capability for resisting the nihilistic moral logic that has invaded contemporary social values. A sharp division from phronesis is used to contrast the pursuit of the human good in civil society with an economic consumerism concerned only with a technical and individualistic calculation and production. In this way, Dunne and others in fact emphasize the importance of phronesis as determining and perceiving the right human end—indeed to perceive that there is a substantive and moral, as opposed to merely utilitarian, end at all—and they downplay suggestions in Aristotle that phronesis may also calculate means (to ends already established). What is needed, today at least, is a phronesis that can provide social life with a more substantive moral compass. In a way that places Aristotle and Plato relatively close, the poets are to be kept clearly separated from the realm of social morality.

A somewhat more complex view, however, is provided by the communitarian ethicist Alasdair MacIntyre, who gives Aristotle's notion of phronesis the more modest role of *applying* socially constituted moral virtues to the particular contemporary situation. Phronesis on this reading is focused, unlike in Dunne, on the *means* to already traditionally established and constituted ends (the ends constituting the *polis*). Indeed, MacIntyre views social ends as perhaps even more deeply already conditioned than does Aristotle, for they are not transparent through examining the facts of human nature but already constitute the very language itself for examining goods from a particular traditional point of view. For MacIntyre, "there is no standing ground, no place for enquiry, no way to engage in the practices of advancing, evaluating, accepting, and rejecting reasoned argument apart from that which is provided by some particular tradition or other."[11] In this way, MacIntyre reinterprets Aristotle to suggest that "phronesis is the exercise of a capacity to *apply* truths about what it is good for such and such a type of person or for persons as such to do generally and in certain types of situation *to oneself on particular occasions.*"[12] Phronesis is the means by which the "truths" inherited from moral tradition are brought to bear specifically on our own particular present situation.

What, then, becomes of *poiêsis?* Although MacIntyre himself has relatively little to say about this distinct intellectual virtue, one can detect a certain implicit distinction between phronesis and poetics precisely around the means and ends of moral life. Although the ends of phronesis are already determined by traditions, traditions are themselves in fact somewhat plastic. Traditions transform—and can be transformed—over history. Traditional ends are not just inert deposits from the past but also "arguments" which have to be made and remade—that is, produced—over against rival traditions. "A living tradition then is a historically extended, socially embodied argument, and an argument precisely in part about the goods which constitute that tradition."[13] Not only are goods "tradition-constituted," but also traditional goods themselves are, we might say, "constituted" through a process of extended historical discourse.

Even if MacIntyre does not explicitly put it this way, the suggestion is that while phronesis applies the right means, traditional ends themselves are in a certain limited sense "poetic" creations. It is this formation or development of moral ends that appears to be precisely what MacIntyre's own ethical writings attempt to accomplish, being not just histories of traditions but also efforts to reconstitute given traditions in a coherent and meaningful way. This is obviously vastly different from modernist Kantian and Romantic conceptions of "poetics" as subjective expression. Rather, in a more Greek sense, the process of traditional argumentation *produces* conceptions of the social good, which phronesis, by contrast, then applies to the individual situation. Indeed, when traditions undergo what MacIntyre calls an "epistemological crisis"—a fundamental breakdown of coherency—this, he says, "requires the *invention* or *discovery* of new concepts and the framing of some new type or types of theory."[14]

The result in MacIntyre is that the self's project of forming what he too calls a "narrative unity of life" is poetic at least in the limited sense of taking place on the basis of traditional goods which themselves have been formed over time.[15] As he puts it, "the unity of a human life is the unity of a narrative quest," a quest which is not existential in nature but shaped decisively by its larger historical community.[16] "The key question for men is not about their own authorship; I can only answer the question 'What am I to do?' if I can answer the prior question 'Of what story or stories do I find myself a part?'"[17] The self's teleological quest is constituted by the particular social identity, roles, and responsibilities formed *in it* by a tradition. MacIntyre's clear anti-individualism rests in fact on this strong sense of traditions having been formed prior to phronetic judgment itself. "I am never able to seek for the good or exercise the virtues only *qua* individual.... [W]e all approach our own circumstances as bearers of a particular social identity."[18] Or, more strongly: "It is *always* within some particular community with its own specific institutional forms that we learn or fail to learn to exercise the virtues."[19] But, interestingly enough, the whole apparatus here of bearing a social identity rests on a starting point that individuals—like MacIntyre himself as a historical ethicist—can in fact have an important role in forming.

What is also interesting in MacIntyre, on this point, is that despite his self-avowed Aristotelianism, he is in fact well steeped, however implicitly, in a deeper tradition of the poetics of tragedy, the tradition of Homer and the tragic poets. For as he says in the beginning of *After Virtue*, a meaningful life, at least today, places selves in a situation of strangely paradoxical conflict. The "catastrophe" of virtue in which modernity has cast us is one in which the very "language of morality" has been lost. "We have—very largely, if not entirely—lost our comprehension, both theoretical and practical, of morality."[20] Traditions and hence moral communities have utterly broken down. We are called, therefore, to a massive poetic work of cultural transformation. We might call it a sociohistorical catharsis. This task is radically "tragic"—and hence profoundly "poetic" in Aristotle's sense—because the very social conditions in which we are steeped militate against the formation of coherent moral traditions in the first place. I come back to this tragic question shortly.

The truly radical nature of this historically transforming task has been perhaps most fully developed by the Christian Aristotelian communitarian ethicist Stanley Hauerwas, who is otherwise quite close to MacIntyre. I say "radical" because Hauerwas blends Aristotelianism with the historically disruptive theological hermeneutics of Karl Barth. Thus, Hauerwas's "narrative theology" is intended to "help Christians rediscover that their most important social task is nothing less than to be a community capable of hearing the story of God we find in the scripture and living in a manner that is faithful to that story."[21] Modern liberalism, in Hauerwas's view, tries to live according to "no story," or at least no public and historical story, whereas what is really needed is "a true story" that transcends this fragmented world. Moral narration again originates beyond free selves, but now in the divine. "What is crucial is not that we find some way to free ourselves from such stories or community, but that the story which grasps us through our community is true."[22] What is a "true" story? One that "provides a pilgrimage with appropriate exercises and disciplines of self-examination" and that "can provide integrity in a manner that does not deny the diversity of our lives."[23]

While Hauerwas thus shares MacIntyre's desire to locate practical wisdom within historical traditions, he gives human beings the more humble task, not of creating traditions over time, but of responding to the Word "created" solely by God. Because of Hauerwas's Barthianism (as opposed to MacIntyre's Thomism), the larger narrative or quest itself is formed only in response to God's revelation, resurrecting or renewing human historical nature as such. Indeed, Hauerwas's christological orientation leads him to say that a narrative unity of life can be based only (at least for Christians) on "the story of a man who had the authority to preach that the Kingdom of God is present," so that "the truthfulness of Jesus *creates* and is known by the kind of community his story should form."[24] It is God (in the form of Jesus) who creates the very narrative on the basis of which we may know that the narrative is true. This means, ultimately, that the self's creative role lies less in the formation of tradition itself (as still in MacIntyre) than in living up to an already "true" tradition through discipleship, struggle, and moral growth. Poetics comes into the picture in the significantly more limited practice of "the growth of character," which starts from and utterly relies upon accepting a true tradition's revelations. "It is only through a narrative which we learn to 'live into' that we acquire a character sufficient to make our history our own."[25] Moral creativity means, simply, in a deeply passive or receptive sense, "to be the story."[26]

These contemporary perspectives share Aristotle's sense that poetics and phronesis are ultimately distinct, even if the latter two, from MacIntyre and Hauerwas, also provide poetics with a secondary teleological moral role (in Hauerwas's case even more secondary than in MacIntyre's). However much poetics plays a role in evolving or listening to traditional narratives, good action itself is subsequently fixed by what this history has produced and determined. We do in fact find a greater role in communitarianism for poetics than in Aristotle. Perhaps this role is attributable, in part, to a heightened contemporary sense that histories and traditions themselves are multiple, conflicting, and open to interpretation, as opposed to Aristotle's own clearly Greek assumptions about good human nature.

But this sensibility does not lead, in these ethicists, to any notion of moral practice as freely, individually, or actively creating one's narrative unity for oneself. This unity is created instead by tradition, however much tradition itself may be open to transformation. Poetics has a role in moral life, but only as phronesis's handmaiden. Once one has formed or accepted a coherent moral tradition, moral practice itself is then preconstituted in its aims and possibilities. Phronesis is primarily the established good's passive reception and application to particular situations. Only once an individual has made the leap into accepting one moral story or another as "coherent" or "true" may she then begin to exercise the limited freedom of applying teleological ends to herself. This does not mean that such contemporary Aristotelian perspectives lack a conception of the self. It means, rather, that the self—the phronimos—is subordinated, in moral terms, to historical goods which have in one way or another already been created.

Why is this Aristotelian separation of poetics from ethics, even where there exists some relation, finally indefensible? As I argue in chapter 1, moral traditions are not the sort of things that human beings simply fit themselves into. In passively inhabiting them we also actively form their meaning for our own present lives. Texts like Aristotle's *Nicomachean Ethics* or the Bible, for example, present us only with *proposed* worlds of meaning, worlds that require not only creative ordering within themselves, but also creative interpretation into my own narrative meaning. MacIntyre and Hauerwas can read out this creative narration of the contemporary world because they conflate what

Ricoeur above calls "traditionality" and "traditions": the moral historicity that directly effects consciousness and distinctly structured moral texts. Traditional texts are not simply expressions of our already given historicity (a historicity which MacIntyre thinks we have lost and Hauerwas thinks is revealed in the church), but distanciated objects in the world that demand our own creative interpretation into moral meaning. This tension of historicity and textuality within traditions opens up the possibility that traditional goods are not merely inherited from the past, but belong, as I argue in chapter 1, to the larger project of the free self's creation of its own narrative identity. Creative tele-ological narration cannot simply be opposed to free selfhood.

Furthermore, these Aristotelian perspectives cannot therefore account for what later in this chapter I call human "radical evil" or "sin": that is, the inscrutable human freedom to choose wrongly, to destroy one's own good oneself, to use freedom against its own created possibilities. MacIntyre assumes that the fundamental moral problem lies in the conflict (or disap-pearance) of traditions as such, a problem that relegates the question of moral selfhood to a strictly secondary status. He risks ending up with a rather Hegelian view that the "rivalry" of traditions will itself eventually produce traditions of a more coherent and true nature, leaving individuals the chiefly receptive task of then applying them properly to their own lives. This fails to account for, even as it presupposes, selves' deep poetic moral responsibility.

More surprisingly, given his sharper allegiance to the Pauline and Au-gustinian dimensions of the Christian tradition, Hauerwas fails to locate the moral problem in the human will either. For Hauerwas, the key moral problem is what he calls "self-deception," meaning the human tendency to follow stories that are *not true* (or even to follow no stories at all). "Our sin lies precisely in our unbelief—our distrust that we are creatures of a gra-cious creator known only to the extent we accept the invitation to become part of his kingdom."[27] In a sentence that directly contradicts my own thesis, Hauerwas claims that "our sin—our fundamental sin—is the assumption that we are the creators of the history through which we acquire and possess our character."[28] Hauerwas is here opposing a fundamental tenet of much of the very Christian tradition he claims to represent: that human fallibility lies not in its historical conditions alone but in its own free self-enslavement, its deliberate and hence radically evil choice. The deeper question is not whether we are living according to the right narrative, but why we inevitably fail in our primordial capability *to narrate*.

Moral Tragedy

These difficulties within contemporary Aristotelianism around the relation of ethics to poetics can be addressed in part by looking "behind" Aristotle, as it were, into a still more ancient Greek notion that Aristotle himself was apparently trying to move beyond: the moral poetics of tragedy. Like Plato, Aristotle wanted to establish moral life on a more rationally ordered foundation than the dominant Greek moral tradition out of the poets. While Aristotle recognized tragedy as the height of poetics, many of his Greek contemporaries and predecessors saw tragedy as also addressing humanity's deep moral nature. The poets from Homer and Hesiod to Aeschylus, Sophocles, and Euripides viewed moral practice as tragic through and through, indeed resting on a certain tragic wisdom. I want to show here both that the teleological (and Aristotelian) good presupposes a certain hidden tragic moral depths, and that these moral depths themselves involve not only a sense for human finitude but also an inchoate (though incomplete) poetics of moral creativity.

That Aristotle's ethics assumes a sense of moral tragedy that it nevertheless does not thematize is an argument that has been made by a different strand of contemporary Aristotelian ethical thought than the above communitarianism, led most prominently by the American philosophical ethicist Martha Nussbaum. Nussbaum claims that Plato and Aristotle both, although Plato much more sharply, are opposed to the direct inclusion of poetics in ethics because they seek what she calls a "goodness without fragility."[29] They want to found moral life on a form of social "rationality" that will free it from the vicissitudes of fate and fortune. Aristotle's efforts to unite happiness with virtue are at bottom a project to show that the teleological good is something rational, that well-raised human beings can bring about for themselves by good action. Nevertheless, Nussbaum claims, Aristotle better than Plato does still retain an opposed, even if chiefly implied, sense for "the fragility of goodness." Nussbaum's own efforts lie along the lines of developing a more tragically informed Aristotelian ethics that tempers our sense of rationalistic self-mastery with a poetic moral wisdom about human vulnerability, passivity, and dependency.

The chief function of tragic poems, plays, and (she adds) novels, for Nussbaum—which in a similar way to Aristotle are the epitome of poetics—is to provide a unique and important training in what she calls "moral attention." Tragic works teach us "the loving perception of each particular" in the complex actual persons and situations that surround us.[30] This capability for moral attention is not just a poetic means to virtue but is of the very essence of the end of practical wisdom itself. For goodness depends necessarily on selves overcoming their habits of "moral obtuseness" and "simplification" of others and sharpening, through literary narratives, their capabilities for "moral perception," "moral imagination," and "moral sensibility."[31] These phronetic capabilities are not, as in MacIntyre, means for "applying" already historically established moral ends, but part of the very practice and completion of moral life as such. Moral wisdom consists precisely in the capability for attention to and perception of tragic finitude. "Stories cultivate our ability to see and care for particulars, not as representatives of a law, but as what they themselves are: to care deeply about chance happenings in the world, rather than to fortify ourselves against them; to wait for the outcome, and to be bewildered—to wait and float and be actively passive."[32]

Tragedy particularly teaches us a sense for human vulnerability. To narrate one's own story in the world is to face the exigencies of contingency, power, fortune, and luck. As Aristotle himself says of fortune, "a happy [virtuous] man will never become miserable; but even so, supreme happiness will not be his if a fate such as Priam's [whose sons die in battle] befalls him."[33] Nussbaum adopts a German line of thought from Hegel to Hölderlin and Nietzsche that takes this view further and sees tragedy as not just accidental to moral life but part of the very ontological human moral condition.[34] This tragic condition Nussbaum calls our vulnerability to "external contingency."[35] By this she means that, like the characters in many Greek tragic poems and plays, all of us are profoundly conditioned by historical circumstances beyond our immediate control or liking. "Circumstances may force me to a position in which I cannot help being false to something or doing something wrong; that an event that simply happens to me may, without my consent, alter my life"; likewise, tragically, "it is equally problematic to entrust one's good to friends, lovers, or country and to try to have a good life without them."[36] The more we attend concretely to others and to the larger moral situation around us, the more we realize our happiness is part of larger narrative adventures whose outcomes are not entirely in our own hands.

The classic example of moral tragedy in this sense—the subject of intense debate from Hegel to Nietzsche, Heidegger, Irigaray, Nussbaum, and others—is Sophocles' 441 B.C.E. play, the *Antigone*. We will have occasion to return to this brilliant depiction of the poetics of moral life at several points also in the following chapters (examining, for example, Irigaray's and other feminist readings of the play around questions of social power in chapter 4). Let us pause here to see what it might teach specifically about the poetics of teleological *phronesis*.

The story itself is simple. A young woman, Antigone, defies the laws of her city, Thebes, by burying her dead brother Polyneices, despite his having died fighting as a traitor for Thebes' enemies in an effort to usurp kingship for himself. Antigone buries him out of filial piety. The actual king of Thebes, Creon, however, who is also Antigone's uncle, first prohibits then condemns the burial for the good of the city. His power and intractability lead the defiant Antigone eventually to commit suicide, an act then followed by the suicides of Creon's son Haemon, who is in love with Antigone, and then Creon's wife Eurydice, distraught over her son. Creon, who in some ways is the central character the play follows, and whose position is not entirely unsympathetic, is finally forced to face up to his own lamentable narrowness and hubris. "Oh, the awful blindness of those plans of mine," he cries at the end.[37] His final tragic words are these: "Lead me away, a vain silly man who killed you, son, and you, too, lady. I did not mean to, but I did. I do not know where to turn my eyes to look to, for support. Everything in my hands is crossed. A most unwelcome fate has leaped upon me."[38]

Nussbaum adopts a Hegelian reading of this play in one respect: that it illustrates the potentially profound conflict of alternative moral points of view. "We have [in the play] two narrowly limited practical worlds, two strategies of avoidance and simplification. In one a single human value has become *the* final end; in the other a single set of duties has eclipsed all others."[39] But

Nussbaum disagrees with Hegel's larger point that such conflicts represent the movement of history as such, that they are merely "unmediated *Sittlichkeit* [ethical life]" on the way toward the greater synthesis of (in this case the Greek) historical Spirit (*Geist*).[40] For Hegel himself, "each of these two sides realizes only one of the moral powers [Antigone's family duty or Creon's state obligation], and has only one of these as its content; this is the element of one-sidedness here, and the meaning of eternal justice [in which these would be fully mediated] is shown in this, that both end in injustice just because they are one-sided, though at the same time both obtain justice too."[41]

Nussbaum's argument is not that Hegel thereby obscures the characters' creative moral freedom—a point we will come to shortly. Nor is it that Hegel overrides the fundamental moral problem of "otherness"—a point we will come to in later chapters. Nussbaum's argument, useful in our present teleological investigation, is that any such totalizing mediation of historical moral powers fails to learn the lesson of the play itself: that human moral life is not just secondarily but *inherently* vulnerable to fortune and luck. What Creon finally learns (too late for him, but not necessarily too late for us, the play's audience) is the danger of all "projects of harmonizing and synthesizing" and "the terrible power of unconstrained contingency."[42] The moral of the play is not that "the family" must finally become sublated in "the state" (as Hegel claims), but that moral action in any sphere requires attending to the particularities and contingencies of those around us. Neither Antigone nor Creon fully succeeds in this moral task—as, indeed, can none of us—but Creon's blindness is more profound and disastrous because of both his greater power and his greater incapability for perceiving the moral worlds of those with different stories.

Useful though I find Nussbaum's account of the need for a tragic poetic attention in moral life, I would also argue that it still remains, much as in Aristotle, chiefly related to a kind of passivity: the perception or reception of the stories of others. The play itself arguably points to a further more active and creative dimension of tragic poetic wisdom. This dimension will help us see, in a way that the still somewhat Hegelian perspective of Nussbaum does not quite do, how tragedy plays a role not only in perceptiveness toward others but also in selves' active constitution of their moral worlds.

Let us recall (as indeed does Nussbaum herself) the most famous lines of the play, sung by the chorus just as the above tragic forces are beginning to unfold:

> Many are the wonders [*deina*], none
> is more wonderful [*deinon*] than what is man.
> This it is that crosses the sea
> with the south winds storming and the waves swelling,
> breaking around him the roaring surf.
> He it is again who wears away
> the Earth, oldest of gods, immortal, unwearied....
> He has a way against everything,

and he faces nothing that is to come
without contrivance.
Only against death
can he call on no means of escape;
but escape from hopeless diseases
he has found in the depths of his mind.
With some sort of cunning, inventive
beyond all expectation
he reaches sometimes evil,
and sometimes good.[43]

These lines are sometimes mistakenly read as simply praise of human inventiveness. Hans Jonas quotes these very same verses toward the beginning of *The Imperative of Responsibility* to suggest humanity's remarkable capacity for technological power (and hence, he goes on to argue, humanity's great moral responsibility).[44] The strange, perhaps even absurd, disharmony in these lines, however, is that human inventiveness and creativity are being held up here just as the great evils of the play are beginning to unfold—indeed, just as the hearts of Antigone and Creon are becoming hardened to their very different aims. Included in what is "tragic" about human life is that, inscrutably it seems, humanity's own uniquely creative abilities "reach sometimes evil, and sometimes good."

Nussbaum rightly points out that the word "wonderful" [*deinon*]—in the line, "none is more wonderful than what is man"—is for the Greeks, and especially in this play, deeply ambiguous. It can mean either admirable, brilliant, and unsurpassed or, alternatively, strange, out of place, incomprehensible, even fearful and terrible.[45] While the first meaning is perhaps the more evident one at the early point in the play at which these lines appear—and fits more readily with our contemporary sensibilities about the admirable powers of humankind—the second slowly takes over as the play progresses through the awful stubbornness of Creon, the passion of Antigone, the resulting triple suicides, and Creon's final heart-wrenching lament. Nussbaum's conclusion is that "the human being, who appears to be thrilling and wonderful, may turn out at the same time to be monstrous in its ambition to simplify and control the world. Contingency, an object of terror and loathing, may turn out to be at the same time something wonderful, constitutive of what makes a human life beautiful or thrilling."[46] As the chorus itself concludes, "practical wisdom [*to phronein*] is the most important constituent of human good living [*eudaimonia*]"—practical wisdom, not exactly in Aristotle's sense of the intellectual ordering of habits, but in the more deeply tragic sense of attunement to vulnerability and finitude.[47]

But does such a reading fully appreciate the claim in the above poem that what is "wonderful" in this sense about humanity is precisely its poetic capability, its ability to "invent" new things and to "face nothing that is to come without contrivance," continually to act "beyond all expectation"? If tragic poetry is a response to our own limitations of moral understanding, then human creativity may also—however ambiguously—be part of the answer. Such moral creativity is modeled, not on the narrowed inventiveness of the characters themselves, which remains inescapable, but, in contrast, on the broadening cathartic experience of the audience in witnessing the tragic poem itself. The distinction between human contrivance which "reaches evil" and that which "reaches good" may find a clue in the distinction between the failed pursuits of Creon and Antigone and the ever fresh possibilities opened up *for us* to include both their points of view at once. Such a possibility is not completed in the story of the play as such; the play brings no closure. The creation of moral inclusion can take place only in the stories of the lives of the departing members of the audience. The audience is, indeed, encouraged to entertain such a possibility by the play's own chorus, which performs something of a mediating role between players and audience. The chorus's conclusion, specifically, is to advise a certain activity of *phronêsis* that creates new meaning out of the conflict. The chorus is what instigates us to bear the weight of the characters' tragedy but also, and at the same time, to reflect critically on the meaning of the narrative as a whole. We are encouraged to view human life as not only filled with narrowness and contingency, as Nussbaum argues, but also, and even more radically, open nevertheless to "reaching good" through the cathartic creation of new depths of meaning.

The modern tradition of thought about moral tragedy from Hegel onward, which in the end even Nussbaum does not fully escape, is that human life is in one way or another ineluctably *finite*. Arthur Schopenhauer, for example, reads the *Antigone* as illustrating "the triumph of wickedness, the scornful mastery of chance, and the irretrievable fall of the good and the innocent."[48] Nietzsche claims Greek tragedy is about the powers "beyond good and evil" of authentic human historicity.[49] Heidegger reads Antigone's plight as an example of a new historical "destiny"—the destiny of the home and hearth (*hestia*)—making its phenomenological "appearance" in the world.[50] Freud was interested in Oedipus (Antigone's at once father and brother) as a symbol for the tragic conflictedness of the human unconscious.[51] Bernard Knox develops on Freud to read the *Antigone* as a tale of humanity's unavoidable erotic entanglement.[52] While differing from Hegel's reading of the play as about the clash of the historical forces of family and state in important respects, what is retained in such readings is a sense for Greek tragedy as pointing to human historicity, passivity, and destiny.

In chapter 4 I look at some of the more promising recent interpretations of this play, and of moral tragedy generally, in postmodern feminist critiques of this entire Hegelian project. But because today, thanks to modernity, we are generally so convinced of the power and efficacy of human freedom, there is still great value in reading a tragic play like the *Antigone* as reminding us, even on the level of the teleological good, of moral contingency, luck, and fortune. Any sense in which we freely create our own narrative ends must keep in view our also being inevitably enmeshed in the always already created histories and communities on which self-creativity depends. We moderns and postmoderns often assume that following our deepest moral convictions will lead (at least in the long run) to the creation of an ever more just and harmonious social order. On this view, the self's creation of narrative meaning can appear relatively unproblematic. Indeed, the term "tragedy" today often connotes only situations in which bad things happen undeservedly to good people, as in premature death and earthquakes. Or, as the literary theorist Terry Eagleton claims, tragedy simply means "very sad."[53] It is more difficult for us to grasp tragedy as darkly ironic, as springing from the ambiguous "wonder" (deinon) of human creativeness as such.

But in the end, even Greek tragedy itself is capable of pointing also in the direction of a deeper kind of moral poetics in the activity of cathartic self-transformation. This kind of practical wisdom arguably underlies Aristotle's own theory of phronesis as deliberating well in situation—despite Aristotle's explicit denial of a direct connection. Such a capability would go beyond the above communitarian formation and application of consistent traditional narratives. The desire for a coherent larger story by which to live one's life is precisely the tragic problem: as illustrated most dramatically in Creon's application of the goods of the city to the particular situation thrown up by Antigone. True practical wisdom involves not just receiving given narratives from the past, but also actively and creatively refiguring them in response to the tensions, fragility, conflicts, and incommensurabilities of the present. If there is any call for us to apply a reflective deliberative capability to moral habits—which is the heart of Aristotle's theory of the intellectual virtue of phronesis—it should be here in the tragically tutored reshaping of those very habits themselves. The creation of coherent moral communities, however important, must always take second place to the creation of coherent narratives of the present situation, narratives attentive (as in Nussbaum) to that situation's fullest possible particularity and complexity, but narratives also actively and cathartically responsive to it.

Our conclusion from this investigation into tragic moral wisdom is that phronesis can be understood, from a poetic point of view, to require a strange, unsettling, and apparently endless detour of radical narrative self-transformation. The practical wisdom involved in forming a good life—both for oneself and in community—must face and form responses to its own blindness and contingency. What we learn from tragic plays like the Antigone is not just to attend to the particularities and fortunes of those around us, but also to do so in a way that changes our own stories as well. The difference between human inventiveness reaching evil and that reaching good involves (even if it is not reducible to) the difference between narrative closure and simplification and narrative openness to catharsis. There is no narrative framework that can resolve this human conundrum in advance, no matter how coherently, traditionally, or even divinely constructed. The only solution available to us merely finite and limited creatures is to become ever more profoundly capable of creating new narratives of the good in relation to one another. This capability for poetic self-formation is both passive and active at once: receptive to the finitude of the situation at hand and inventive of its ever more inclusive possible meaning.

Narrative Intentionality

This is where we may once again find assistance from Ricoeur. Ricoeur's value for our inquiry concerning the good is to help us more accurately describe this more active, formative, creative, and free dimension of the self's capability for teleological self-narration. The transition needs to be made between the above Aristotelian and pre-Aristotelian senses for narrative conditions and their implications for a free narrating self. Ricoeur does not, in my view, fully appreciate the deep passivity articulated in Aristotelianism and in moral tragedy itself—a point to which I return later. But he does better explain what it means to say that each self has a certain innovative capability *to form* its given finite world in the direction (however endless) of its own narrative unity of life. Ricoeur's poetics of the will, as I argued in chapter 1, describes the self's strange capability for inhabiting the *tension* of finitude and freedom—in all its many manifestations—so as to refigure for itself its own narrative identity. The question from a teleological point of view is how such a poetic self may thereby be capable of refashioning its ambiguous and fragmented historical situation in the direction of a new and greater (if never complete) sense of narrative unity.

The key notion here—a notion that stands at the root of Ricoeur's entire moral project in each of its different phases—is that of "ethical intentionality." Revising Husserl's phenomenology of perceptual intentionality, ethical intentionality refers to the self's fundamental "desire to be" in the larger world to which it belongs.[54] As Ricoeur puts it,

> I will call [teleological] ethics ... this movement (*parcours*) of actualization, this odyssey of freedom across the world of the works, this proof-testing of the being-able-to-do-something (*pouvoir fair*) in effective actions which bear witness to it. Ethics is this movement between naked and blind belief in a primordial "I can," and the real history where I attest to this "I can."[55]

This rather abstract ethical "I can" or "capability" is neither a fitting of freedom *into* the world nor a Promethean imposition of freedom *upon* the world. Rather, it is a passive-active capability for attesting to oneself through a real history specifically of one's own. My body, my traditions, my social relations—these are to be taken up, ethically speaking, into my own actualization in the world.

This "desire to be" begins to take on a poetic form in Ricoeur insofar as the values and aims within which freedom may be realized need to be infused with the self's own evolving sense of meaning:

> [F]ollowing Josiah Royce and Gabriel Marcel, I should say that values are not timeless ideas but suprapersonal existences, thereby stressing that their appearance is tied to a definite history on which I collaborate actively with all the power of my dedication, briefly, *a history*

which I invent. Yes, that is the paradox of value: it is not completely
a product of history, it is not invented, it is recognized, respected,
and discovered—but only to the extent of *my capacity for making history, for inventing history.*[56]

This "history which I invent" does not realize freedom in the existential sense
of the expression of freedom *in spite of* history. Nor does freedom simply "join
up" with history as already constituted. Rather, freedom must traverse a
continual "hermeneutical circle" of recognizing and valuing history as it is
and simultaneously engaging in remaking history for oneself.

Let us again take the example of the body, which is so easily reduced, in
terms of the moral good, to merely a passive raft of needs. To be sure, the body
appears to the self in the first place as always already constituted by a biological history of evolutionary adaptation, human functions and needs, gender
and age, personal attributes and health, and socially received meaning. But it
is also, at the same time, *my* body—*someone's* body—capable of being taken up
into meaningful efforts at self-realization in the world. Eating, for example, is
more than just a reaction to an involuntary impulse. It is also an intentional
practice endowed with meaning for the particular eater by such activities as
choosing particular foods over others, dining with family and friends, and
taking up culinary traditions and cultures. Even unconsciously repressed
Freudian desires, as Ricoeur argues in *Freud and Philosophy: An Essay on
Interpretation*, have "meaning" only to the extent that they become available to
the self's own intentional projects, such as in the "working through" process,
psychoanalytic catharsis, dream interpretation, projection, sublimation, and
identification.[57] A meaningful human existence as a biological being does not
mean simply acting according to biological drive. It means refiguring nature,
genetics, the id, desire, and so forth into ever more coherent teleological
intentions. As Ricoeur puts it, "happiness is not given in any experience; it is
only adumbrated in a consciousness of direction."[58]

It is not until his later thought, however, that Ricoeur develops this notion
of ethical intentionality in specifically narrative terms. Here, the notion of a
"narrative unity of life"—explicitly recast from MacIntyre—is used to describe
the involuntary-voluntary self as it forms and refigures its aims and ends over
time. A narrative unity of life, for Ricoeur, is the intentional fulfillment by the
self of its "desire to live well with and for others in just institutions."[59] This
"desire"—more rounded than the simple "desire to be" above—incorporates
the fullest possible range of teleological dimensions of selfhood: from the
body to the psyche, family life, career, community, economic well-being, and
political purpose. It is "narrative" in the sense, not just that it receives its good
from these conditions themselves, but also that it actively and creatively refigures them into an ever deeper unity of meaning for itself.

This narrative good thereby has, for Ricoeur, three dimensions that parallel the three moments of his previously discussed hermeneutical arc and,
more generally, of his poetics of the will. The first dimension has to do with
narrative passivity, and here Ricoeur comes closest to MacIntyre and the

notion of the preconstitution of the moral good by "internal goods" received through a "teleology immanent to the action."[60] Among such internal goods Ricoeur includes not only drives, experiences, and habits but also, as the means to interpret these, "standards of excellence which allow us to characterize as good a doctor, an architect, a painter, or a chess player."[61] Each of us is already *narrated* before we begin—or even could begin—to narrate ourselves.

Even here, however, Ricoeur finds a protoreflexivity, a beginning to freedom, that he claims is missing in the ethics of MacIntyre. MacIntyre's view of tradition-constituted goods, Ricoeur claims, fails to account for the needed "return . . . to life along the multiple paths of appropriation."[62] Even as they shape me historically, traditional conceptions of goods and their instantiations within communities and practices must also be taken on as *my own*. "In appraising our actions [as part of a history of practices], we appraise ourselves as being their author."[63] However much the practices of being a good physician, for example, are defined by the standards of excellence established by the larger medical and social community, they are in each and every instance also the practices of a singular self who inhabits and lives within them as her own. Only in this way do practices begin to gain meaning and physicians become good instead of poor ones.

The second and more voluntary dimension of a narrative unity of life Ricoeur calls "life plans." Ricoeur finds this element more evident in Aristotle himself than do his communitarian interpreters. A *phronimos*, as we have seen, may be someone who is good at judging not just good means to already established ends, but the nature of this end itself. Phronesis can involve deliberating freely on the meaning and nature of *eudaimonia*, excellence, happiness per se.[64] While the human good may be fairly clearly posited in abstract generalities about "happiness," concretely it requires great wisdom to see what it would actually look like in the world. Ethical intentionality becomes actively *narrated* insofar as received goods are placed in the service of personal ideals. Such life plans project possibilities for a "higher degree of integration of actions in global projects, including, for example, professional life, family life, leisure time, and community and political life."[65] Selves must form the stories of which they are already a part in the direction of deliberately formed stories of their own, constituting a range of voluntarily chosen possibilities for realizing oneself in the world. A physician, for example, has to make ongoing choices about such things as how to balance patient care with financial gain, professional life in relation to family, medical goods in relation to larger social goods, and diverse interpretations of the very meaning and purpose of advancing human health. Such voluntary self-narration, as Ricoeur puts it, "designates the person as a whole, in opposition to fragmented practices."[66]

But these involuntary and voluntary poles of the narrative good stand finally in tension with one another. One arises out of the self's historically received past, the other projects its ideally desired future. An actualized narrative unity of life can be sought only in the refiguration of the self's past and its possible future in an ongoing narrative present. "Practices and life plans [are finally] put together by the anticipation of the narrative unity of life."[67] This narrative unity is no metaphyisical "presence" of the self to itself through already conceived ideas of moral being. Neither does it rely on a narrative history which it only has to apply to particular situations. Nor, however, finally, is a narrative unity of life merely chosen at will, a simple description of life plans, or reducible to a moral idealism.

Rather, such narrative wholeness is an interpreted direction of meaning in the here and now of the complex and fragmented historical present. It is a wager and a task, an unfolding sense of developing narrative coherency within the self's fullest possible temporal thickness.

> While the notion of life plan places an accent on the voluntary, even willful, side of what Sartre termed the existential project, the notion of narrative unity places its accent on the organization of intention, causes, and chance that we find in all stories. The person appears here from the outset as suffering as well as acting, subject to those whims of life which have prompted the fine Hellenist and philosopher Martha Nussbaum to speak of the "fragility of goodness," the fragility of the goodness of human action, that is.[68]

Narrative unity is a task of realizing life plans in relation to one's actual and messy historicity. Ricoeur's rare mention here of Nussbaum makes a telling qualification. The fragility of goodness should prompt not just a sense of human finitude and vulnerability; it should prompt also "action" in the sense of the self's deliberate reshaping of its given world for itself. Narrative unity belongs, in the end, to real selves responsible for forming a meaningful identity in their own world. To quote Ricoeur again: "Freedom is less the quality of an act than a 'way of life,' a bios, which does not occur in any single act but expresses itself in the degree of tension and consistency which permeates a course of existence."[69]

The fundamental human capability that makes possible any such self-unifying narration is the capability for what Ricoeur calls estime de soi, or "self-esteem." This capability is not psychological but normative: we should esteem ourselves as capable of narrating our own existences meaningfully and coherently in this world. For Ricoeur, self-esteem is "the new figure in which attestation appears, when the certainty of being the author of one's own discourse and of one's own acts becomes the conviction of judging well and acting well in a momentary and provisional approximation of living well."[70] As the ability to actualize chosen life plans in relation to one's given historical situation, self-esteem means being able to make judgments of the "adequation between our life ideals and our decisions."[71] It is that which allows us not only to project ideal life plans but also, and even more importantly, to make genuine efforts to realize them in a narrative unity of life in the concrete situation of the here and now. As Peter Kemp has succinctly put it, self-esteem in Ricoeur is the affirmation, in terms of the moral good, of one's own "narrative competence."[72]

At the same time, since one's own narrative good necessarily involves others, self-esteem includes also the capability for esteeming others, for exercising what Ricoeur calls "solicitude" (*sollicitude*) toward others as participants in one's life story as well. Solicitude is not yet a deontological capability for respecting others in their very otherness—a capability I discuss in chapter 3. Rather, it is somewhat like Nussbaum's attentiveness to others in their narrative particularity, or, more generally, Aristotelian friendship. My own good life includes participating in larger goods both with and for others. Fulfilling the dream of being a good parent, for example, involves care and attention to the particular life of one's child. Absent such solicitude, I would no longer be good at fulfilling parenthood as part of my own life story.

Again, however, attention or friendship is no mere reception (or perception) of the good of others without one's own free and creative interpretation. Rather, it is the inclusion of others in one's own narration of a more expansive and socially coherent life. "To self-esteem, understood as a reflexive moment of the wish for the 'good life,' solicitude adds essentially the dimension of *lack*, the fact that we *need* friends."[73] Others are not so much useful to narrative unity as necessary, in that human beings are social animals. "I cannot myself have self-esteem unless I esteem others *as* myself. 'As myself' means that you too are capable of starting something in the world, of acting for a reason, of hierarchizing your priorities, of evaluating the ends of your actions, and, having done this, of holding yourself in esteem as I hold myself in esteem."[74] A meaningful story of my own life could not be formed without narrating the particular and distinct meanings of the stories of others around me, and without those others also participating in narrating the stories we share. *My* narrative unity is also a narrative unity participated in by others.

Ricoeur also sees self-esteem as including a third-person capability for treating others with what he calls a "sense of justice."[75] This again is prior to any deontological meaning of the term. As in Aristotle, it suggests the ability to participate in the shared narrative aims of entire societies. A physician cannot be a good physician without taking part in a range of third-party institutional structures from hospitals to medical insurance companies to societal laws. Each of us belongs to a vast web of social narratives which we must both enter into sympathetically and interpret meaningfully for ourselves. Ricoeur compares this sense of justice to Aristotelian "equality" (*isotes*): the need for proportion in the distribution of social goods. My own good can be pursued only in proportion to the good of others. But Ricoeur again insists that such participation expresses a capability of selves for narration. A sense of justice means not just taking on a social role but also making a creative contribution to an ongoing and organic social story. Each other member of an institution or society is also such a socially narrating being, so that they "provide . . . to the self another who is an *each*."[76] The self is capable of shaping its own narrative unity only as the member of a world shaped by a plurality of other such self-narrating selves.

In the end, we find that Ricoeur's concept of the good of narrative unity is a more hermeneutically and poetically sophisticated development of his ongoing concern with ethical intentionality. The "desire to be" is ultimately the aim to narrate oneself meaningfully and coherently over time within the fullness of history and society. It is here that we find a first ethical meaning of Ricoeur's larger "poetics of the will": in the self's capability for a passive-active narration of its own complex relational life. The historical and anti-individualistic notions of narrative unity in MacIntyre and Hauerwas allow only a limited poetic creativity in choosing and retelling already told traditional stories. These stories are simply *applied* to the present situation. Nussbaum more fully appreciates poetics as a moral capability, but it still remains chiefly passive: the imagination and perception of the narrative particularity of others. But Ricoeur shows that, in the end, no received narrative component of moral life does not also, at the same time, demand to be *narrated by* a capable self. Narrative goods finally belong to "selves" as those beings in the world uniquely capable of having and forming narrative meaning. Presupposed in all narrative history, truth, and particularity is a free human capability, however actually realized, for creating one's own more coherently storied life.

None of this is to say that Ricoeur sufficiently appreciates the pre-Aristotelian sense in which moral goods are always already steeped in tragic conflict. If he expresses a tension between freedom and finitude, he is less clear about a further implicated tension within teleological finitude itself. Ricoeur's discussion of moral tragedy occurs only in relation to social systems, as we see in chapter 4. Here, at least, I think we can say that MacIntyre and Nussbaum—even more than Aristotle—have a sense for moral tragedy that is worth retaining in our teleological poetics. MacIntyre sees clearly how one's existing historicity is itself a story of tension and development by which the self is fundamentally blinded and limited—a moral history with a kind of "intentionality" of its own. Ricoeur looks in this respect like a great deal of contemporary Continental thought, which is so anxious to avoid history's Hegelian totalization—its reification of an all-consuming *Geist*—that it insufficiently appreciates the ways in which history itself does in fact impose concrete narrative parameters and limits upon meaning, limits that qualify and can even destroy moral meaning as such.

This imposition is tragic in the sense that, to a certain extent, the world we construct for ourselves is a world already constructed in a narrow and oversimplified way. Don Browning has criticized Ricoeur around biology, arguing that narrative self-realization rests on not just claiming one's body as one's own but also recognizing the realities of "underlying regularities of human needs and basic capabilities that must both be satisfied, exercised, and prioritized if we are to live well with others in just institutions."[77] More generally, we might say that constructing a narrative unity of life is a question of not just weaving together diverse elements of our history, but also perceiving and facing this history's own inner tensions, realities, and conflicts. The Ricoeurian good might involve deeper poetic dimensions if it were more clearly "realist" in this tragic and finite sense. The poetic capability should involve investigating and acknowledging the very historical resources and horizons out of which narrative aims arise in the first place.

Nor does Ricoeur fully appreciate Nussbaum's argument for the role of a tragic sensibility in perceiving the distortions within which our narrative worlds are already embroiled. Our tendencies to oversimplify the moral universe blind us to its deepest tensions and complexities. The feminist writer Helen Buss criticizes Ricoeur along such lines by arguing that Ricoeur's focus on "self-esteem" as the fundamental ethical problem does not adequately account for women's experiences of selfhood in a history of patriarchy. At least as important as Ricoeur's question "Who am I?" is the question, as Buss puts it: "How can I be? That is, how can there exist a way of being that makes me an 'I' who then becomes capable of self-esteem, and who can then esteem another?"[78] My very history itself may limit my options for self-narration within it, forcing, for example, the Antigones of the world to suicide as the only avenue of coherent self-narration. I advance a more developed feminist critique of Ricoeur in chapter 4 around questions of social power. But even here we can see that, if selves are to create a narrative unity of their lives, they must face the tragic discordancies and limitations of the very historical conditions on the basis of which such a good may be created at all. This problem will prompt us eventually to propose an even more radicalized form of narrative self-creativity than Ricoeur here imagines, one that is not only a capability but also a primordial affirmation.

The Serpent Within

Ricoeur can, however, despite (even because of) these drawbacks, help us press the problem of the free poetic narration of the good toward some of its most profoundly mysterious depths, its depths of "radical evil." Ricoeur's discussion of moral evil is, in effect, a trenchant recasting of the notion of radical evil in Kant, but broadened to include not only a deontological but also a prior and perhaps even more fundamental teleological dimension. The question of radical evil takes our discussion of moral creativity to its implied religious limits. The question is not just how freedom may realize itself (or come to be) in the given historical world around it. The question is also why freedom fails in this primordial human task in the first place, and how therefore it may be revived. If humanity is capable of creating a meaningful narrative unity of life in the world, it also inscrutably defeats this capability by choosing, for no meaningful reason, not to (not, at least, as fully as it could). Our actual sense of narrative incompleteness and meaninglessness is only partly attributable to the tragic disorder of the world around us. Ultimately, if we are indeed free to create a narrative unity, our failure to do so is also a sign of a kind of original poetic human guilt—not in the sense of actual historical wrong, but in the more primordial and paradoxical sense of humanity's ability to turn its creative narrative freedom away from its own very purposes and possibilities.

In *Religion Within the Limits of Reason Alone*, Kant sets out a novel humanistic account of "radical evil" that places a largely Pauline and Augustinian view of the self-enslaving will at the presupposed "limits" of ordinary human reason. Kant, a champion of moral rationality, nevertheless appears to have rejected the reigning theodicies of his day, put forth by influential thinkers like G.W. Leibnitz and Christian Wolff, in which a philosophical *explanation* is offered for evil by making it all part of God's mysterious plan. This, to Kant, negates the very phenomenon of moral evil itself, since moral evil involves, at least in part, human freedom turning against its own freely self-given moral law. Kant wishes to tackle head on the question or "antinomy" of how moral freedom can be both perfect and imperfect at once, how it can both ground the moral law and yet cause the moral law's defeat. This is indeed deeply paradoxical.

What Kant specifically insists is that "there is . . . for us no conceivable ground from which the moral evil in us could originally have come."[79] Moral evil, as he repeatedly claims, is ultimately "inscrutable" [*unerforschbar*]. It is implicitly a free choice of the will, and yet the free will is the very foundation of the moral law that evil rebels against. Human freedom inexplicably violates its very own purpose and meaning. Humanity defeats its own humanity. Moral evil does not, for Kant, simply visit us from without, but is something we paradoxically visit upon ourselves. The moral law begins in humanity, but humanity is also its downfall. Moral evil can only be described, at the limits of rationality, as the mysterious use of freedom against freedom itself, freedom's voluntary enslavement to nonfreedom.

Evil is "radical," for Kant, therefore, not in the sense that it is everywhere in history (for this would deny morality its free grounds), but in the sense that it lies at the very limits of moral reason itself. It cannot be described in terms of any explicable maxim, because "it corrupts the ground of all maxims."[80] Since radical evil defeats moral autonomy, it can only be postulated negatively as a human "propensity" [*Hang*], the inexplicable propensity *not* to act according to our own human nature. Evil "remains inscrutable [*unerforschbar*] to us, because this propensity [*Hang*] itself must be set down to our account."[81] What is inexplicable is that the will is somehow freely capable of making immoral choices in the first place, thus negating the very grounds of its own moral freedom. The term "radical" does not refer to any strength or power of evil in the finite historical world, or even to any kind of finite inevitability. The term "radical" means "inscrutable": a strange and inexplicable freedom at the heart of humanity to defeat its own moral freedom as such.

Kant did not, of course, make up this view of moral evil entirely by himself, but can be situated, in fact, within a broad tradition of Augustinianism. Like Augustine, Kant refused to reduce evil to some non-human Manichean or merely historical force in the universe, but insists that humanity freely corrupts itself. Evil is a *self-enslavement* to the phenomenal world of passion for which freedom alone is ultimately responsible. Thus, as Augustine says, "the evil of mutable spirits [i.e., human beings] arises from the evil choice itself, and that evil diminishes and corrupts the goodness of nature. And this evil choice consists solely in falling away from God and deserting him, a defection whose cause is deficient, in the sense of being wanting—there is no cause."[82] While

Augustine's idea of God is very different from Kant's, as is his sense of original sin persisting over history through the seed of Adam, they both claim that human evil is a *privation* of human freedom enacted by human freedom itself. Kant even adopts the Augustinian language of the "perversion of the will."[83]

This problem of evil leads Kant to posit a profound "antinomy" within human moral freedom itself. On the one hand, it seems (from the experience of moral wrong in the world) that freedom inscrutably defeats itself. In this case, Kant says, it stands in need of "atonement" from some higher source, namely God. Freedom in this case calls out for a kind of "ecclesiastical faith."[84] On the other hand, any reliance of freedom upon a higher source appears to annul freedom itself, which as the very ground of moral life cannot rest upon some higher power alone. Thus, "the question arises: What, in the use of our free will, comes first (not physically, but morally)? Where shall we start, *i.e.*, with a faith in what God has done on our behalf, or with what we are to do to become worthy of God's assistance (whatever this may be)?"[85] Kant's answer to this antinomy is of course that the latter (freedom) must ultimately precede the former (faith) if the paradox of moral evil is to be kept in view. Faith in God, in any moral sense, can only be conceived of as a "pure moral faith"—not that humanity will be rescued from evil by a higher power, but that there still exists an ultimate goodness within human moral freedom itself. The self "must believe that he must first improve his way of life, so far as improvement lies in his power, if he is to have even the slightest ground for hope of such a higher gain [as atonement]."[86]

Do we not find, in fact, in Kant's notion of radical evil, what could be called a proto-poetics of the will? Kant insists that the self should not wait around for freedom to be reformed by God, but must of necessity *make* its own freedom once again morally worthy. The self "must first improve his way of life." If the moral law has been inexplicably corrupted, it can be saved only by freedom's own re-creation of itself, its own radical self-reformation and renewal. This is not to say that Kant's critics do not have a point that his solution to radical evil is ultimately unsatisfying. The response to freedom's inscrutable self-defeat is to have faith in the very same freedom that is already acknowledged to have defeated itself. The argument is circular at best. At worst it is a sign of the impossibility of grounding moral life in freedom alone. Our own account will come back to this problem, in part, by relating freedom primordially not just to itself but also to human finitude. But it remains plausible to suggest, nonetheless, that even in Kant's highly philosophical and autonomously grounded moral self, there is an "inscrutable" sense in which the self must "create" its own moral being. Prior to the realization of moral freedom in the world is a more paradoxical freedom—affirmable only by a humanistic faith—to reform moral freedom itself.

Ricoeur (to my knowledge, uniquely) takes such a conception of radical evil into the realm of moral teleology. In this way, one could argue, he revives in a newly critical way something of its more ancient meanings in Paul and Augustine, who as premodern thinkers are in fact primarily concerned with the human good (broadly speaking). But Ricoeur also has the benefit of having been tutored by the philosophical rigor of Kant. This synthesis, if I may put it that way, is accomplished in Ricoeur by the notion that radical evil lies at the heart, not just of freedom alone, as in Kant, but of the self's both free and finite *capability* for narrative self-formation. "The inscrutable," he says, referring to Kant, must be more broadly conceived as "the limit-experience of an impotence of our moral power."[87] Radical evil becomes "the *incapacity* belonging to the capable man, the incapacity that does not abolish capability but presupposes it as the very thing that has ceased to be available to man as we known him historically."[88] Such "incapacity," original to the human being as such, is attached in Ricoeur to everything from speaking and narrating to teleological self-fulfillment and (as we shall see) deontological respect. In general, "there is something broken in the very heart of human action that prevents our partial experiences of fulfilled achievements from being equated with the whole field of human action."[89]

This broadening of radical evil is possible for Ricoeur because freedom is understood to constitute itself only in relation to passivity, according to his own post-Kantian philosophy of "the will" as simultaneously voluntary and involuntary. Moral evil is not the defeat of freedom alone; rather, it is the defeat of the fallible and tensional relation of freedom to finitude. It consists most generally in humanity's failure to realize its own intentionality of being in the world. Ricoeur's closeness to Augustine on this point is evident in the fact that Augustine is also interested in freedom's realization in its actual world. As Charles Mathewes argues, evil in Augustine involves a wide range of questions involving the relationship of human freedom to human nature.[90] The human "will" is not reducible to human freedom alone. Instead, for Ricoeur, "human being can surely be defined as a 'capable subject'—a subject capable of speaking, of acting, of narrating, of allowing responsibility for its actions to be attributed to it. But is this capacity itself really simply available to us? Does not evil consist in a radical incapacity?"[91]

Ricoeur makes this argument most extensively in his 1960 *The Symbolism of Evil*, where he claims that evil infects the human good by reducing the free will to what he calls "the servile will." This Pauline notion can be recaptured, according to Ricoeur, not philosophically but only symbolically, for it is at this point that the self becomes inscrutable to itself. The servile will is a "stain" on the self, a "defilement" of freedom, a paradoxical "self-enslavement." Re-interpreting Pauline images of humanity as a "body of sin" or "servant of sin," Ricoeur claims that

> the symbol of the enslaved body is the symbol of a sinful being who
> is at the same time *act* and *state*; that is to say, a sinful being in whom
> the very act of self-enslavement suppresses itself as "act" and relapses
> into "state." The body is the symbol of this obliterated freedom, of
> a building from which the builder has withdrawn.... A "yielding" of
> myself that is at the same time a "reign" *over* myself—there is the
> enigma of the servile will, of the will that makes itself a slave.[92]

Ricoeur's point is not, of course, that the body as such is sinful. It is that "body" symbolizes the self-enslavement of human freedom, for it is one of the clearest ways in which selfhood can be experienced as "state" divorced from "act." "Sin" is a paradoxical self-enslavement involving the "unavailability of freedom to itself," the "yielding of myself to captivity," the "superimposition of servitude on self-determination."[93] Evil is not the victory of finitude over freedom but, rather, the collapse of their primordial relation, in freedom's voluntary self-enslavement to passivity.

Ricoeur finds a powerful narrative symbolization of such radical evil in the mythology of the fall of Adam. Adam symbolizes, for Ricoeur, humanity's "loss of the bond with the origin," its own free break from its more primordially given freedom in the Garden of Eden.[94] The fall is inscrutable because it is from the goodness of creation in which human freedom has already been perfectly fulfilled. Evil is not a force of history but a radical break more primordial than history: humanity's defeat of its own humanity at history's origin. Thus: "The etiological myth of Adam is the most extreme attempt to separate the origin of evil from the origin of the good; its intention is to set up a *radical* origin of evil distinct from the more *primordial* origin of the goodness of things."[95] Adam symbolizes evil's paradoxical bursting forth onto the scene of an already good human existence. It is a choice made by human freedom in violation of its own primordial goodness. Ricoeur concludes that "the cause of man's fall is not the human libido, but the structure of finite freedom. It is in this sense that evil was *possible* through freedom."[96]

The defeat of human teleological freedom is consummated, finally, in God's (again mythological) curses: that women will have pain in childbearing, men will have to toil over the earth, and both will die (Genesis 3:16–19). Setting aside for future chapters the obvious moral problem here with gender, including the further curse that women will be ruled over by their husbands, let us note with Ricoeur that most of these curses involve otherwise good dimensions of our existence: reproduction (directly related to the command to "be fruitful and multiply"), tilling the land (again a form of "productivity"), being created out of the dust to have God's breath and spirit of life. The real curse, according to Ricoeur, is that we enslave ourselves to existences that fall short of the joy and happiness already possible in this world, a realization within finite existence for which freedom is primordially capable. "Work ceases to be joyous and becomes toilsome, placing man in an attitude of hostility toward nature. The pain of child-bearing darkens the joy of procreation," and "even death is altered: the curse is not that man shall die ('for dust thou art, and to dust shalt thou return'), but that he shall face death with the anguished awareness of its imminence; the curse is the human modality of dying."[97] In each case, human radical evil ushers in the defeat of an authentic realization of human freedom in the world.

Such efforts to symbolize radical evil in terms of the good are a distinct advance over the above Aristotelian perspectives on the moral problem, as well, in fact, as over a great many contemporary moral teleologies such as out of sociobiology and psychology that do not think through the profound problem of human moral freedom. If it were possible to inscribe evil within a traditional narrative, as Hauerwas claims, then it would no longer involve humanity's own inscrutably free choice. The difference between a "narrative" of evil and a "mythology" of evil is that the latter explicitly points to evil's primordial inexplicability in merely historical terms. It refuses the temptation of any kind of theodicy or global inner coherency, whether narrative, metaphysical, evolutionary, sociological, or psychological. Rather, it places moral evil at the ultimately inscrutable origins of our own very humanity. This, for Ricoeur, is precisely the point of the Adamic symbolism: to show that human evil is historically inexplicable, since it is humanity's paradoxical self-defeat of its own very humanity. The human moral problem is not the lack of a "true" narrative, or any narrative at all, by which the fragments of our lives may be rendered coherent. The problem of moral evil involves a primordial self-enslavement of the free human capability for *narrating* in the first place.

At the same time, however, can we not detect even in this mythological world something at least akin to a pre-Aristotelian sense for moral tragedy? Tragedy could never supplant radical evil because it emphasizes the victory over human freedom of human finitude: in the forms of fate, luck, destiny, and fortune. But this does not mean it does not presuppose in some way freedom's self-defeat. There is something profoundly tragic in our failure to realize ourselves in the world. The self's defeat of self-narration is deepened by situations in which there are already distortions in the narratives that selves have to work within. While Antigone and Creon are both ultimately responsible, from the point of view of radical evil, for their own narrative self-destruction, Antigone finds herself in the more profoundly tragic situation, because she is more narratively constrained than Creon by her patriarchal world. For her, a narrative unity of life faces steeper historical odds. Or today, a cancer patient needing expensive medical treatments may primordially be responsible for not being able to find a meaningful new narrative for her life, but at the same time her problem is greatly exacerbated by the tragic limits of medical care and insurance available to her. Even if our lack of narrative unity is ultimately attributable to our failed realization of freedom in the world, the sheer brute finitude of the world also contributes to this failure by its already tragically distorted narrative realities. Our poetics of moral narration should not lose sight of this vital cathartic dimension.

Ricoeur himself does not explore such tragic possibilities, but he at least opens up ways to begin to approach them. Consider again the symbolism in the Adamic myth of the serpent. Ricoeur reads the serpent as representing the fact that "every individual finds evil *already there*; nobody begins it absolutely."[98] This is not to suggest some kind of Manichean evil power. Rather, the serpent is quasi-human, speaking in human language and seeming to understand human ways; it symbolizes something profound and passive within humanity itself. "The Evil One is never anything more than a limiting figure, which denotes the evil that I continue when I, too, begin it and introduce it into the world... the evil for which, nevertheless, *I* am responsible."[99] Evil is "already there": although I perform it, in another sense I have already become its slave, already given in to its temptation.

For Ricoeur, this passivity is largely limited to the sense that freedom itself has given up its fullest capabilities. But could we not read the myth as also involving a very concrete human tragedy? What could be called "tragic" here, admittedly superimposing Greek upon Hebrew sensibilities, is that there is something serpentine and alive already within us that we experience as a powerful reality in our moral world. What is especially peculiar about the serpent is that it signifies an inscrutable fact of evil that is both human and nonhuman at once. In fact, the serpent not only talks but is also part animal: it arises from the world of brute nature. Its own curse involves a return to its own animality in having to move about the earth on its belly (and eat the dust from which *adam* itself is separated by God's breath). Its curse involves an endless *tension* with humanity, through the establishment of "enmity between you and the woman, and between your seed and her seed" (Genesis 3:15). Although the biblical traditions here do not speak in these terms, the symbolism of the serpent suggests not only freedom's own unavailability to itself, but also its tragically confronting a world that has become strange and disordered in and of itself. The lies of the serpent are not only freely accepted by ourselves, but also built into the fabric of our given human historicity that it is part of freedom's job to resist and overcome. Human freedom borders on the inhuman insofar as it becomes lost to itself.

In this way, the radical evil at the heart of the self's incapacity for narrative unity may be understood in an even more fully poetic sense. It involves not only the human failure *to narrate* its world in a meaningfully coherent way, but also its failure to do so in a world that is itself already *narrated* incoherently to begin with. The very narrative histories and languages (the serpent speaks, but untruthfully) on the basis of which we are to create narrative unity are themselves tragically disordered. Forming one's life into a narrative wholeness is faced with a radical tension from both directions at once: freedom *and* finitude. Freedom enslaves itself to only narrow and finite stories. At the same time, these stories are themselves already distorted by the historical conditions out of which they have arisen. The failure moves at the same time along both directions of the voluntary-involuntary polarity that constitutes narrative meaning. Even the symbolism of Adam and Eve, however much it tells us about the moral problem, is itself bound up with a social history that is filled with patriarchal and hierarchical distortions. We cannot fully trust even the language we use to symbolize evil. The most radical conclusion we may draw from our failure to create narrative unities of our lives is not just that freedom is self-defeated. It is that this failure, being human, is active and passive at once: active in each of us endlessly repeating the failure freely for ourselves, passive in the larger culminating history in which human failure becomes enshrined and self-sustaining over time.

Originary Affirmation

Even if such tragic dimensions of radical evil may be folded into our account through Aristotelian and pre-Aristotelian means, Ricoeur remains instructive as we now move toward imagining what kind of primordial moral poetics may be able, finally, to provide such radical evil a response. For like Kant, Ricoeur refuses to throw the fallen free will finally upon the mercies of God, or even upon the mercies of any traditionally preconstituted interpretation of God's desired good. Rather, he finds in the Genesis mythology what he calls an "originary affirmation" of the teleological capability of the human moral self.[100] This affirmation resists evil because while evil is original to humanity, the capability for goodness can still be posited as *more original still.* Before humanity's fall lies (symbolically speaking) its Creation. Such an originary affirmation of human moral freedom in the world is not a metaphysical axiom or a historically constituted value, but a matter of radical moral faith. It predates, as it were, meaning and narration as such. It stands as a mythological positing, in the face of evil, of a human capability for goodness at all. It will fall to us, in conclusion, to ask what this primordially given Creation has to do specifically with narrative creativity. But Ricoeur at least shows why some such primordial ethical capability must be posited—not as part of a moral tradition, but as presupposed in the possibility for moral traditionality and meaning at all.

In the face of radical evil—and all its attendant suffering, sadness, and disappointment—lies what Ricoeur calls an "absolutely primitive...joyous affirmation of being-able-to-be [*pouvoir-être*]."[101] As Theodore Marius Van Leeuwen describes it, Ricoeur's religious writings rest on the affirmation, the wager, the attestation that "existence and being are ultimately meaningful."[102] William Schweiker, partly influenced by Ricoeur, has similarly argued that "the moral meaning of Christian faith" is "the transvaluation of power [in the world] through the experience that it is good to exist."[103] If human freedom unaccountably turns against itself in this world, this very action need not destroy—indeed, it ultimately implies—a still more radical capability for human freedom to be something that is good. There could be no free "turning away" from the capability for good were there not something—however mysterious and covered over—to turn away *from.* The admission—the confession—of radical evil is already, in a way, an implicit affirmation of some still more radical capability for goodness.

Ricoeur describes such an originary affirmation in the paradoxical—and, in postmodernity, controversial—language of "gift." Although we *receive* this gift through the passivity of faith, the gift itself received is nothing other than our own freedom *to give*—in this case, to give meaning to our own fallen existences. (Further senses of "giving" emerge in the next chapters: giving to others, giving in society.) The gift belongs to an "economy of the gift"—itself a paradoxical phrase implying the self's both receiving something and actively participating in giving. Ricoeur is building here on the ontological conceptions of faith in Schleiermacher's "feeling of absolute dependence" and Tillich's "ultimate concern." If he agrees in part with Barth's conception of the Wholly Otherness of God (see chapter 1), he still insists that the "meaning" of the divine gift is ultimately also given by the human. Ricoeurian originary affirmation expresses a primordial faith that human freedom can affirm itself as given to itself as good, in spite of its own evil self-destruction. Faith may be placed in an "originary giving of existence" that affirms human freedom's ultimate capability for giving meaning to its world.[104]

This gift does not, according to Ricoeur, add anything substantive to the conception of the good as a narrative unity of life. It functions rather as the good's liberating ground in the face of evil.

> The ethical function of the gospel is best understood if we keep in mind the ethical dynamism. I propose saying that the Gospel *reanimates* this whole dynamism from its point of its departure. I think we go astray when we ask what possibly novel values, imperatives, or laws the Gospel adds. It seems to me that the strategic level where the evangelical morality operates is precisely that of the ethical intention.[105]

What is given through this originary affirmation is not a specific direction for ethical intentionality but a renewal of the possibility for ethical intentionality itself. The "desire to be" is not overwhelmed by non-being. Moral faith's function is to regenerate, not any particular story of goods, but the human teleological capability itself.

> I think that the verb "to save" primitively means "to liberate (*délier*) freedom" and as a consequence to put freedom back into motion, to restore its original dynamism to it. Kant understood this when he said that the function of religion is to regenerate freedom. The problem of regeneration is not at all that of legislation. It is a question of healing freedom at the level of the incapacity of its capacity.[106]

The originary affirmation is not ultimately of God, history, tradition, the Bible, or any particular narrative; it is of the primordially given human capability for giving itself meaning in the world in the first place.

Ricoeur again puts this ultimate capability mythologically. He finds a radical expression for the goodness of humanity in the claim in Genesis 1:31 immediately after humanity's creation: "God saw everything that he had made, and behold, it was very good." In *The Symbolism of Evil*, Ricoeur situates this originary affirmation as more primordial still than Adam's original fall:

> To posit the world as that *into which* sin entered, or innocence as that *from which* sin strayed, or again, in figurative language, Paradise as the place *from which* man was driven, is to attest that sin is not our original reality, does not constitute our first ontological status; sin does not define what it is to be man; beyond his becoming a sinner there is his being created.[107]

Faith, in fact, draws its meaning, in this way, first of all from sin itself. It is that which, in relation to sin, is more radically original still. Faith does not eliminate history or wipe out radical evil but, rather, *exceeds* historical sin. It is radical evil's own ultimate presupposition—on the far side, as it were, of its actuality.

Sin may be "older" than sins, but innocence is still "older." The "anteriority" of innocence to the "oldest" sin is, as it were, the temporal cipher of a profound anthropological fact. By the myth [of Adam] anthropology is invited, in the first place, to gather all the sins of the world into a sort of transhistorical unity, symbolized by the first man; then to put the stamp of contingency on that radical evil; and finally to preserve, superimposed on one another, the goodness of created man and the wickedness of historical man, while "separating" the one from the other by the "event" which the myth tells of as the first sin of the first man.[108]

This "event" describes original sin as a fall *from* a still more original human goodness. Both evil *and* innocence lie at the symbolic origins or limits of history as we actually experience it. But innocence can be affirmed, through the mythology of faith, as the more primordial reality.

Almost forty years later, in *Thinking Biblically*, Ricoeur extends this line of thought further by pointing out that Genesis 2–3 juxtaposes humanity's "separation" from God's goodness upon the "foundation" of actual human history. Ricoeur notes several distinct moments of "separation" from God: Adam's initial "already dependent" creatureliness (having not made himself but having been made by God); God's forbidding Adam's eating of the tree (separation through moral "limit"); the development of specifically *human* functions, different from God's, like naming the animals and sexuality (Ricoeur asks: "Does not the man, in his cry of jubilation, celebrate the woman without naming God?"); and only then the separation of the fall itself by choosing the serpent over God, followed by the expulsion from the Garden of Eden in which humankind's separation is finally consummated.[109] Each of these distinct separations (assuming the two creation stories here can be read together) illustrates the nature of the divide that separates human history overall from its original Creator.

And yet, at the same time, each separation founds or inaugurates something primordially good about humanity in actual history. Humanity breathes God's spirit; it can name through language; it can take joy in interpersonal and sexual relations; it is capable of knowledge of good and evil; and, in the end, it has a real history which it can constitute for itself through its own consciousness of time, meaning, and death. In this way, the myth depicts not just a loss of innocence but also "a founding event" having "the energy of a beginning" concerning the origins of human capabilities as we know and experience them in this world.[110] These origins are not only falls from God but also traces of humanity's lost but still more original meaning. They chart, as it were, the turning point from goodness to evil, and hence— from this side of the Garden of Eden—the trajectory of possible ways back from evil toward goodness. Evil is in the end not simply *opposed* to goodness but also a signpost toward the goodness that has been lost. As in Augustine, we can approach our own primordial goodness only in the end through the confession of sin.

What should we make of this concept of "originary affirmation" which I am claiming is the ultimate origin of Ricoeur's theory of the teleological good? Its great advantage is that it allows us to speak of a self-narrating human *capability* even in the face of the free self-enslavement of radical evil. As in Kant, ethical life remains grounded through and through in ethical freedom, for it is ultimately each one of us who is called to act with moral responsibility. But beyond Kant, this free capability can now be applied to the human narration of goods. If we can narrate a story like that of the creation and fall of Adam and Eve—in other words, if we can mythologize our own radical evil as preceded by our own still more radical createdness as good—then this very capability for *radical* narration can, paradoxically, be affirmed as good. It is only through narrative symbolism, in the end, that such an affirmation could be made, for only such impossible narration allows us at once to separate the origins of evil from good while at the same time ordering them sequentially. Mythology uses time to symbolize our own primordiality. And mythologizing is something we human beings can do.

Indeed, one could argue that Ricoeur resolves Kant's problem of radical evil better than does Kant himself. For radical evil is the problem of why human freedom is simultaneously the ground of moral life and its defeat, at once perfect and imperfect, good and evil. From a Kantian philosophical point of view—"within the limits of reason alone"—all we can finally say is that radical evil is inscrutable. But from the point of view of a hermeneutics of religious mythology, we can entertain the impossible possibility that freedom, while both good and evil, is nevertheless *still more primordially* good. Radical evil belongs to an original Adamic prehistory, but it signifies a fall from a distinct and still more original Adamic prehistory that is rooted in the goodness of Creation. Such a humanistic affirmation is no mere "ecclesiastical faith" (in Kant's phrase) in which freedom is thrown upon the mercies of God. Rather, it remains an affirmation of human freedom itself, but now as still more primordially good than evil. Mythology, from this angle, allows one to acknowledge the absolute originality of evil in human life while at the same time positing its lesser originality than goodness. The antinomy of human moral freedom cannot be resolved by philosophy alone, which simply presupposes it, but only by a hermeneutical poetics able to express the limits of the inscrutable primordiality of faith. This originary affirmation opens us up to our own impossible possibility for liberating ourselves from our own self-captivity, however much this possibility evades us in actual thought and history.

Interlude on Givenness

It should be clear by now why we could not accept any notion of this "gift" of original human goodness as a gift that is only received passively. Hauerwas finally succumbs to this antihumanistic temptation in arguing that the gift, for him, is a "Christian narrative" after which to pattern one's life. He claims that "to learn to be God's creatures means we must learn to recognize that our existence and the existence of the universe itself is a gift."[111] But this means, for him, that "theology is the discipline that attempts to juxtapose the various images and concepts of the language of faith in order to form a coherent pattern."[112] Here, perhaps, Hauerwas's Aristotelianism finally leads him into the tragic effort to secure a form of "goodness without fragility": a goodness that overcomes human frailty and fragmentation once and for all in a "true story." This effort is at odds, however, not only with what one may learn from tragic wisdom itself (not to rely too much, as Creon did, on grand social narratives), but also with Christianity's own myth of the fragility and brokenness of humankind at its very historical origins. Such a notion of the divine gift is clearly far, at any rate, from a Ricoeurian view of the gift as not a narrative per se but a human narrative capability, affirmed only through myth: the capability for goodness in the world despite human radical evil. Although Hauerwasian perspectives claim to tell the "true" Christian story, they do not reach Christianity's mythological depths as a reply to the self-enslavement of moral freedom.

At the same time, a more trenchant critique of the notion of "gift" is made by the poststructuralist analyses of Jacques Derrida and his followers. Although we cannot here do this larger conversation the justice it deserves, it is worth making it a brief reply, since it touches on the very possibility or capability put forth by Ricoeur for human meaning-making as such. For Derrida and others touch on what it means to say that "gifts" are ultimately "impossible" *qua* gifts. Our question is whether they may not still remain, even more radically prior to their actual impossibility, and from a poetic moral point of view, an "impossible possibility."

Derrida's argument develops upon the anthropologist Marcel Mauss's claim that the "economy of the gift" witnessed in potlatch societies such as those in Polynesia and Melanesia in fact encircles gifts within a logic of exchange. In this archaic economy, Mauss claims, a gift is not a free donation but, rather, "'exchange-through-gift' is the rule": anything given to someone else places that person under an automatic responsibility for a return, thus creating webs of social hierarchy and community.[113] Derrida's radicalization of this thesis consists in asserting that *anything* given as a gift under *any* circumstances immediately cancels itself out by giving something back to the giver. Even a gift from God, insofar as it is understood as given freely, is strictly speaking "impossible."

> [A]s soon as a gift is identified as a gift, with the meaning of a gift, then it is canceled as a gift. It is reintroduced into the circle of an exchange and destroyed as a gift. As soon as the donee knows it is a gift, he already thanks the donator, and cancels the gift. As soon as the donator is conscious of giving, he himself thanks himself and again cancels the gift by re-inscribing it into a circle, an economic circle.[114]

Derrida's point is not that no such thing as a "gift" can take place, only that gifts, by virtue of the fact that they cancel themselves out, cannot properly be described under the phenomenon of *giving*. The act of giving deconstructs itself, since giving is always also a giving back, a receiving of something in return.

This thesis has been developed in two ways by Derrida's followers. First, Dominique Janicaud, in an extensive critique of what he calls the "theological turn" of French phenomenology (in thinkers like Ricoeur, Levinas, and Marion), argues that there can be no such a thing as a "gift" from God at all, whether of creation, existence, covenant, love, grace, goodness, or anything else. Such a gift would have either to lie beyond the realm of phenomeno-logical investigation or to cancel itself out in God's consciousness of having given and in the self's own thankfulness for it. Such a gift could neither be freely given nor freely received, for it is in fact not "free" at all.[115] Second, and more recently, John Caputo and Michael Scanlon have argued that if "the gift is impossible," then this *itself* makes it an expression of a certain possibility for "faith," faith in "impossibility" as such. In this case, since it deals with impossibility, "deconstruction is structured like a religion."[116] This second approach seems to me the more promising of the two. One could argue it is where Derrida himself was headed toward the end of his life.

However, while I am sympathetic to this deconstructive skepticism about gifts in the world, I am more convinced by the richer and more symbolically worked out conception of the religious "gift" by the phenomenologist Jean-Luc Marion. In reply to the Derridean notion that gifts are strictly speaking im-possible, Marion argues that "givenness" (*donation*) lies at the very root of phenomenological meaning as such. Insofar as phenomena in the world "appear" to us, they are thereby also, and primordially, "given" to us. Indeed, in an important sense, as phenomena, they "give" themselves. Even the notion of the radical impossibility of the gift, one could say, is something "given" to experience. In an exchange on gifts with Derrida, Marion argues that, in a more originary way than any cancellation of gifts *within* the world (a Maussian claim he has no reason to deny), "givenness remains an immanent structure of any kind of phenomenality, whether immanent or transcendent."[117]

The original "gift" that can allow of no "return" is, on this view, the very "givenness" of the world itself. "Givenness" has a radical "precedence" over beings in the world, even over *différance*. It "exceeds" even Being as such. For it is the primordial characteristic of the human experience of any phenome-non at all.[118] Herein opens up the task, for Marion, of the phenomenology of religion, which in Marion's words is to "think impossibility." "The incom-prehensible, the excess, the impossible, are part and parcel of our experi-ence."[119] Indeed, some sort of primordial gift is the impossibility at the heart of the very possibility for meaning as such. We do not have to fall back onto a Christian historical narrative, in which the gift can be only *part* of the story, or a true as opposed to false story, to grasp our own and our world's primordial givenness. We can say that all meaning, however fragmented or coherent, even the meaning of historicity or time, is in some sense "given" in the world to consciousness.

Marion does not work out what such "givenness" might mean specifically for the teleological good. (He does, however, speak of its significance for "love" toward the other, as a kind of gifted generosity—a subject of our next, deontological chapter.) But he at least shows that "gift" is a possible human experience—indeed, part of the very grounds of the possibility for human experience itself. To say that a gift is "impossible" is to imagine it as only a part of human meaning, while in fact it can describe a dimension of human meaningfulness as such.

This brings us back to Ricoeur's notion of the "originary affirmation" of the self, the affirmation that selfhood is primordially, even if not historically, given to itself as good. It brings us back to this affirmation, however, in a more critically defensible way. This gift comes, not just from religious poetic language, but from a more phenomenologically radical source: the experience of givenness itself. We can call this source "God" (or as Marion himself prefers, to indicate its impossibility, "G⊠d"). But what "God" means in this case is a possible impossibility. Such a mysterious impossibility is able to be described, not because we can fold it into consciousness, but because it lies at the origin of the possibility for human consciousness itself. If it is true that a gift from God is impossible—as in a way deconstructionism is right to claim—this does not rule out its possibility in the sense of primordial origin of meaning.

The Gift of Creativity

What, then, can we say, finally, about the human gift—in the face of its own radical evil—for teleological *creativity*? In what impossibly possible sense might selves be capable of creating the good of their own narrative unity? Here is where even the profound poetics of Ricoeur must finally give way to something more. I have already argued in this chapter that Ricoeur's concept of narrative unity can be deepened by relating it to certain pre-Aristotelian considerations of the givenness of moral tragedy. The good is most radically a problem of the tension not only of historicity and freedom but also, and at the same time, of historicity's own inner disproportionalities. At the same time, we now confront the further limitations of Ricoeur's choosing to separate his philosophical from his religious writings, now in terms specifically of the good. (Ricoeur's reasons for this separation are discussed in chapter 1.) The mythical possibility for an originary gift of createdness needs to be related to its impossible possibility in this world. The question that faces us, in radical poetic terms, is the exact nature of the teleological human capability that must originarily be affirmed.

In Ricoeur's philosophical ethics, this capability is for narrating one's fragmented temporal world in the direction of a greater meaningful whole. In his biblical hermeneutics, however, the capability remains significantly more abstract. It is the capability for freedom in the face of self-enslavement. Here, the term "poetics" refers chiefly to the textual worlds themselves by which religion helps us imagine such human limits and possibilities, rather than to any kind of radically creative capability for this world's narration by selves. Biblical poetics in Ricoeur describes human createdness rather than human creativity.[120] We can perhaps say of Ricoeur's religious ethics what David Tracy has said of liberation theology: that it finally "retreats into . . . symbolic vagueness [and] premature announcements of paradox, scandal, and mystery."[121] Ricoeur does not press his more complex philosophical notion of narrative unity into any kind of comparatively passive-active capability at humanity's radical mythological limits. Here we are asking about what we might call moral creativity's impossible *possibility*. The fully primordial dimensions of human moral creativity consist in a primordial freedom, not only to liberate oneself from self-enslavement, but also, and more concretely, *to create* one's own ever more radically harmonized and inclusive narrative world.

To describe this primordial poetic teleological possibility, let us return to the mythology of Adam's Creation and ask what it might affirm about human creativity now understood as in the Creator's image. Or, in other words, let us ask what the giving Creator may symbolize about not only our gift *from* Creation, as in Ricoeur, but also, in the end, our own just as primordial gift *of* creativity. In what sense is this poetic gift not only received from our origins but also constitutive of the very phenomenological experience of moral capability itself? What could it mean for us to have a gift *for* creating narrative unities within our world? And what might this creative capability suggest for a radicalized moral poetics that can respond to the hidden passivity of moral tragedy?

What does this Creator do? It is not altogether clear that it creates ex nihilo (a theological notion developed later in early Christendom). God is said to exist in a world already populated by other god-like beings ("Let *us* make humankind in *our* image, according to *our* likeness," Genesis 1:26) and by things in the world itself like "the darkness," "the deep," and "the waters" (Genesis 1:1–2). But this Creator does create out of these mysterious and chaotic elements—we might even say: out of this primordial passivity—a certain worldly wholeness, a certain order and unity of Creation. Creation itself—as both a product and an activity—is directed toward a mysterious cosmic harmony. In addition, God not only creates time (the separation of darkness and light on the first day), but also creates *over* time, in the six days of creative activity. Thus we could say, without stretching the point too far, that the Creation in Genesis 1 is precisely the creation of a "narrative unity": in this case, the narrative unity in both space and time of the entire cosmos. Creation here has as its teleological end (however much things descend into chaos after Adam) its own narrative unity of life that is symbolized ultimately by a day of "rest." Narrative unity is a primordial Sabbath.

If humankind is originally affirmed here as created "in the image" of *this* God, human beings may be said ultimately to aim at such a narrative wholeness and rest for themselves. Prior to the fall (mythologically speaking) humanity is an image of the Creator of the whole as such, the Wholly Other as Creator of the Whole (or, indeed, the Creator as Wholly Whole). The ancient Jewish conception of the "imitation of God" by observing the Sabbath (as mentioned in the previous chapter) may be read in a mythological sense to suggest precisely some such impossible possibility for "imitating" the world's primordial narrative unity. The Sabbath is not just rest as such, but rest resulting from the labor of creation. It is the perfection of creative activity. So also might humanity's rest not be a merely passive cessation of activity but, rather, a perfect passive-active creation of order amid chaos. Even God's act of Creation confronts the plurality of "the darkness," "the deep," and "the waters" of the world with an exercise of intentional narration over time. How much more for us, then, is the rest and wholeness of the ethical Sabbath still yet a task to be accomplished. No one can anticipate its actual narrative end, but each of us may feel its primordial urgency.

But human creativity in imitation of God is also experienced as a command, the first and most primordial command there is: "Be fruitful and multiply, and fill the earth and subdue it" (Genesis 1:28). This command predates, as it were, the negative, prohibitory command not to eat of the fruit of the tree of knowledge of good and evil. It also predates the commands at Sinai: not to kill, not to steal, and so on. This prior command has been read in many ways over history, including as a license for humanity's exercise of power over nature or as affirming the importance of biological reproduction. But it can also be read as affirming, in a more radical way, humankind's own world-creative capability. Fruitfulness and multiplication are precisely what the Creator itself exhibits or symbolizes in its Creation of the world. Beyond the literal procreative meaning of this command is a symbolic possibility that we too are called to create a narrative unity and rest in our own world. As part of a myth that projects something of our now lost original humanity, this command claims that the disorder, fragmentation, and meaninglessness that we actually experience is not our ultimate reality. Ultimately, we are the kinds of creatures who can narrate the meaning of our existence, and narrate it in the direction of wholeness and unity. The inner teleological perfection of this narrative capability is the active drawing together of complexity. Before the fruit of evil is human fruitfulness. Before that which we actually make of our given creativity is the gift of creativity itself.

This does not mean that procreativity cannot thereby itself add symbolic meaning to this primordially creative task. As images of God, human beings are in a way like God's children. We may "grow up" to in turn create "offspring" in the likeness and image of ourselves. Such offspring, I submit, may be conceptualized in moral terms as our own very humanity. The humanity of human beings has yet to be created and fulfilled. It has paradoxically already been defeated through the self-enslavement of radical evil. Humanity here would not indicate a merely Kantian autonomous freedom. Rather, it would refer to each self's active-passive capability for narrating the meaning of its own life in the world into ever greater narrative wholeness. The symbolism of procreation is in this way read neither noumenally nor biologically but, rather, phenomenologically in the sense of the radical experience of the human possibility for creating one's own world of meaning. We are, in essence, commanded to procreate ourselves: to bring forth through the labor pains of our own constant self-defeat and rebirth our own deeper humanity. Like having a real child, the human gift for creating its own world of meaning is a gift for new being and new life, for expanding transformation and renewal. Procreating, indeed, may be the sharpest sign that in history we can still exceed ourselves. Humanity has at its Genesis a profound call to narrative generativity. The wager of creating human history anew is a wager both possible and worth making.

In addition, we may note that the Creator creates narrative wholeness in the world not just by action but also by speech. Indeed, speech itself defines action, since each creature comes into being by the simple declarative, "And God said, 'Let there be...'" Even humankind is made by God's *speaking* humankind into existence. One implication is that Creation as such is a spoken act. It is a primordial *logos* or Word that endows the world with meaning and wholeness. If we human beings are called also to the creation of our world, we are called to do so by using our own like capability for the creation of meaning through language. A narrative unity of life arises through the tale each of us can tell of our own world of meaning. From this angle, the story of the Creator creating the world through speech can be read as a story of our own impossible possibilities, as this Creator's image, for ever more radically whole self-narration.

This kind of use of language—not just reflexive but also creative of new and growing meaning—may be peculiar to humanity as such, a distinctive characteristic of human being-in-the-world. It is true that many nonhuman creatures also have speech and senses of narrative meaning, but do they, in addition, participate in this meaning's very creation? The perfection of a creative capability, in the end, involves not just the use of language as such but also its ever new creation: its formation of the diverse and multiple elements in our lives into more radically whole meaning and purpose. The culmination of speech, coming with the rest of the Sabbath, is gained only by the gift of speech itself: that is, the *giving* by speech of newly created meaning. Mythology in particular (as in Genesis) is a radical form of language that calls us back to the radicality, the primordiality, indeed the mystery, of human language itself. There would be no need for mythologies of humanity as created in the image of its Creator if our own linguistic creativity were already perfect. Such mythologies call us back to our as yet unrealized possibilities. As Marion says, we "play redundantly the unthinkable donation"—in an endless and impossible quest, I would say, for ever more radical narrative completeness.

By reading the primordial gift from God as a gift not only *of* created goodness (as in Ricoeur, and as, indeed, in most traditional ethical readings of the myth) but also *to* create goodness, we are also in a position to incorporate a pre-Aristotelian sense for the poetics of moral tragedy. What tragedy lends to this poetic good is not a response to radical evil as the distortedness of our finite freedom. It lends instead a response to the implied distortedness— within finitude itself—of the historical and linguistic situation within which human creative freedom is always already embroiled. Fate decrees that some of us have more resources and greater historical power to pursue our dreams, some greater psychological capabilities for handling conflicts, some greater access through stories and education to the complexities of their culture and language. Like Antigone, many of us must face the historical blindness of others toward us. Or, like Oedipus, many confront profound blindnesses in (and to) themselves. But all of us find ourselves, like Sisyphus, having constantly to begin creating our lives over again. The capability for creating a narrative unity of life involves not only the realization of creative freedom in the world but also the renewal of this broken world itself.

In this way, the formation of a narrative unity of life faces, in part, what is already given in the world. In a certain sense, Heidegger is right to link tragedy with appearance, for appearance signifies the concrete historicity that is always already given to us. Any gift of human self-creativity must be affirmed as more primordial than this givenness of our finitude, because this givenness is itself already distorted and distorting. An authentic meeting of freedom and finitude requires not only the liberation of freedom *from* the world but, in a more complex way, the liberation of freedom *within* the world. The tragic-poetic dimensions of this task refuse moral creativity any escape into Gnostic world-transcendence, or for that matter into an inner-worldly asceticism (as described by Max Weber) in which we dominate the world through its use. To create a narratively whole life involves not only freedom over the world but also inhabiting the cathartic complexities and discordancies of the world as it appears in itself. It is precisely through the multiple and contradictory historical conditions by which one finds oneself already given to oneself—the darknesses and the waters of one's world—that one is able to narrate oneself in the direction of an ever more world-excessive wholeness.

A narrative unity of life is therefore the teleological impossible possibility that stands at the limit or horizon of the narratives we actually tell of ourselves in the world. Its formation does not consist in its historical simplicity. A white supremacist does not have a highly unified narrative of life because his story leaves out so much of its own given historical complexity (quite apart from the deontological violence that it does to otherness). A genuine narrative unity does not make an idol of one's own narrowness, for this (as Creon learns) is tragic indeed. Merely projecting stories already known is never, in this world, enough. Rather, narrative wholeness is forged only insofar as the self can radically re-create the story of its own multiple biological, cultural, and traditional inheritances; its living relations with persons, institutions, and environments; and its own inner conflicts, needs, and aspirations. Ethicists who reflect on narrative unity also face the task of greater rather than lesser inclusion of such largely hidden dimensions of the moral world. As Nussbaum shows, simplicity can be the opposite of narrative unity because it covers over the diverse particularities of the world on the basis of which narrative depth and meaning are created in the first place. Narrative wholeness is an impossible horizon, imaginable only ultimately in myth, challenging us constantly to exceed all that we know, calling us beyond our own inevitable self-fragmentation.

What in the end unites poetics with teleological ethics is the radical possibility that the *tension* of freedom and finitude may be rendered productive of ever more coherent narrative *intentionality*. The "stretching" (*tensio*) of freedom and finitude may give rise to the self's "stretching toward" (*intensio*) an ever greater narrative wholeness. Primordial creativity is concretely completed in a new poetics of the will. "Ethical intentionality" in Ricoeur's sense may now be given the more specifically poetic meaning of the capability for creatively stretching the tensions of human life toward ever deeper narrative unity. Narrative tension is both our problem and our gift, both already given and still yet to be given meaning. It is always already *given*, in one sense, in our radically evil self-enslavement to a tragically distorted world. But it is also given in the more primordial sense of the strange human possibility for *giving* our given world new meaning. The goal of a narrative unity of life is not to erase tension, as we inevitably anxiously attempt to do, but to create out of the real tensions of our lives an ever more concretely realized narrative intentionality in the world.

And what, in the end, does this strange and primordial ethical intentionality actually stretch us toward? What, as we might say, is its *possible* impossible possibility? Here we find the first and most simple meaning of what I am calling ethical "inclusivity." Inclusivity at this point has nothing to with hospitality toward the stranger or sharing social power; indeed, it may frequently oppose them. All we can say about this poetic possibility at the level of the teleological good is that it describes the kind of inclusivity contained within the perfection of ethical narratives. What is to be included are the multiple dimensions of the self's historical existence in a narrative unity of life, dimensions which self-narration as radically evil in fact ignores, distorts, and remains blind to. Inclusivity means "narrative unity"—not of a merely traditional or fictional kind but as what can only appear to us as a primordial, mythological impossibility. Inclusivity as a teleological aim avoids the charge of historical totalization or simplification if it is understood poetically as the perfection of a human narrative creativity. It is a rendering productive of the irreducible tensions of human freedom and finitude, tensions which find rest only in constant self-renewal. We are not created to create our lives according to preconstituted historical patterns. Nor, however, are we created to create them in any way we please. We are created to create a narrative unity in its ever more radically excessive superabundance. Such is the paradoxical impossible possibility, never reached but always beckoning from within, against which our limited human ends are to be judged.

Luc Ferry has said that "if human beings were not in some way gods, they would no longer be human beings."[122] Our conclusion here is that we cannot realize our human telos or good unless we are in some way like our Creator. Aristotle and Plato began the long Western separation of the good from poetics because they sought to relativize the tragic incompleteness of this world under goods that could be considered rational or natural "ends in themselves." In the process of elevating an eternal human reason, however, they covered over humanity's more mysterious and god-like capability for its own fragile world's renewal. This not only affirms, as Ricoeur says, that "all creation is good, and the goodness that belongs to man is no other than its status as 'creature.'"[123] It affirms, even more radically and poetically than this, that humankind has a strange gift, however ill used, for creating its own fragmented world into greater narrative wholeness. History itself cannot give us a story that is already complete. And we paradoxically turn our very narrative capabilities toward this history's even further narrowness and distortion. But within the tension of freedom and finitude always lies the still more primordially human possibility, however excessive of what we can actually imagine, and however scandalously and shockingly, for narrating ourselves with ever greater wholeness.

3

Otherness and the
Poetics of Love

The poet William Wordsworth describes being overcome by love
for his daughter in his 1802 ode, "It is a Beautious Evening, Calm
and Free," as they walk in the fading darkness by the vast openness of
the sea:

> Listen! The mighty Being is awake,
> And doth with his eternal motion make
> A sound like thunder—everlastingly.
> Dear Child! dear Girl! that walkest with me here,
> If thou appear untouched by solemn thought,
> Thy nature is not therefore less divine:
> Thou liest in Abraham's bosom all the year;
> And worship'st at the Temple's inner shrine,
> God being with thee when we know it not.

Wordsworth is not touched by some preconceived theological belief
that his daughter happens to embody. He is touched by his daughter
herself as a fresh revelation of the divine, herself a singular person in
the here and now whom God is with even "when we know it not."
His daughter crashes in upon his thoughts and feelings the way a
wave crashes in from the darkness of the sea upon the shore where
they walk. And this crash makes a sound like thunder, drawing short
his breath and commanding him simply: "Listen!"

And in what does this listening consist? For Wordsworth it
consists in writing a poem that can somehow make this breaking in
of his daughter's divinity a response. To listen, for him, does not
mean simply to use his ears. The great passivity he feels before his
daughter, the dark sea, and the divine within them is an invitation to
remake his own world of meaning anew. It is true in part that his

daughter's transcending beauty drives him simply to imitate, to make a copy, to transfer the experience into poetic description. But there is more to his response than that. He feels he must actively pay attention, listen closely, and configure and symbolize the experience for himself. The poem would mean very little if it were not a testament not only to his daughter's divinity but also to his own self-transformation in her wake. She initiates the cathartic change within him; it crashes in upon him like a wave. But he completes it, or at least struggles to, in his creation of this poem. The command from his daughter is the poetic one to remake his own world of meaning in response to her.

This chapter moves our discussion of moral creativity beyond the teleological realm of the previous chapter, where it concerned the way selves create their own narrative unity in relation to their given social histories. In this chapter, we follow the story of the creative self as it encounters, not its own historical past, but now the call from others in the immediacy of the present. Here we enter the more complex moral terrain of "otherness"—otherness in the sense not just of narrative difference but of absolute alterity, singularity, and nonsubstitutability. While from one angle others are elements within my own narratives of the world, from another they are utterly irreducible to narration as such. They crash in upon my world, disrupting it like the thunder of divinity from without, interrupting how I am used to interpreting and thinking of them. They demand that I "listen" to their strange appearance, allow it to speak for itself from its own origin, as not just different from me but absolutely transcendent of the horizons of my own imagination. The other appears, as Emmanuel Levinas says, as a face of the divine: not a mysterious goodness like that I find within myself, but a command and call from the other's own singular alterity. This change in moral register, for reasons I will explain, I call deontological, by which I mean externally binding, obligational, prohibitory, imperative.

In contrast with much contemporary ethics of otherness, however, my claim is that the command from the other as a face of the divine does not reduce the self to passivity alone but demands its own passive-active creative self-transformation. The other's command is "poetic" in the sense that, however much it originates outside the self, it also requires the self to "create" it a radical response. Moral thought that seeks to account for otherness should not only warn of irreducibility but also provoke ever more radical senses for moral responsibility and renewal. This kind of call to self-transformation is utterly different than that discussed in chapter 2. Just as Wordsworth is moved to a poetic imitation and catharsis in response to his daughter, so too are each of us on some level obliged to re-create ourselves in the ever new face of others in their very otherness.

This poetic perspective helps to address what in my view is one of the most trenchant problems of poststructuralist Continental moral thought today—namely, how the other can appear as a moral demand when it is thought absolutely to overcome my own freedom. To use Kantian language, we find here a profound antinomy. The other arrests, stops, interrupts human freedom, and yet only freedom can finally give the other a response. My claim is that while otherness initiates this new level of moral life, it still requires, from a poetic point of view, my own passive-active, self-transcending moral creativity. What I am called to create is not greater narrative unity, but, in an equally radical yet directly opposed sense, ever greater imaginative responsiveness. The poetic capability called for here is a capability for one's own creative undoing, disruption, and radical reorientation. It is in this sense that moral creativity takes on what I am calling a "negative" dimension. (Only in the conclusion do I return to the precise sense in which these opposed moral poetics are also related.)

I proceed by moving through this chapter from the notion of the deontological freedom of the self to increasing senses for freedom's disruption by the in-breaking of otherness. This movement does not in the end abolish the self, but rather demands of it an ever more tensionally and primordially creative response to the other. First we examine a presupposed poetic dimension within Kant and his contemporary followers, since Kant lies in the background of much of contemporary thought regarding otherness (without of course grasping otherness itself) and yet deliberately separates ethics and poetics. Then I examine how Ricoeur picks up and radicalizes Kantianism in response to the extremity of the moral command issued in by otherness, and Ricoeur's correspondingly disorienting and "scandalous" religious ethics of the love command. This ethics is subsequently critiqued by means of the ethics of the face of transcendence in Levinas, allowing us to take otherness to its most radical religious extreme in which the other commands as itself a trace of the Wholly Other. Finally, I argue for a poetics of love that mediates a Levinasian origination in the Other with a Ricoeurian responsiveness to it, in the radical human capability for *creating* new moral relations to others of a transcendingly self-disruptive kind. The antinomy of freedom and otherness can finally be understood as a moral *tension* demanding the self's excessively creative upheaval.

Poetics in Kantian Ethics

It is well known that Kant separates ethics from poetics even more sharply than does Aristotle. This is because, for Kant, ethics is grounded in the universal law which freedom gives to itself: the law of respect for all humanity. Aesthetics, by contrast, which is modernity's new term for poetics, is for Kant concerned with the judgment of pleasure or displeasure concerning the beautiful and the sublime. This judgment shares with moral action that it is free and that it claims universal assent (to say that a flower is beautiful is to say that others should find it beautiful as well). But it is also entirely *subjective*: that is, it is not a matter of obligation or imperative but of personal and inner taste. When it comes to the aesthetic pleasure I take in art or nature, according to Kant, "I cannot be talked into it by means of any proofs."[1] In moral life, by contrast, freedom is necessarily constrained by a moral law that is rationally objective. In fact, morality demands our putting aside precisely our subjective senses of pleasure or displeasure in order to submit ourselves to the categorical imperative.

At the same time, however, Kant seems to have thought that aesthetic or poetic judgment adds something that his purely formal account of moral life lacks. As David Guyer has argued, we find in Kant the notion "that the aesthetic experience of the freedom of the imagination in response to beauty and of the power of reason in the feeling of the sublime can make our practical [moral] freedom palpable to us, thus supplementing the entirely nonexperiential inference of our freedom from our obligation under the moral law."[2] Guyer even thinks that Kant's third critique (on aesthetics) has as its "ulterior motive" the exploration of how the moral freedom of his second critique (on morality) is concretized in the aesthetic phenomenal "experience of freedom" as such.[3] There is a certain plausibility to the notion that if moral life is the exercise of pure freedom in practical relations to one another, then it will be aided by a poetic sense for how freedom is actually experienced in relation to the beauty and sublimity of the world.

But these considerations of a possible link between Kant's own ethics and aesthetics do not take us to the heart of the problem of how deontological ethics may involve the practice of creativity. Kant's aesthetics is deeply related to—indeed, forms much of the basis for—a Romantic view of creativity that makes it the purely subjective appreciation for nature or the expression of inner artistic genius. This form of "creativity" is at once subjective and highly receptive, an appreciation of beauty as something to be perceived in and of itself, and it is not surprising that Romanticism often opposes art to moral obligation. One can perhaps draw certain connections with Kant's subject-oriented ethics, but the gulf between ethics and such an aesthetics becomes a chasm if ethics is viewed from the point of view of intersubjective relations with the other. It is hard to learn much about otherness per se from the experience of my own inner aesthetic taste. On the contrary, taste would seem to close itself off to otherness as such by reducing otherness to selfhood, even promoting what we might call a *dis*taste of otherness, insofar as otherness offends what is thought to be pleasant and sublime.

A more fruitful tack is to see how Kant's moral thought in fact presupposes, even while claiming to deny, a fundamental relation between agency and passivity, autonomy and heteronomy, the voluntary and the involuntary. In this way we may begin to detect the inner necessity for an active-passive social creativity at the heart of deontological ethics itself. Here "creativity" may be related to the question of moral "necessity" or "bindingness" in the sense of the Greek *deon*. Deontological ethics is generally conceived of in Kantian terms as *self*-binding as opposed to binding from any external constraint like custom, goods, utilitarian benefits, natural desire, or even the divine. But it may be that, in a paradoxical way, both with and beyond Kant, what binds the self is also in part initiated *passively from without*: by otherness in its absolutely singular alterity. In this case, a radically creative tension may be detected in how otherness is necessarily self-binding.

This new kind of tension of freedom and finitude, agency and passivity, is in fact inchoately (although not explicitly) presupposed in Kant's first two formulations of the categorical imperative in his *Groundwork of the Metaphysics of Morals*. The first formulation is a clear assertion of the centrality of autonomy to moral life: "Act only on that maxim through which you can at the same time will that it should become a universal law."[4] It binds the self to others precisely by demanding treatment of others universally as free agents like oneself. The second formulation, however, is more relational. Kant says: "Act in such a way that you always treat humanity, whether in your own person or in the person of any other, never simply as a means, but always at the same time as an end."[5] Here, an implication creeps in that persons are not just autonomous agents but also can be "treated" passively as "means." That is, the moral law requires not just that I treat others also as autonomous agents like myself, but also that I *not* treat others as mere *objects* for my own use, that I recognize in them a certain human passivity. Here we find something akin to what, in the previous chapter, we saw Nussbaum call humanity's profound vulnerability. Except that in Kant this teaches us nothing of moral life's tragic dimensions.

A similar point is made regarding Kant by Ricoeur, around the notion of the moral "will." Kant's *Groundwork* opens by stating that "[i]t is impossible to conceive of anything at all in the world, or even out of it, which can be taken as good without qualification, except a *good will*."[6] By including the qualification "good" in the term "good will"—and the sentence would clearly not make sense without it—Kant presupposes that the will is not necessarily good *in and of itself*. The will is only "good" insofar as it chooses the moral law over other possible uses of its freedom. Ricoeur argues that we find implied here a "real opposition" facing the will between two distinct *influences*: "respect for the moral law" on the one hand and the "impulsion" of desire on the other.[7] The will turns out to be "good without qualification" only insofar as it allows itself to be *passively qualified by* the force of reason rather than the force of desire. The choice is between two possible influences, two kinds of reality to which freedom may subject itself. We could say that there are, in effect, two wills at work: the autonomous, self-legislating will that makes the moral law, and the practical will that gets the final say in choosing whether this moral law should influence action in the world.

The moral will in Kant in fact not only *gives* the moral law to itself but also *receives* it. In legislating itself, the will is both legislator and legislatee. In this case, the moral law is binding not only in the sense of autonomously given to oneself but also in the sense of being a force in its own right to be obeyed. According to Ricoeur, this means we may "doubt the autonomy of autonomy," for autonomy is always bound to something bigger than itself, even if that something is the law it gives itself.[8] Even the autonomous will itself, as sharply articulated in the ethics of Kant, can be deontologically self-binding only insofar as it is also receptive toward, beholden to, or inspired by the majesty and power of the moral law itself.

Contemporary Kantians are not unaware of this problem in Kant and have attempted to address the passive-active dimensions of moral life in various ways. Among the more successful attempts in this regard is the "proceduralist" ethics of John Rawls, which mitigates Kant's idealism with the more pragmatic and concrete contractualism of Jean-Jacques Rousseau and John Locke, a contractualism that recognizes selves' profound moral dependency upon one another. Rawls broadens autonomy, in fact, into a theory of the procedures required for governing social *inter*action. Morality is not based on self-legislated reason alone but on the "considered convictions" that arise when the points of view of diverse selves are all taken into account. What is to be set aside in this new kind of "social contract" is not selves' passivity through desire (as in Kant), but their partiality in realizing desires alongside others. The "original position" on which moral life should be grounded throws a "veil of ignorance" over one's own particular interests in a situation, so that one may pursue instead a fair and just social dialogue about the relative interests of all. The problem is not so much freedom's loss of autonomy as freedom's being used to instrumentalize others against their own desires.

The result for Rawls is a certain sense in which selves are to use their freedom only in fair and equitable balance with the freedom of others. This imperative is articulated through two basic moral principles that should govern intersubjective relations overall, neither of which forgets selves' potential vulnerability to each other. First, "each person is to have an equal right to the most extensive basic liberty compatible with a similar liberty for others"; second, "social and economic inequalities are to be arranged so that they are both (a) reasonably expected to be to everyone's advantage, and (b) attached to positions and offices open to all."[9] The first principle ensures, in a way similar to Kant, the protection of generalized freedoms (freedom of expression, of assembly, etc.), but in a way that protects such freedoms from encroachment by others. The second principle (also known as the "difference principle") requires that inequalities of goods be permitted only if they can be said to further all selves' interests. This latter principle insists that social interactions not advantage some at the expense of others, thus recognizing that selves remain in an irreducible sense socially dependent upon one another. Freedom does not need to be rationalized so much as constrained by mutually agreeable contracts.

But does Rawls appreciate the full depths to which selves may be passively instrumentalized by one another, and hence the depths of their poetic moral irreduciblity and tension? Is Rawls's "other" really "other"? Similar critiques of Rawls are made along such lines by Ricoeur and Nussbaum.

Ricoeur in various places argues that Rawls's procedures rely on a prior passive openness (which Rawls himself fails to thematize) of the self to the other's concrete historical particularity. For one thing, Rawls's proceduralism leaves little room for the possibility of "irreducible conflicts among goods," since "the effect of the formalist nature of the contract is to neutralize the diversity of goods."[10] But even more importantly, the "considered convictions" to be arrived at presuppose that they are considered from multiple points of view: "In the expression 'considered convictions,' the epithet 'considered'... [should mean] open to the criticism of another."[11] This would be possible only if selves were conceived of as capable not only of entering into contracts with one another, but also of responding to other selves' otherness as such, in such a way as potentially to change the self's own interests and perspective. "A procedural conception of justice at best provides a rationalization of a [particular teleological] sense of justice that is always presupposed."[12] Merely remaining behind a veil of ignorance does not open selves to the needed critique of their own interests from alterior points of view that a genuine dialogue among different interests would require.[13]

Nussbaum is also concerned with this fragile and irreducible relation of agency and passivity. As discussed in chapter 2, she views just moral relations as involving not only speaking for oneself but also "attention" to others' concrete particularities. Intersubjective social dialogue must involve, at least in part, the effort to overcome one's own simplifications of the moral situation through the work of a literary and sympathetic moral imagination of differences. Nussbaum specifically criticizes Rawls's theory of "reflective equilibrium." For Rawls, the practice of reflective equilibrium moves the above general principles into actual dialogue in the concrete situation, dialogue in which interests are tested reflectively against one another. Nussbaum insists that what is really needed, however, is a "perceptive equilibrium": the practice of coming to imaginatively shared judgments about moral life's actual nuances and details.[14] This, in a way (although Nussbaum does not say as much), employs something like a Kantian aesthetics of the "perception" of beauty. The point of moral perceptiveness in Nussbaum is precisely to overcome the habitual "obtuseness" that results from failing to be receptive to otherness. Indeed, a "deeper and more inclusive attunement" to others is something that the generalized application of procedures generally obscures.[15]

It is not without irony that we may conclude that Rawls offers, in effect, a more subtle form of utilitarian calculation than that found in the traditional utilitarianism that is Rawls's chief object of criticism. Rawls is right to be suspicious of the possibility that selves, as not just free but also interdependent creatures, will seek to instrumentalize one another for their own ends. But he views the passivity of others as able to be overcome by the self in itself, by following fair principles of discourse behind a veil of ignorance. But behind this veil, is not the self in fact encouraged, precisely, to *calculate*? Even if it were possible to pretend not to know which portion of the goods will be distributed to itself, the self is still encouraged—indeed, required—to make the more subtle calculation of which arrangement of goods would further the self's interests in relation to others if its exact social position were unknown. What is established is a kind of Tocquevillian enlightened self-interest in which I must pursue my own good in a roundabout contractual setting. The social contract is entered into, after all, in classic social contract theory, so as to advance personal interest, not to demand responsibility to otherness.

What is truly lacking in Rawls and much of Kantianism is not a sense for moral freedom but a just as necessary sense for moral tragedy. The tragedy of human moral relations (in part) is that selves' separate interests admit of no rational or anticipated confluence. Indeed, no self is qualified—even from behind a veil of ignorance—to say how interests may be justly proportioned with others in the first place. What Antigone and Creon need, for example, is not clearer moral procedures. Each would apply the same principles of goods as they already do even from behind a veil of ignorance. What they need are greater capabilities for listening to what is different and strange in one another's particular story. As Nussbaum claims, "the good human life is inseparable from the risk of opposition, therefore of conflict.... [T]o unify and harmonize, removing these bases of conflict, is to remove value as well."[16] Instead, genuine social dialogue involves an endless poetic adventure of following the new stories opened up to oneself when others are faced in their concrete particularity. It is ultimately our "loving perception of each particular" that opens us up toward a just treatment of our fellow human beings.[17]

The freedom that each of us should respect and not violate in each other is not, then, in the end, absolutely free. Moral autonomy is by itself an insufficient grounds for moral relations. Freedom must be qualified by receptivity and imagination toward others, and by openness to self-transformation in response to them. Kant's efforts to concretize moral freedom through aesthetic taste is doomed to fail. It reveals the limits of grounding moral relations in moral freedom alone. If aesthetics is to enter the picture of moral life, it must introduce into the world of the self a profound and discomforting passivity. Perception of the other needs to be more than a freely made judgment of taste; it needs also to involve a reception of otherness in its strange and unpredictable alterity. Tragically, the other depends on my capability for imagining their otherness as such, a capability that I never perfectly fulfill. Wordsworth's daughter may share with Wordsworth a certain autonomous freedom, but she also overcomes and even defeats his freedom through her absolutely irreducible singularity in the world. The fundamental reason Kantian ethics consistently divorces ethics from poetics is that it refuses to acknowledge moral freedom's debt to the overwhelming reception and disruption of the other. In this way, it obscures moral freedom's necessary tension with moral finitude.

The Problem of the Other: *Do ut Des*

This conditioned relation of selves to others has been taken up by discussions of ethics in contemporary Continental phenomenology. Perhaps the key problem addressed here is how moral freedom is limited by otherness as such. With a few exceptions in Continental ethics today like Alain Badiou,[18] otherness of this radically self-disrupting kind is *the* moral problem. The towering figure here is Levinas, who argues that the otherness (*l'altérité*) of the other is a voice that commands absolutely, as if from the God of Mount Sinai, "You shall not kill." The other is a trace of the Wholly Other, the hyperbolic origin of moral life that utterly disrupts and negates selves' interests and being in the world as such. For Levinas, the other is not just different from me but the very face of Transcendence, the form in which the unfathomable God is revealed, an epiphany that reduces me to absolute passivity before it. The other person exceeds not only my own interpretation of it but (beyond even Heidegger) language and being as such.

I return to Levinas in detail later on. For now, it is important to note that the problem of otherness has a larger French and now Anglo-American context. For Jean-Paul Sartre, for example, independently of Levinas but around the same time, otherness took on the explicitly secular meaning of the struggle for the other's authentic expression in a world of mass bourgeois sameness. Levinas sharply criticizes Sartre for locating the experience of otherness in freedom rather than in passivity, but they still agree that otherness transcends essence and disrupts moral rationality. For Jacques Derrida, who in moral terms is deeply indebted to Levinas, otherness is *différance*—not just difference, but difference endlessly deferred, the difference of surprise and the never-ending trace that continually deconstructs my view of the other's presence, introducing in its place the other's absence. For Luce Irigaray, more recently, otherness in our patriarchal world means first of all the female. These and many others attest in different ways to the virtual obsession in post–World War II French moral thought with otherness as the antidote to modernity's perceived reification of autonomy and its consequent reduction of humanity to sameness, totality, and hegemony.

Such ideas have acquired a growing force in Anglo-American ethics, too, where the powerful hold of the Kantian analytic tradition led by Rawls has been placed into sharp question by a sense for moral life as radical disruption. John Caputo, for example, chiefly following Derrida, has vividly interpreted the problem of otherness as having to do with being "taken hold of from without, seized by something else . . . [a] heteronomy, that disrupts me, that is visited upon me, that knocks me out of orbit."[19] Similarly, the English writer Simon Critchley, chiefly following Levinas, describes otherness as "the putting into question of the ego, the knowing subject, self-consciousness."[20] More concretely, Alphonso Lingis, the English-language translator of Levinas, says in his own ethics that "this *other community* forms not in a work, but in the interruption of work and enterprises. It is not realized in having or in producing something in common but in exposing oneself to the one with whom one has nothing in common: to the Aztec, the nomad, the guerrilla, the enemy."[21] From this "Continental" point of view, moral life is less a question of the laws of freedom than of exactly the opposite: the disruption visited upon and arresting freedom by alterity.

In what follows, I argue that the problem of otherness does not replace the problem of moral freedom but, rather, qualifies it in a radical and fundamental way. My own view is that the above-mentioned forms of "otherness" do not so much reduce selfhood to pure passivity as introduce into moral life a new and more complex level of passive-active moral tension. Although otherness is sometimes thought to destroy any sense of moral selfhood altogether, this is only true of particular forms of the moral "self" such as the autonomous or calculating ego of modernity. By now, however, this "ego" is all too easy and large a critical target. The more interesting and paradoxical problem, at least from a poetic point of view, is how the other can remain a moral concern when it ultimately demands something *of me*, some kind of self-disruptive or self-transcending response. I am called by the command originating in the other, from this angle, not just to self-negation, but also to self-transformation, self-creation—however passively this call is first received. As Kearney has asked, "How is one to be faithful to the other, after all, if there is no *self* to be faithful?"[22] A more complex view of the moral self, I argue, allows us to see otherness as instigating within the self a poetic crisis or tension. It is from this other-self tension (very different from the narrative tension of the previous chapter) that the self is called toward moral self-creation of a negative, disruptive kind. The poetic "intentionality" of the previous chapter is replaced with what I will call a new poetic "distensionality."

Here is where we may once again find initial assistance from Ricoeur. Although Ricoeur is sometimes thought to misunderstand the other as a figure of the self, and although I will agree that this is true up to a certain point, he is in fact concerned with the complex problem of how moral otherness, in all its absoluteness, imposes a unique *involuntary* demand on the *voluntary* responsibility of the self. The other, for Ricoeur, can represent even a face of the Wholly Other God—but even God demands our own interpretation of God for ourselves. Ricoeur's theory of otherness is part of a larger poetics of the will in which "will" can constitute itself meaningfully only because it finds itself always already constituted from without. Although, therefore, Ricoeur was a colleague of Levinas in the 1960s at the University of Paris X at Nanterre, and although he was one of the first to explore the problem of otherness in moral life, he nevertheless continually refuses to allow otherness to overwhelm selfhood. Rather, the question is how otherness stands in irreducible tension with the self's capability for making it a response. (I return to Levinas himself later in this chapter.)

Ricoeur agrees with Levinas that the moral problem here is characterized first and foremost by violence: violence to otherness by the imposition of sameness. He claims, however, that violence is not just the refusal to accept passively the disruption of the other, but also an *active* choice to take advantage of the other's own passive vulnerability. It is something for which selves are guilty and must be held responsible for committing, however much the prohibition against violence originates in the other. Violence itself is strangely active-passive. It consists in "the diminishment or the destruction of the power-to-do of others."[23] It includes, for Ricoeur, a "descending slope . . . from influence, the gentle form of holding power-over, all the way to torture, the extreme form of abuse."[24] But in each case it is neither a conflict of two agencies (as in Kant), nor a call to pure passivity (as in Levinas), but rather a deepening of the self's problem of being an agent and a patient in moral life at once.

This means that for Ricoeur otherness introduces into human relations a profound and unsettling aporia or paradox. The paradox is that it is exactly the same "self" who does violence to the other who is nevertheless called upon to undo it. The other relies for nonviolence on the response of selves when it is precisely the response of selves that is the problem. As Ricoeur puts it, otherness raises the problem of the *asymmetry* of human capability or "power":

> [Violence is] the fact that, by acting, someone exerts a power over somebody else; thus interaction does not merely confront agents equally capable of initiative but agents and patients as well; it's this asymmetry within action as interaction between agents and patients which gives way to the most decisive ethical considerations. Not that power as such implies violence; I say only that the power exerted by someone on somebody else constitutes the basic occasion for using the other as an instrument.[25]

It is not that selfhood per se causes violence, but that selfhood is violence's *occasion*. It would be possible for selves not to do others violence, even if they inevitably do. As Kearney interprets Ricoeur on this point, selves "run the *risk* of reducing otherness to selfhood."[26] It is the fact that others depend on selves for nonviolence that makes violence possible in the first place.

This paradox makes violence an inscrutable human choice, a figure of what we have been calling human radical evil. The problem of the other cannot simply be explained as the outcome of worldly desire or interest. It is also, and at the very same time, a paradox of human freedom being used against humanity itself. Radical evil in this sense takes on a different face than it did in teleological terms in chapter 2, where we described it as an Augustinian self-enslavement of the will to its own narrow ends. Neither Aristotle nor Augustine was explicitly concerned with the problem of moral otherness. Rather, Ricoeur here follows instead the Levinasian sense for evil as the disobeying of the other's moral command. This arguably more Hebraic sensitivity has to do with estrangement from the divinely given covenant. But in Ricoeur it remains an estrangement or disobedience that brings responsibility also upon the freedom of the will.

Ricoeur develops this dimension of moral evil specifically around ways in which the Bible problematizes the meaning of the golden rule. In Ricoeur's view, both Jewish and New Testament interpretations of the golden rule reveal its inherent impossibility, or at least our own inevitable falling short of it in human history. The golden rule, "Do to others as you would have them do to you," is prey to what Ricoeur calls a "logic of equivalence."[27] It can be interpreted to advise the merely *instrumental* norm to do to others *because* you would have them do to you. Rather than treating others with the inherent singularity each of us normally claims for ourselves, we inevitably also, when it comes to others, keep an eye out for what doing for others may gain for us in return. "The golden rule, through its [fallen] demand for *reciprocity*, remains within the parameters of the *lex talionis*: an eye for an eye, a tooth for a tooth. Understood this way, the golden rule just says, 'I give *so that* you give' (*do ut des*)."[28] *Do ut des*: do for others so that one may eventually gain a reward in return. Do for others so that either they will do for you, or, ultimately, God will provide deserved blessings. Is not this logic the false equivalency criticized implicitly in the story of Abraham and Isaac and explicitly in the book of Job?

Ricoeur's point is in effect to refuse to separate violence as something passively inevitable through interest and being in the world from violence as something inscrutably, sinfully posited by human freedom. Both must be thought at once. To reduce another to my own instrumental aims is actively to take advantage of the other's inherent human passivity in relation to the world. At the same time, to fail to receive passively the other's command against violence is to fail to act differently than I could. The problem is not that freedom overcomes passivity (or, as in Kant, the reverse), but that the two fall out of tension with one another. Instrumentalizing others is not just the way of the world but also, and at the same time, a form of radical evil. It implicates the self in making use of its will in doing violence to the will of another.

This does not mean that violence is reducible, for Ricoeur, to a Kantian violation of human freedom. "Do to others as you would have them *do to you*" refers the self to its own experience of passivity, its awareness of the possibility for having violence *done to* itself. Violence goes against a required double substitution: you should place yourself in the place of the other as a passive recipient of your own actions. Violence raises a mirror to the self in revealing the other as another self like oneself. But the other, in this case, is not just another free agent but also, like me, and most importantly, able to have violence passively done to it. The golden rule is no mere rule of universalizability, therefore, but rather raises a more profound moral problem. It "lays the stress not only on the conflictual side of interaction but on the asymmetry between what someone *does* and what *is done* to someone else. In this sense, the formula of obligation does not bring side by side two agents, but an agent and patient of action."[29] This asymmetry between self-agency and other-passivity undoes the deeper possible interconnectedness of human agency and passivity as such. Indeed, for this reason Ricoeur claims a preference at times for Hillel's negative formulation of the golden rule in the *Babylonian Talmud*: "Do not do unto your neighbor what you would hate him to do to you."[30] This formulation emphasizes more sharply one's own vulnerability— what one would "hate" to have others do to oneself—so that this vulnerability should be recognized also more clearly in the other.

Ricoeur illustrates this strange paradox of violence to others, this radically evil instrumentalization of the other's will, in a variety of ways. One is the idea of *vengeance*, which he interprets as a "logic of equivalence" now regarding not goods but harms. Vengeance claims to "do justice" by an exchange of violence itself. In response to the harm another does to me, reducing me to its instrument, vengeance claims justice lies in returning an equivalent harm to the other. Of course, vengeance is clearly visible in acts like ethinic cleansing and "taking justice into one's own hands." But it is also more subtly present even, for example, in penal systems, which inevitably slip into some level of retributive vengeance of society. It is not that punishment for crimes lacks a utilitarian function—say in dissuading further crime or keeping criminals off the street. It is only that, in the process, retributive justice also instrumentalizes a human being's otherness for larger societal ends. Doing justice cannot help but fall short of full respect for the criminal's singular alterity, however much justice should still be done. According to Ricoeur, "even in the most just punishment" the implication is made that a criminal act may be redressed through a like exchange, while in fact the crime belongs solely to the criminal and the harm done could never receive a totally "just" return.[31] To suggest any less is to suggest that the guilt of the crime can be erased.

In an address delivered in a memorial at a synagogue in Chicago to the six million Jewish victims of the Holocaust on Yom Ha-Shoah, Ricoeur claims that here the understandable desire for vengeance nevertheless tends to undermine the irreducible particularity of the crime's victims. Vengeance makes the finally reductive claim that the horror of the suffering can be made some sort of equivalent recompense. Instead, the violent nature of the crime is ultimately preserved only by refusing such a logic:

> The task of memory [in this case] is to preserve the scandalous dimension of the event, to leave that which is monstrous inexhaustible by explanation. Thanks to the memory and to the narratives that preserve this memory, the uniqueness of the horrible—the unique uniqueness, if I dare say so—is prevented from being leveled off by explanation.[32]

The unique singularity of the victims in this case can in fact be memorialized, not through an exchange of vengeance, but only through a poetics: in this case, lamentation. "The lamentation reveals the murderers as murderers and the victims for what they are: namely, the bearers of a lamentation that no explanation is able to mitigate."[33] Lamentation is memory put into psalm. Only in this way is the otherness of violence's victims preserved against even the most well-meaning efforts at recompense—even if such efforts may otherwise serve a useful purpose—because only in this way is the radical task undertaken of remembering the victims in their own particular singularity and not just as accidents of history or desire.

Of course, on this token the entire philosophy of utilitarianism is sharply critiqued as well, and not just on Rawlsian grounds that it undermines justice as fairness. Utilitarianism is nothing more than the rational codification of humanity's failure to grasp each other's otherness. Ricoeur argues that utilitarianism rests finally on a "process of victimization" in which "the maximization of the average advantage of the greatest number [comes] at the price of the sacrifice of a small number."[34] Any effort to rationalize systems of human exchange, however tolerant and free, is doomed to marginalize not only some others but all others *qua* other. Each other becomes (and submits itself to becoming) an instrument in a system of calculated exchange. Contemporary market capitalism is the most obvious example. It is built precisely around "practices of exclusion" that reduce oneself and others to commodities.[35] The point is not that such systems should not be constructed. It is that in constructing them we should be aware that they always fall short of respecting the otherness of the very persons of whom they are comprised, so that "justice" to the other always requires something more.

The key problem raised by otherness is not, therefore, on this account, merely the self's reduction of otherness to sameness. Violence is more than the assertion of free selfhood, more even than the self's refusal to be knocked out of its own accustomed orbit. In the end, violence cannot be reduced to what Levinas calls "the *conatus* of beings," the "being" of beings as such, the way of the world absent Transcendence.[36] The key problem is that the self falls short of responding to otherness with the radicality of which it is ultimately capable. Violence violates not only otherness but also the violator's own primordially created humanity. The problem could not consist only in the self's failure to reduce itself to the non-being of passivity, since violence is also an act, something for which selves remain inscrutably responsible. It is not just a function of finitude but also of free radical evil. We can know this because violence does to others what we would ultimately not want done to ourselves. It turns us against a primordial sense for humanity that lies deep within each one of us. Even though I inevitably and inscrutably fail to do so, it is still only an *I* who is capable of making the orphan and the stranger a nonviolent response.

If there is something tragic about this all-too-human situation, it is that our freedom to make others the required response not only defeats itself through sin but also experiences itself as always defeated already. This experience is ultimately false, but it is also very real. It is as though the Furies conspire to pile vengeance upon vengeance and blindness upon blindness so that humanity may never realize its own responsive ethical potential. Few of us would not gladly end all wars, feed the poor, and welcome the stranger, but none of us reaches very far in escaping the narrow horizons that implicate us in such violence's perpetuation. If Creon forcefully undermines the justice of protecting Thebes with his blind drive for revenge against its traitor, neither is Antigone entirely free of violence in refusing to consider the needs of her state, however just her own particular cause. Her act of suicide, however noble, is also in part an act of bitter vengeance. It would be tempting, indeed, to attribute violence to the being of the world as such, were it not that humanity is not just passive but also free to act differently.

And so however much violence to otherness may arise out of the finitude of the world as such, out of the conditions of interest and sameness, and however much we may be able therefore to give it some explanation, it remains the case also that selves bear a primordial responsibility for it and therefore are radically called to overcome it. As Mohandas Gandhi saw, hearing the voice of those done violence is also a deliberate and patient practice of self-discipline, however endless and humbling. It is a moral task that *belongs to me*. Because of the sinful and tragic nature of the problem, this call must appear to us as a summons to something historically impossible. And yet, as we will now see, it is a call also to a radical human possibility.

How Much More

Ricoeur's response to this problem of otherness is instructive because it insists on the necessity of not just self-disruption but also self-transformation. The other demands a response, and this response must be made by a self, a self who is now called to hyperbolic self-renewal. This kind of responsiveness Ricoeur calls "love," which he interprets as neither a subjective feeling nor an explicable reciprocity but a disorienting moral command. Love is related to what in his philosophical writings Ricoeur calls "respect" for the self (*respect de soi*), by which he means not just Kantian respect for selves' autonomy but the refusal to do violence to others in their genuine otherness from oneself. There, Ricoeur argues that "respect is self-esteem that has passed through the sieve of the universal and constraining norm—in short, self-esteem under the reign of the law."[37] Respect is respect for the other's own singular intentional capability. The "universal and constraining norm" here is not just freedom itself but freedom incarnated in the passivity of the world in each other's irreducible narrative particularity. Rather than pursuing this revision of Kant, however, our task here is to see how, in response to radical evil, love commands the self still more radically and transformatively.

According to Ricoeur, love in fact rests on faith—faith in the ethical sense from the previous chapter of the originary affirmation of created human goodness. The economy of the gift that begins in the gift of humanity to itself demands, in a second moment, that this gift also be *given* to the other in its otherness. Ricoeur interprets Jesus' command to "love one another" to mean this: "because it has been given to you, you give in turn."[38] Because I have already been given the gift of primordial existence and goodness, I am to give to the neighbor a correspondingly superabundant regard. Ricoeur is in a sense taking up a classic notion of grace as something that in being received also obliges the receiver to fulfill overflowingly in the world. But this graceful giving of love is understood not just as the bounty of God, but also, in moral terms, the bounty of the self in its primordial capability for giving to the other. An analogy could be drawn in this respect to Marion's view of gift as jubilation: "To return the gift, to play redundantly the unthinkable donation, this is not said, but done.... Only then can discourse be reborn, but as an enjoyment, a jubilation, a praise."[39]

But in Ricoeur love is also a command. It reflects not only praise of God but also the responsiveness demanded by other human beings. If the problem is that selves tend to reduce one another under their own utilitarian "logic of equivalence," then love replies as a countervailing "logic of superabundance." The purpose of love is to overturn, so to speak, the tables in the marketplace. The utilitarian calculation "I give *so that* you give" is disrupted in a new excessiveness: "I give because it has been given to me."[40] I give to the other because I have already been given an originary affirmation. The other demands a response that exceeds all possible calculation because the other is also, like me, absolutely and primordially good. However, this implies not just equity but excess. No matter how much I might admire or detest another, every other is ultimately a creature of God whom I am commanded to love more than I can actually imagine.

In the widest possible sense, in fact, the love command identifies the neighbor with "Creation" as such. "The sense of our radical dependence on a higher power thus may be reflected in a love for the creature, for every creature, in every creature—and the love of neighbor can become an expression of this supramoral love for all creatures."[41] This means that no amount of ordinary respect for the other finally matches the excessive regard which the other in fact deserves:

> [E]ach response [by Jesus to his followers] *gives more* than that asked by ordinary prudence. The right cheek? The other also! The coat? The cloak as well! One mile? One mile more! Not just this, but even that! It is this *giving more* that appears to me to constitute the point of these extreme commands.... This logic of generosity clashes head on with the logic of equivalence that orders our everyday exchanges, our commerce, and our penal law.[42]

The love command turns humanity's rootedness in creation into an outward demand to *give more* to each other, to exceed our always insufficient and faulty generosity. The love command as a religious phenomenon is inherently excessive.

Such a view would remain within the orbit of a now discredited conception of love as self-denial and "other-regard" were it not part of a larger moral symbolism. Reinhold Neibuhr's ethic of love has been criticized, for example, for denying the importance of love for oneself. In Ricoeur, the love command is a limit-expression in the same sense as for all sacred symbolisms. It is not a theologically reasoned social possibility but a mythologically disruptive *impossible* possibility. Its function is not to replace ordinary senses of human justice, to offer up an alternative norm, but to convict justice and respect themselves of falling short of their own most radical ideal. Like faith in one's own primordial goodness, it responds to human sin as a "hyperbolic corrective" that sets humanity back in the direction of its own more original course.[43] Thus, the love command is made precisely to the self, the self as capable of recognizing in love its own primordial obligation as a human being. Love is a giving more, to others, of the disruptive affirmation one is already called to give to oneself.

The sharpest expression of this excessive command, according to Ricoeur, is Jesus' saying to "love your enemies" as formulated in Luke 6:27–28: "But I say to you that listen, Love your enemies, do good to those who hate you, bless those who curse you, pray for those who abuse you."[44] The logic of superabundance here has analogies to the excessive pronouncements of the prophets, love in the Song of Songs, other gospel sayings like "give to everyone who begs from you," and Paul's constant reference to the "how much more" demanded of the spirit.[45] "Love your enemies" is paradigmatic, however, because it places the accent of love squarely on the other's alterity. The enemy is the one who most decidedly does *not* give your love any return, but on the contrary presses forward with its own violence. Love given to the enemy least anticipates a return. It flies in the face of the logic of return itself.

The command to "love your enemies" immediately precedes Jesus' formulation of the golden rule: "Do to others as you would have them do to you" (Luke 6:31). As we have seen, the golden rule is in Ricoeur's view inevitably reduced, despite even our best intentions, to a logic of equivalence: *do ut des.* Jesus' "juxtaposition" of hyperbolic love and the golden rule functions, according to Ricoeur, to rescue the latter from its inevitable disintegration in a mere logic of reciprocity. The love command reveals ordinary human justice's intrinsically radical implications. Doing to others as you would have them do to you is an ambiguous and corruptible saying, but it can also become revealed as a radical impossibility that remains for us nevertheless also our deepest human possibility. Thus, according to Ricoeur, "what is called 'Christian ethics,' or, as I would prefer to say, 'communal ethics in a religious perspective,' consists, I believe, in the tension between unilateral love [loving even enemies] and bilateral justice [the golden rule], and the interpretation of each of these in terms of the other."[46] The love command is, in short, a *tension.* It is not a law but a call to a human primordiality that has inscrutably been lost but can still animate new behavior.

The result is that the love command acknowledges the absolute alterity of the other, but still requires that one make the other a response. "Love converts justice to its highest ideal."[47] It functions to steer justice toward the ever wider inclusion of alterity.

> Is there then any incompatibility between the golden rule and the commandment to love? No, if we see in the commandment to love a corrective to rather than replacement for the golden rule. The commandment to love brings about a *conversion* of the golden rule from its penchant toward self-interest to a welcoming attitude toward the other.[48]

Such a conversion is necessary because of violence. It introduces crisis and tension into one's regard toward the other. Selves inevitably fail to embrace one another's "singularity and nonsubstitutability."[49] Taking a phrase from the Jewish thinker Franz Rosenzweig's *The Star of Redemption,* Ricoeur finds in the love command the primordial declaration from the other to myself: "love me!"—a declaration the self never absolutely fulfills but can still hear and give a response to.[50]

Ricoeur finds concrete examples of the living reality of this tensional love command in various quarters. Politically, for example, one has the act of pardon: "Even international politics can be touched by love in the form of unexpected acts of pardon, as exemplified by German Chancellor Willy Brandt falling on his knees before the Holocaust monument in Warsaw or King Juan Carlos asking pardon from the Jews for their expulsion from Spain at the end of the fifteenth century."[51] More recently, Pope John Paul II has asked pardon for the Catholic Church's complicity in the Nazi regime. Here is acknowledged a failure to hear the voice of the other and an effort to give otherness something greater of its due, however impossibly in the end. Love can also make its way into jurisprudence: "I would even say that the tenacious incorporation, step by step, of a supplementary degree of compassion and generosity in all of our codes—including our penal codes and our codes of social justice—constitutes a perfectly reasonable task, however difficult and interminable it may be."[52] Or economics:

> The law of exchange is not eternal. Ethnology [as in Mauss] tells us
> of an economy of the gift more ancient than that of exchange; it tells
> us of festive events on which human beings competed against one
> another with their generosity and munificence. Is not our task at the
> national level, and even more at the international level, to bring about
> the economy of the gift within a modern context? Is not our task
> to rectify by some positive interventions, the inequality that results
> precisely from our application to all our economic and commercial
> relations of the logic of equivalence?[53]

This excess of generosity toward others, this going the extra mile, this superabundant extension toward one's friends and enemies alike, is everywhere defeated in human life and yet remains its interminable task.

It is thus that Ricoeur begins to help us see how the apparently impossible problem set by otherness—whether one could ever actually give it a response—is met with a still more radical possibility for self-transformation. What Ricoeur sometimes refers to as his "poetics of love" or "poetics of agape" suggests that, in the face of the other, the self can still make its own self-transcending response.[54] Ricoeur himself does not in fact connect love to his early anticipated poetics of the will. And the term "poetics" here appears to refer more to the necessity of the appearance of the love command in symbolic and religious language—to describe its hyperbole and superabundance—than to self-creativity as such. Nevertheless, it is evident that the "how much more" owed to the other is also the self's own "giving more" than it can possibly imagine: giving to the other in such a way that the self's participation in worldly violence is itself transformed in the direction of love. The love command recognizes that the human imagination is always already bound to reduce otherness to its own finite calculations. And so it commands in response that the human will itself, as at once passively caught up in and actively embracing of violence, turn ever more superabundantly toward its other. The command is not fixed or static; it is for the self's radical and continuous moral conversion.

Levinas's Command

Before we can draw any conclusions concerning the self's responsibility to create, however, there is a problem with Ricoeur's account that must be overcome and that has not gone unnoticed by his critics. This problem is that, however hyperbolically Ricoeur may interpret it, the love command still does not on his interpretation *originate* in the other as such, the other as a face of the Wholly Other. It is more accurate to say that for Ricoeur love is given to the other from the self, originating in a prior faith in the self's own human created goodness that is then applied to the other as another such self. One might say that Ricoeur replies to the ordinary exchange of the world with something like a hyperbolic religious exchange: "I give because it has been given to me." I am to love the other, not as itself the absolute origin of the command, but as part of my own winding path toward redemption. I love the other in order to return the gift I have received, not to the other per se, but to my own Creator. Indeed, the very notion of inscribing the other within an "economy of the gift" cannot help suggesting a certain logic of equivalence of its own, however much this new "economy" resists radical evil by originating in God rather than in the world.

Richard Cohen has made the most sustained critique of Ricoeur along such lines by arguing, using Levinas, that Ricoeur's origination of ethics in self-esteem denies the original nature of the other's command inherently. Cohen mistakenly argues that Ricoeur has no place for religious "hyperbole" at all, since he focuses only on Ricoeur's philosophical writings.[55] But he is right to suggest that in a certain sense Ricoeur "misses accounting for the prior impact which is at once the impact of alterity as such and moral obligation."[56] Although, as we have seen, Ricoeur does not reduce *all* of moral life to the obligational level, when it comes to this level he does in fact not fully appreciate how otherness is morally originary *qua other*. The "impact" of the other on the self should not be limited to its analogously being another creature of God like me. It is not first of all *I* who gives to the other (my superabundant love), but *the other* who gives (the command) to me, the other as a trace of the Wholly Other in and of itself. Our movement from the Kantian self to the radically other is in other words not yet complete. Their tension is deeper still than Ricoeur imagines. Beyond the other as commanding my response is also the other as the moral command's very origin.

Levinas and Ricoeur in fact share a great deal, a fact which commentators like Cohen sometimes gloss over. Both engage in lifelong projects to reorient Husserlian phenomenology around religious ethics, and for this reason share primary responsibility for what has been called French phenomenology's "theological turn."[57] Although Levinas is frequently interpreted into secular terms, there is no doubt that his own writings have a profound and explicit religiosity, however different this may be from more traditional (in his case Jewish) theology or dogmatics. In addition, both Levinas and Ricoeur resist what they perceive as the antiethical, as well as the antireligious, developments of post–World War II French existentialism and structuralism. In particular, both feel these movements cannot respond adequately to the depths of human evil that was revealed so forcefully in examples like Auschwitz and Stalinism.

What is more, despite their different conceptions of otherness, both agree that it is a response to alterity that is called for by moral evil. Morny Joy has argued that "it is in this relationship to the other, with its connotations of absolute responsibility and humility, that Ricoeur and Levinas most resemble each other."[58] Although it is now well known in religious ethics that otherness can be a moral term, Levinas and Ricoeur were already sowing the seeds of this vineyard in the 1950s and 1960s. Anglo-American ethicists have come to this term *l'altérité* only recently, but it has a long and complex history already, some of it mentioned above, in which both Levinas and Ricoeur are deeply immersed. And both argue, somewhat uniquely in fact, that its mystery and depths require a response of a transcending religious order.

With these similarities in mind, however, the differences become all the more striking. Although they are many, those that especially concern us here have to do with the *kind* of command which otherness is said to visit on the self. What makes Levinas's view useful for us is precisely this command's origination in the other, not as recommended to me by my own feeling of givenness by the divine, but as *itself* the divine's unmediated voice. Levinas, unlike Ricoeur, calls ethics "first philosophy." What he means is that the call from the other is not heard through any prior phenomenological, hermeneutical, or even theological lens, but is precisely the very origin and ground of being, language, and action as such. The trace of the primordial can appear to us only, according to Levinas, through the ethical command of the other not to do it violence. How we might interpret or act on this command can only be secondarily derived from it.

The roots of this view in Levinas lie in how he understands religious *language*. Ricoeur, I have argued, views "the naming of God" as taking place first in sacred texts. Texts name God before we, in turn, receive this name and interpret it into our own actual lives. For Levinas, however, *all* language, whether explicitly sacred or not, and whether enshrined in texts or spoken directly, expresses a single prior and hidden Voice of Transcendence. Language as such "signifies" or "witnesses to" a hidden Wholly Other. This is because anything that belongs to the realm of "the said" (*le dit*), or actual words and texts in the world, announces an invisible and transcendental "saying" (*le Dire*) behind it. "Saying states and thematizes the said, but it signifies it to the other, a neighbor, with a signification that has to be distinguished from that borne by the words in the said."[59] Language, in other words, is a trace of the transcendental dimensions of otherness. Indeed, "the said" is said, in Levinas's later *Otherwise than Being, or Beyond Essence*, to represent the other's "betrayal," for it inherently falls short of expressing the other's hidden depths of "saying" in its alterity.[60]

Unlike Ricoeur's reliance on biblical language to reveal God, Levinas therefore generally uses sacred texts much more loosely. While Levinas does make liberal use of such biblical terminology as "witness," "prophesy," "command," "the chosen one"—and above all Abraham's response to God: "Here I am!"—he in fact refers directly to the Bible itself in his best known writings generally only in footnotes. What is important is not the language itself or its "sacred" status so much as the infinite "saying" that lies behind it. As John Caputo has observed, in Levinas it is not the Torah that ultimately signifies divinity, but the "archi-Semitic" "stranger" who is the "desert wanderer" behind its pages.[61] Or, as Edith Wyschogrod puts it, for Levinas "language is in its very foundations ethical,"[62] so that language *about* ethics can be no more than ethics' imperfect invocation of the primordial origin to which it bears witness. The trace of God is "manifested," not in certain hyperbolic texts and not others—a distinction Ricoeur clearly draws—but in language's hyperbolic moral "saying" as such by the other.[63]

As a result of this view of language, a second difference from Ricoeur emerges in Levinas's view of God. For Levinas, the divine is not a limit-experience disrupting selfhood from all sides, but a Transcendence "beyond being" witnessed only in the face of the other. As we have seen, Ricoeur views God as having many names: "The originary expressions of faith are complex forms of discourse as diverse as narratives, prophesies, laws, proverbs, prayers, hymns, liturgical formulas, and wisdom writings. As a whole these forms of discourse name God. But they do so in various ways."[64] Levinas is in a sense much more singularly monotheistic. God only appears in the face of the other as Other. God is only ultimately the God of the invisible ethical command. As Mark Wallace has pointed out, unlike Levinas Ricoeur appears "to subsume legal discourse to a wider concern for the panoply of other, nonlegal discourses that generate the surplus of meaning,"[65] while Levinas sticks singularly to the God of the saying of otherness. While Levinas does use a variety of expressions for the appearance of the divine—such as "the Transcendent," "the Infinite," "Absolute Exteriority," and "otherwise than being"—these all point to one and the same phenomenon: the ethical Wholly Other.

The result, in moral terms, is that while Ricoeur places the moral command within the context of a larger act of "naming God," Levinas reverses religion and ethics so that what comes first is the hidden ethical "voice" that comes directly *from the other*. What is original in Levinas is precisely this ethical command. Moral life begins in the saying of the other as Other that brings into the world the "breathlessness of the spirit," "the breathlessness of inspiration."[66] The other person is the only trace of the unpronounceable Absolute. All our efforts to name God, including in and through sacred texts, are for Levinas ultimately "cut short in the wind of alterity."[67] The meaning of religious symbolism always lies beyond the words themselves in the Wholly Other whose true manifestation is the ethical face of the other immediately before us.

Moral life finds its *origin*, therefore, according to Levinas, not in the self—as ultimately in Ricoeur—but in the other *qua* other. As Levinas summarizes it: *"L'absolument Autre, c'est Autrui."*[68] For complicated reasons, in Lingis's English translation, *"Autrui"* or the other person is capitalized as "Other," while *"l'absolument Autre"* or God is not (while in the French, of course, both are capitalized).[69] Thus the phrase is translated: "The absolutely other [God] is the Other [the other person]." The point, however it is translated, is that God or Transcendence enters the world precisely and only in the ethical mode of the other person. The other person *is* the direct yet invisible "face" or "voice" of the commanding God. "The Infinite orders me to the neighbor as a face, without being exposed to me."[70] This face of the other is not its physical appearance but, properly understood, "the glory of the infinite" which is revealed to me absolutely and unmediatedly "without dialogue."[71]

What, then, does this absolutely original "other" face command? According to Levinas, the other says to me, as if from Mount Sinai, "you shall not kill."[72] This divine command is not, as Ricoeur interprets it, a hyperethical corrective to my own ordinary sense of justice. Rather, it is the absolute origin of justice itself. It reveals "a debt contracted before any freedom and before any consciousness and any present."[73] The face of the other is a command precisely because it originates, not in any sense of selfhood or understanding, but in an infinite alterity. It refuses reduction to any human experience of being in the world. Ethics originates prior to freedom in what freedom can only experience as pure exteriority. The command from the other is both invisible and absolute.

Evil, therefore, is radical in a different sense than in Ricoeur. It is not tied to an inscrutable self-defeat of human freedom. Rather, evil lies in the being and interests of the world as such. Short of the moral command, ordinary moral life appears for Levinas to be self-interested and instrumentalizing through and through. Despite his opposition to Kant's grounding of the moral law in freedom, in fact, Levinas in a certain sense accepts Kant's absolute separation of moral law from interest. But in a more radical way, Levinas equates interest itself with human being in the world. At the outset of both his major works, Levinas argues that human "being" itself—as opposed to otherness which is "otherwise than being"—is entirely captive to "war": to a violent drive to reduce otherness to sameness. On the first page of his early book *Totality and Infinity*, Levinas attacks the entire course of Western philosophy since Plato as captive to such a metaphysics of being: "The visage of being that shows itself in war is fixed in the concept of totality, which dominates Western philosophy."[74] Evil consists in the totalizing nature of *being as such*. Anything short of absolute otherness is violence and war.

This view is sharpened further at the beginning of *Otherwise than Being*, where Levinas associates human "being" or *esse* with "interest" or *interesse*. "War is the deed or drama of the essence's [being's] interest."[75] Without the hyperbolic intrusion of the command from the other, originating only in the other as such, moral life becomes "the struggle of each against all," "the clash of each against all in which each comes to be with all, becomes reciprocal limitation and determination, like that of matter."[76] "Reciprocity" here is not just a logic of calculation; it is the law of being a self. What we have been calling the logic of equivalence is the logic of being as such. Levinas appears here in a sense as a world-denouncing prophet. We think we are living good and holy lives, but in fact human being itself is mired in the totality of violence. No action begun in oneself can escape this blasphemous condition.

Unlike in Ricoeur, therefore, the other is not to be *given* a gift of love by the self, but, on the contrary, it is the other who *gives* the command. The stranger, the widow, the orphan in my midst is not just another person in the world but also "the epiphany of the face" that originates ethical life as such.

Ethics rests in "the way in which the other presents himself, exceeding *the idea of the other in me*."[77] Only in its absolute exteriority to me can the face of the other cut short the war and violence of being in the world. "The ethical, beyond vision and certitude, delineates the structure of exteriority as such."[78] The command from the other exceeds not just utilitarian reciprocity but all possible being, words, and understanding.

It is this which leads, especially in his later *Otherwise than Being*, to Levinas's extreme assertion—which my own account will finally question— that the only way for the self to be ethical in the world is through its "pure passivity." If there is any tension between human agency and passivity, this is strictly secondary to the ethical originality of the other. Agency and freedom in myself are not to be converted but opposed. The self must be reduced to the other's "hostage."[79] It should "substitute" itself with the other.[80] The epiphany of the face commands a radical moral "subjectivity" that is not freedom but rather "subjection" to the other, a "responsibility" that is not enacted but a purely passive "response."[81] The self must in fact take on "a passivity more passive still than the passivity of matter," a passivity more passive than being.[82] If being is war, otherness commands the possibility "against my will" for ceasing my part in the killing.[83]

If it seems paradoxical, as Levinas himself fully admits, that the moral subject is defined precisely by its subjection to otherness—that acting ethically should be absolutely passive—this is finally because the "other" is not just another person but also, and at the very same time, a trace of Transcendence. This, we might say, is Levinas's reply to the antinomy with which we began, the antinomy of responsibility and alterity. Like Abraham before God, our response to otherness can be made only in the passive mode of saying "here I am." Levinas interprets this as follows: "here I am (*me voici*) for the others."[84] In saying this, the "I"—the French *me* not *je*—is both grammatically and ethically in "the accusative."[85] Because I am only capable by my own will of violent interest, the ethical command disrupts my very being from without. The other is not, as in Ricoeur, the command's object, but, first of all, its giver. *L'absolument Autre, c'est Autrui*: the Wholly Other *is* the other. This means that the self commanded to give a response can do so only in the passive mode of submission and self-denial.

There are several advantages to Levinas's conception of the moral command if we are to understand the creative tensionality at the heart of the relation of self and other. First, Levinas provides a more coherent way to speak of the command from otherness both philosophically and religiously at once. There is no split here, as in Ricoeur, between ordinary respect for the other as another person and disruptive regard for otherness as such. Levinas eschews misleading scruples about "cryptotheology" with a directness that ultimately gives religion greater ethical meaning for today. In Ricoeur this split makes the love command something one hears only through a prior faith, only after having already accepted a gift of God's superabundance as operative in human life. Levinas more successfully integrates religious language into philosophical ethics because he locates the radical ethical command in human moral relations through and through. Since this root of moral life is now transferred from the modernist self to the antimodernist other, it becomes possible to link humanity as other rather directly to a Wholly Other. Cohen claims that it is here, in fact, that Levinas's ethics has its greatest value, for it "raises the priority of the encounter with the alterity of the other, ethical priority, to the status of the very humanity of the human." For Cohen, "Levinasian thought...is precisely the humanism of religious humanism, the only humanism worthy of its name."[86]

Second, I think Levinas more fully articulates what I have been calling evil's dimension of tragedy. Tragedy is not a term used, of course, by Levinas himself; indeed, he is explicitly opposed to much of the Greek ethical worldview. This, however, is because Levinas equates Greek ethics chiefly with Platonism and its location of ethics and transcendence in Being. However, if prior to Greek philosophy were the tragic poets, and if (as claimed above) Greek philosophy tried to overcome the tragic poets' sense for goodness' fragility, then prior to the Platonic order of being may be found a certain tragic wisdom concerning the violence of being as such. To say that the world of *esse* is inherently a war of *interesse* is to suggest a similarly tragic inevitability of moral disorder and chaos in even the best-intentioned human efforts to live well in the world. It is to suggest also a certain necessity for moral catharsis, for being's openness to radical and unknown renewal. In this regard, Levinas's prophetic denunciation of the world may not be entirely unlike the tragic poet's accusation of humanity's blindness. The prophets are after all in a sense tragic figures, announcing new social possibilities in a world itself unwilling to hear them. Even when we think we are being just and good—indeed, *because* we think we are being just and good—in fact we perpetrate violence.

But third, and most important of all, Levinas shows why the moral tension of self and other must finally originate in the other, not in the self. Whatever role we might feel inclined later to restore to the self, it must be a role of secondary responsiveness. Levinas's notion of the other as itself giving the moral command is finally unavailable even to the tragic poets. The other as Wholly Other is not to be used for any self-redemptive purpose whatsoever. Rather, God *is* the other. The only return I could possibly make to such a God would be through the negativity of nonviolence. The other should never lose its absolute strangeness, as a stranger not only to myself but also to the world, a strange wanderer through this inhospitable vale of tears. There should be no presumption of a prior and already received grace which the self may bestow on others at will, since this again reduces the other to my instrument. Such a presumption has provided the occasion for all manner of religiously justified violence against "others" in the past and still in the present. To resist the self's subtle violation of otherness, it is necessary at least on some level to assert that the other commands me, not just as another creature of God *like myself*, but as witnessing to the ethical God in a wholly original and primordial way.

Otherness as Creation

Does this wholly original command from the other, however, destroy any possible sense for the self's responsive moral creativity? Does it give the lie to any self-creative other-self tension? I will now argue that it does not. On the contrary, the other's command calls the self to a still more radically passive-active self-transformation than even imagined in Ricoeur. Prior to Sinai is the Creation. Levinas is right to insist on the other's absolute moral primordiality, but wrong to say that this reduces the self to an absolute passivity. The command from the other could not be *ethical* were it not on some level a command requiring my own primordially free and creative response. The paradox or antinomy of otherness and selfhood is fully addressed only through the notion of a poetic other-self tension. Even God must be "given" or "made" an interpretation by the self, however invisibly originary and Wholly Other God may remain. Is not Levinas's entire body of work precisely his own creative interpretation of otherness? And is it not finally addressed to me, to you, to human selves as capable, in the face of others, of transforming ourselves in loving response?

The extremity of the other who commands as if from Sinai not to kill and the more limited command articulated by Jesus to love your enemies are only opposed if we neglect their common symbolic roots in Creation. We now find that it is not just the self who is created in the image of God, but also—and just as absolutely—the other *qua* other. From a deontological point of view, the other appears as an altogether different kind of image of the Creator. And this means, or so I now wish to argue, that the other also, in a different way, *creates*. What the other creates is not a narrative unity of life but in a way precisely its opposite: a command for the world to give it a nonviolent response. This command *originates* in otherness. The other *makes* it as a trace of its primordial Maker. It is precisely the other—and not some God disembodied from the being of this world, nor any God of the self—who, as itself a likeness to God, "makes" this command to me. The other as Wholly Other "creates" the command to love by virtue of its own primordial human originality.

This means that creativity in this deontological register is more complex than in its teleological sense discussed above. Moral creativity is now doubled. The other creates a command, in effect, for the self to re-create itself in response. The other appears to the self as more than part of the self's historical world or even the self's own ultimate narrative possibilities. But this appearance does not rob selfhood of moral responsibility. The will is imperfect and always fails to give the other an adequate response. But this does not mean it is not still called toward its own deontological perfection. This perfection is love. But beyond Ricoeur, the love of the self toward the other is realized only to the extent that the command created by otherness is given the response of hyperbolically creative self-renewal. The poetics of love is the impossible possibility for "making" the other a response, "making" now in the negative sense of undoing oneself self-disruptively, unraveling one's own violent being in the world.

In what sense, first of all, does the other as other "create"? Clearly not in the same way as the self creates its own narrative good. Kearney argues in *The God Who May Be* that a distinction can be made between "person" and "persona," the former representing the phenomenological manifestation of the latter, which itself remains utterly mysterious. "Each person embodies a *persona*. *Persona* is that eschatological aura of 'possibility' [as opposed to actuality] which eludes but informs a person's actual presence in the here and now. I use it here as another word for the otherness of the other."[87] Such a "persona," if indeed it exists, is more than simply God's trace on earth. It is attached, ultimately, to a person. Otherness as persona occupies a mediating position between the other as person and the other as God. It is something like the "image" or "likeness" of God that we explored through Genesis: neither God Godself nor humanity as we actually know it in this world, but humanity's primordial, impossible possibility. The other too can be affirmed mythologically as some kind of original mirror of the divine. Except that "persona" ascribes such a primordial possibility, not to myself, but to the other in all its irreducible otherness. This "otherness" can be claimed to exist within "the other" I actually see before me as a matter of mythological possibility.

In this case, otherness may be not just a bald Transcendence with which the other is infused but also a primordial human capability of its own, something the other originally *does*. However much my interpretation of the other clouds or channels how otherness appears to me, each singular other still cuts through language and being in and for itself, thus in a sense activating its own absolute moral command. Its "saying" behind all that is said is its *own* saying, in the image of the one who says all being as such into existence. If God is the other, as Levinas claims, then the other is also in a sense God-like. I do not give this command to myself, but neither does it come from a God abstracted from another person. It comes, precisely, from each particular other as another human being in the world. It is given by the other as an image or mirror of Transcendence in the here and now.

What the other primordially "creates" is not divorced from the other's meaning as a person in this world. The problem addressed by otherness cannot be conceived of as this world's being as such—at least not if it is to retain its ethical sense of a problem posed by another actual person. The problem is that being has devolved into violence—perhaps, to some extent, all being—when in fact being is not originally so made. The other commands as a voice of God struggling for meaning within its own historical particularity. What it creates is not just a denunciation of the world but also, and more radically, a demand for some form of radical worldly renewal. Since it is the same God who both commands nonviolence and created the world, the command cannot ultimately oppose the world altogether. The stranger, the widow, and the orphan bring something new *into* the very world that does them violence. What they bring—what they "give"—is the possibility that this world may be re-created in a still less violent way. The other's command is original, not in the sense of transcending this world, but in the sense of *making possible* this world's own more radical transformation and renewal.

Let us take the example of an infant born today in sub-Saharan Africa to a family already unable to feed itself, in a community lacking potable water and a country mired in debt to foreign governments, where the majority of children die before the age of five from malnutrition and easily preventable illnesses like diarrhea and measles. (According to UNICEF and the World Health Organization, the number of such preventable deaths in children each year around the world currently averages almost eleven million, or thirty thousand children a day.) This infant is the victim of many converging forces in its life over which it has absolutely no control. It is done violence by the rest of humanity on a scale most of us can barely imagine.

And yet, does not this infant, helpless though she remains in historical terms, still "create" something? Does she not create from the primordial depths of her humanity a radically new command and responsibility? Before the infant's birth, this particular command did not exist, for the infant was not yet a human being to whom violence had been done. Yet now that she is here and another human being, she is herself an originating source that makes such a command in the world. She not only commands nonviolence but also in a way *creates* this command herself. While she can barely act in any way to feed, protect, or shelter herself in this world, she can still act in this primordial sense. The impossible possibility is not just to hear God's prohibition of violence, but to hear its singular manifestation in the world-creative power of this particular infant. The infant herself, and not some universalized God, finally creates the ethical command. The point is not that infants are somehow immune from doing violence (they too participate in some small way in the violence of fallen history), but that even such a little one as this, who would seem to have no creative power in the world at all, should in fact be heard as world-creative in an originary and radical sense, through her command that the world no longer do her violence.

Levinas is right that otherness is irreducible to the world of being, but the other from Sinai is also the image of the Creator in humanity, capable of scandalously instigating something new in the world. Otherness is not purely Transcendent but also immanent, meaningful, disruptive to the world as it happens to be concretely. Its claim is not general or abstract but particular and singular. It makes not just a religious but also a worldly moral demand. Otherness disrupts by bringing new light to the darkness of self-sameness, new form to the chaos of violence, a new story where before was only the silence of the void. The other's command not to kill is not a command into a void but a command for world transformation. The invisible breath or spirit of the other is a generative, tensional, creative life force. It commands the cessation of the tragic and evil violence by which its vulnerability in the world is already reduced to an instrument.[88]

One could argue that Levinas himself largely neglects this sense of the other as an image of its Creator because he follows the vast majority of biblically oriented ethicists in history in associating the notion of "image" with *graven* images, or idols. For Levinas, it is by making worldly images or idols of others, in fact, that selves reduce them to selves' own worldly interests. He directly opposes worldly "image" and transcending "face": "The face of the other destroys and surpasses at every moment the plastic image that it leaves behind."[89] But the deeper Genesis symbolism of humanity as an "image of God" offers another way to speak about the other's "face." When ethics is no longer separated from poetics, "face" is revealed as "image" in this profound primordial sense. This image symbolizes the face of the other as a face of original moral Creativity. Here, the Infinite is revealed as infinite possibility for world renewal. Its call is the call of one who breathes life and spirit ever anew into the world, breathes "breathlessly" as the Creator breathes life into Adam. This other is an image of its Creator in a different sense than is the self. It does not open up the possibility for narrative unity but, in fact, destroys it. But it still creates, nevertheless, in the sense of demanding the world's ever less violent transformation.

The Creation of Love

Such creativity on the part of the other would lack moral meaning altogether, however, were it not to demand a response specifically of the free moral self. The other suffers violence because, as Ricoeur shows, it is still in part, however much it transcends and commands the world, also vulnerable to the reductive activities of selves. Part of the call to the self is for the self's own ever more excessive moral imagination, the imagination to hear the voice of the other as an image of the Creator. But more than this, the self must be affirmed as ultimately capable, in actual moral practice and thought, of transforming its own (in part freely chosen) violent worldly existence. However much the moral obligation begins in the Levinasian other, it still must end in some kind of Kantian freedom to act differently. Phenomenologically speaking, the command from the other still in some sense *belongs to me*, is *my* command in the sense of given to me.

Our poetics of moral obligation must hold these two polarities of other-origination and self-response in relation to one another. It can do so, finally, because moral creativity arises precisely out of the *tension* between the two. The pure passivity imposed by the other gives rise to a responsive passive-agency demanded of the self. This tension remains in this world irreducible, unbreakable, impossible to overcome. Yet it is in the end a radically self-creative response from selves that the starving infant, the widow, and the stranger finally demand. It is because the command instigates a tension that it demands in turn a creative response.

What the other in fact creates in the world is not just a disruptive command but also the necessity for selves to respond to it by re-creating their own worlds anew. The command of the other for nonviolence introduces a radical new tension into the heart of selves that demands their own creative self-undoing. This passive-active poetic response can be described with the word

"distentionality": the capability in selves for remaking their own moral horizons in response to the self-disruption commanded by the other. Distentionality contrasts with the "intentionality" of chapter 2, indicating a
different kind of self-creativity of a negative or centrifugal kind. If teleological
in-tentionality means "stretching toward," deontological dis-tentionality
means literally "stretching apart." The self is called to stretch apart its practices and understandings in the world in response to the sheer alterity of the
other. Such is the new and very different figure in which passivity and agency,
finitude and freedom, givenness and giving may be rendered poetically productive. To distend oneself is to re-create one's own existing world of meaning
and practice in new ways that exceed beyond all expectation one's own
complicity in violence.

This self-transformation begins in confession, for it is a change in the
very first instance in response to my own sense of radical evil, of falling short
of the other's command. Think of Derrida's ironic response in *Circumfession*
to his most attentive friend and interpreter Geoffrey Bennington:

> [H]e knows everything about the "logic" of what I might have written
> in the past but also of what I might think or write in the future…
> so that I should have nothing to say that might surprise him still
> and bring something about for him, who you would be tempted to
> compare to Augustine's God when he asks whether there is any
> sense in confessing anything to him when He knows everything in
> advance.[90]

Far from being Augustine's God who knows "everything in advance," we are,
like Bennington, in fact deaf to each other's otherness by our own chosen
and created self-circumscription. Bennington does an admirable job of
"creating" a text describing Derrida. But its poetic task could never succeed,
for Derrida could always create something new. But more radically, in moral
terms, the other creates not only texts but also the infinite command not to
do it violence. The first creative act in response must be the self's confession
of radical evil, its own claiming of free complicity in this violence, and hence
its claiming a capability for acting differently that it fails to realize. Confession is a partly creative act because it forms a radicalized perspective on one's
own being in the world and subjects it to a new and decentered interpretation.

This dimension of creative self-agency is arguably implied even in Levinas's extremism about the self being reduced to pure passivity. We must reject
what in the end is Levinas's Kantian dualism of agency and passivity, however
much he reverses Kant and places evil in the former and the moral law in the
latter. After traversing obligational ethics from Kantian freedom at the beginning of this chapter all the way to Levinasian passivity toward the end, we
are now in a position to see how these are secretly related: through a passive-
active moral tensionality. The command from the other for a transformed
world is always also, at the same time, a command for self-transformation. And
the command for self-transformation is always also beholden to the confession
of inadequacy to the original command from the other. This returns us in a

roundabout way to the circular and passive-active poetics of Ricoeur, but this poetics will now have to be radicalized accordingly.

Ricoeur's own critique of Levinas in fact takes us part of the way along this path, and it has nowhere to my knowledge been provided an adequate Levinasian response. According to Ricoeur, "the theme of exteriority [in Levinas] does not reach the end of its trajectory, namely awakening a responsible response in the other's call, except by presupposing a capacity [in the self] of reception, of discrimination, and of recognition. . . . Must not the voice of the Other who says to me: 'Thou shalt not kill,' become my own, to the point of becoming my conviction?"[91] Or, as Ricoeur asks Levinas, "*Who* testifies [to the glory of the Infinite], if not the Self, distinguished henceforth from the I by virtue of the idea of the assignment of responsibility?"[92] Any "testimony" regarding the Other involves also an "attestation" of the self's own capability for making it a response.[93] From a Ricoeurian point of view, any phenomenology of the other ultimately demands some level of attestation, for all meaning and possibility in the world, including the meaning of meaninglessness and impossibility, is ultimately *for* someone. Even God Godself lacks meaning without interpretation into the world of a (however disoriented) self. The absolutely original command from the Other is no exception to this phenomenological necessity.

Kearney puts this matter even more sharply in *Strangers, Gods, and Monsters*, where he argues that the command from alterity should avoid equally both "the modern idolatry of the ego" and "a new [postmodern] idolatry [of] the immemorial, ineffable Other."[94] This latter idolatry consists in taking otherness as the whole and end of the moral story. In fact, responsibility to the other is never reducible simply to the self's passive prostration before it. It always also involves, however disruptively and imperfectly, the act of making what Kearney calls a "practical judgment." This non-idolatrous, passive-active practice allows for "interlacings of alterities" into some new meaning.[95] Indeed, part of moral judgment in response to others involves "our need to differentiate . . . between good and evil aliens," between the otherness of the orphan and the otherness of the Nazi doctor.[96] Otherness is found not just in the strangers to whom we do violence but also in monsters of all varieties and stripes.

Kearney indeed suggests that selves are called by others to enter, rather than to attempt to transcend, moral finitude's powerful, murky, and uncharted waters. This responsivity toward otherness is for him of the essence of humanity itself: "Human existence is always hovering about those frontiers that mark the passage between same and other, real and imaginary, known and unknown. Indelibly marked by finitude, the human self has never ceased to ponder its boundaries or to image what lies beyond—namely, those strangers, gods, and monsters that populate its fantasies."[97] The other can remain absolutely other and still command, indeed open up, my own larger moral possibilities in this world. Such other-self "boundaries" are what I am calling poetic moral "tensions." Facing otherness is not just a disruption of human life but part of the fabric of how the self transforms itself in the direction of ever more radically responsible human meaning.

Ultimately, what selves are called to create, in response to the command created by the other, is not *no* being in the world but their own ever more profoundly *distended* being in the world. The capability for self-creativity, in this deontological sense of responsiveness to others, is a capability for the self's own distentionality or stretching apart of itself. I use this peculiar term to indicate the complex and secondary sense in which the self may re-create itself ever less violently in response to the originating command created by the other. The command from the other produces in the self a hyperbolic tension or stretching to which the self can respond only by its own reflexive un-making, disjoining, deconstructing, distending. Responsive self-transformation rests on the paradoxical possibility that the self can be immobilized by the command against violence from the other, and yet, on this very basis, creatively exceed and reinvent itself in its own ever radically less violent practices.

The creative tension here, contra Kant and Levinas both, is therefore passive and active at once. The other reduces me to a primordial passivity beyond any ordinary passivity I experience in relation to nonhuman objects in the world. Yet I remain somehow, and just as mysteriously, capable of creating the other a new response. It is within this nexus of passivity and agency that the self can distend itself anew. This tension repeats at a new level, as it were, the nexus of the self's primordial creativity as such, in which it is given to itself absolutely passively and yet in the originally active mode of being able to give itself new meaning. But now the self is called to self-creativity of a negative kind that originates outside itself in the other. No longer trapped within its own conditions of sameness, but neither held hostage to otherness as such, the self is freed by otherness to stretch beyond its own given being in the world into being in the world of an ever more profoundly responsible kind.

Love can thereby move beyond Ricoeur's giving of a primordial gift to the other, which in a certain sense still deprives the other of its originality, to a more complex and self-disruptive gift given to the other that the other originally gives me the command and the freedom to give. Love is first of all created as a possibility within the self by the other's absolutely irreducible voice. Genuine love avoids instrumentalization, even the religious instrumentalization of using the other to return myself to God, only insofar as it begins in alterity as such. But love is still given as a response to the other by the self, the self as a human being ultimately and mysteriously capable of transforming its own actual violent historicity. The gift is not returned, in this case, to my own primordial givenness, but to the other as creator of the command, the other as infinitely demanding the gift from me. This return is actually impossible to complete, yet still a possibility toward which I am endlessly called. I do not finally become the other's hostage, because it is still ultimately up to me to exercise my freedom to create a response. I can still choose to continue the course of violence. Indeed, I inevitably to some degree will. Nevertheless, I am impossibly capable of renewing myself in such a way that my complicity in violence begins (ever again) to become undone. The beginning initiated by the command from the other demands an ever new beginning from myself. The moral beginning is in effect doubled. My own new beginning is like the new beginning announced as possible by the prophets. The other as an image of the Wholly Other creates in me, in a way, the ever renewed possibility for imagining and creating my own new world.

What is finally tragic about this particular creative moral tension is that it faces the self with its own inevitable self-entanglement in the finite conditions within which violence is perpetuated. Creon commits violence, but on some level this commission is simply the continuance of the duties which have already fallen upon him as king. In a certain sense violence is fated, and so therefore is each self's continuance of it. It would be possible for Creon to undergo a cathartic self-transformation in which he understands how defending his city could take place without violating rites of family burial. But in fact we can understand why he does not, and indeed the tragic movement of the play depends on the reasonableness of his inherited duties. Were he simply a fool or a tyrant the play would only be a morality tale, and it would not press us to consider moral life's implicit tensionality. As it is, we, like Creon, face the very real tensions of freedom and finitude throughout our lives that our relations to others introduce. The starving infant demands that we undergo the catharsis of transforming our actual lives in the world. It will not suffice that we accept the pure passivity of becoming knocked out of our accustomed moral orbits. Rather, we find ourselves, each one of us, confronted with a profoundly tragic moral tension. We both can and cannot respond. We find ourselves called to the impossible possibility of a radical moral conversion.

But this returns us again to the Kantian problem of radical evil. Ricoeur, we saw, redefines the radical evil at the heart of our incapacity for responding to others as the inscrutable choice to love others, not for themselves as others, but for what loving them might bring us in return. The logic of superabundance is a reply to its own fallen logic of equivalence. But we are now in a position to deepen this problem of evil into a matter of primordial human tension. Instead of perfecting freedom in creating the other a fully singular response, we disobey the other's moral command and continue to participate freely in violence. Violence remains ultimately our own free choice. Adolf Eichmann was able to organize the torture and murder of countless Jews in part because he felt he was "only following orders," in which case he rendered himself entirely unconscious, not only of the other's exterior command, but also of his own other-responsive capabilities. Yet this choice is still his own. All of us, to lesser degrees, refuse to acknowledge our responsibility for violence and hence inscrutably deny our own freedom to re-create our own moral world. The logic of equivalence is also a logic of stasis, of our failure to take responsibility for ever more excessive self-renewal, of the refusal of other-self moral tension.

These tragic and evil dimensions of non-self-creativity can be united under the symbolism of prophesy, already so effectively used by Levinas. Prophesy, we might now say, finds part of its roots in the mythology of Creation. It calls us back to make ourselves not just images of our historical selves (icons) but primordial images of our Creator. As Jeremiah asks rhetorically, after Jerusalem has been overthrown: "Where are your gods that you have made for yourself?" (Jeremiah 2:28). Prophesy makes a moral appeal to a still more primordial God than the gods humanity actually clings to. What prophesy commands, from a poetic point of view, is the re-creation of historical finitude in response to this strange prophetic "other" who announces the truly Wholly Other God. The prophet is the other who confronts each self with that self's own both radical violence and still more primordial and mysterious possibility for moral self-renewal. Ethical life always needs its prophets to spur us beyond our inevitable moral complacency. Prophesy is creative inherently. The job of the social ethicist is always in part, not unlike the job of the artist, to raise such tensions within what has come morally to be taken for granted. It is no accident that prophets often meet with violence, for it is in part violence which they are exposing and fighting against. Their claim appears in fact ultimately impossible to those who, like all of us, are mired in idolatrous finitude. And yet prophesy at least names this idolatry for what it is and convicts us of our own incapability for giving it a full response.

The creative "distention" to which selves are finally called is not, therefore, the negation of their being in the world, but in a more reflexive way this world's still more radically other-responsive renewal. To respond poetically to otherness in this way is to stretch oneself *apart*, to exceed oneself by creating one's own actual world to be different, to realize one's creative capability more fully in relation to alterity. Such creativity is different, although no less hyperbolic, than teleological intentionality, or the creative movement that stretches us *toward* a narrative unity of life. To stretch apart means to transform oneself in response to a transformative call already issued by another. It means to undo my world in some yet unknown way that can include the stranger I would normally have turned away, the infant I have not helped to feed, the poor and the vulnerable whom my own narrative world obscures. No one is free of this task. At the same time, no one is not in need, to some degree, of this responsibility being taken toward them by other selves too. But the task itself, however impossible to complete, still calls on humanity's mysterious and primordial possibility for exceeding itself by re-creating its own being in the world.

In the end, we may once again return, at least obliquely, to the example of the mythology of Adam and Eve. For these first persons symbolize not only "humanity" as such, but also two singular and distinctly other others. Before using their freedom to disobey God, they still more primordially live together with one another in the Garden of Eden. I look at the larger implications of gender and patriarchy here in chapter 4. But for now it is possible to suggest that this myth projects a prototype for what later the prophets and Jesus will command that human relations of self and other should re-create. It is a prototype of irreducibly other human beings still capable of living in a peaceful paradise with one another in absolutely nonviolent love. As Adam declares in jubilation in the first poem of the Bible: "This at last is bone of my bones and flesh of my flesh" (Genesis 2:23). And as the author concludes: "And the man and his wife were both naked, and were not ashamed" (Genesis 2:25). The juxtaposition of these lines suggests an image of the purely naked responsiveness that is impossibly possible toward the humanity of others. Even despite the actual human condition in history of violence toward and covering over of otherness as such, perhaps we too, like those primordial others as imagined before the fall, are ultimately created to create one another an immediate joyous response. The authors of this text doubtless did not mean for it to be interpreted in exactly this way. But read through the lens of the command from Sinai, and in relation to humanity as the image of Creativity, it can suggest a primordial human capability for giving our naked tensionality with each other a still more nakedly creative response. The point is not to overcome the tensions of otherness, but to inhabit and render them productive of ever more radically other-inclusive meaning.

This, in fact, is what Wordsworth seems to have been striving after in the poem to his daughter with which we began. She crashes in upon him with the primordial disruptiveness of the sound of thunder, commanding him simply to "Listen!" But he in turn, rather than simply being silenced or having his thoughts swept out into the turbulent darkness of the sea, responds with a cry of jubilation: "Dear Child! dear Girl!" This at last is bone of his bones and flesh of his flesh (indeed literally so, as his daughter). She reveals to him the divine, the Creator creating the thunder and the crashing seas around. She is the image of her Maker precisely in her at once absolute and particular otherness. Yet Wordsworth can create in turn his own particular loving response. He is at once the real father, the author of the poem, and the figure in the poem who so responds. But in each case, the response consists in a radically self-disruptive transformation of his own moral horizons in the world. He too participates in a self-transcending creativity—a passive-active Creation—in his all too imperfect efforts to create this seemingly small yet infinitely powerful child a response.

4

Ideology and the Art of Reconciliation

In his "Letter from Birmingham Jail—April 16, 1963," Martin Luther King Jr. argues that racial oppression in the American South could be fought only by heightening its underlying tensions in order to provoke the creation of new structures of society: "Human progress never rolls in the wheels of inevitability; it comes through the tireless efforts of men willing to be co-workers with God, and without this hard work, time itself becomes an ally of the forces of social stagnation. We must use time creatively."[1] King did not think a just world could be brought about simply by understanding or applying fixed principles of justice. Those with power have convinced themselves of their right to it, those without it of the inevitability of their oppression. Nor did he think, however, as many in this situation claimed at the time, that justice would work itself out within history itself if just given time. Rather, it had to be taken up actively as a transcending human cause. When he says "we must use time creatively" and as "co-workers with God," what he means is that we—both oppressed and oppressor—have a moral responsibility to stand up to the inevitable forces of historical stagnation and ideology and submit ourselves and our larger social world to ongoing social transformation.

King's work implies a third and still more complex dimension of moral creativity beyond the teleological and deontological dimensions explored above. Since this dimension has no such convenient label, I propose to call it "practical" in something like the sense found in certain liberationist, political, feminist, discourse, and other ethics: praxis, work, social dialogue, and ultimately eschatological horizon and direction. We are not dealing here with the kind of teleological "practices" that I argue in chapter 2 are secondary to a narrative unity of life. Nor do I mean the deontological "practical" of applying general principles to particular cases, for as I show in chapter 3, our moral poetics clearly rejects the one-sided move from universality to particularity. Rather, the term is meant to suggest a new angle on moral life. It indicates the problem not just of coherent narratives or of facing others but of ideological oppressions within entire social-historical systems. The question has to do with how selves act as members of larger groups to transform the always already distorted social systems of which they are implicitly a part.

Such considerations involve a different relation of the poetic moral self to time. The emphasis must be placed here on the future. Or, more accurately, it must be placed on the future of the present, the future as present action's ongoing horizon of expectation. The previous teleological creation of a narrative unity of life makes a new ethical intentionality principally out of the fragments of one's life as already historically given. However much it also opens toward a possible future, its center of gravity lies in the possible new present that may be created out of the past. Responsibility to the other *qua* other is primarily a distention of selfhood in the immediacy of the present itself, however much, here too, a certain nonviolent future is also implied. But transforming entrenched historical oppression "extends" moral creativity—it stretches it *out*—most decisively of all in the direction of a hyperbolically uncertain time to come. It takes up the past, and it confronts the injustices of the present, but it is most profoundly oriented toward what may come to be in a world created by all. Intentionality and distentionality give way here to an always unfolding extentionality. In a way, this makes this third dimension of moral creativity even more challenging, complex, and mysterious than those discussed above.

I argue that moral creativity here takes on the sense of a "new creation" of what is to come. While such an anticipation or promise of the future may rely on a sense of originally created goodness in the primordial past, and while it will include a notion of the Wholly Other in the present, its focus is on an eschatological human destiny that none of us can fully imagine and that has yet to come about. This end is unending, unfolding, opening even more inscrutably than before. It returns us once again to mythologies of Creation, but now insofar as Creation projects an impossible possibility at the end of time for the New Creation of society. Eschatological ethics of the kind employed by King and others also requires, despite facing forward, as it were, humankind's primordially creative capabilities. Moral practice and reflection are called to challenge the world from the perspective of what the world could be transformed toward.

Our previous considerations have in fact already started us down this new and more complex poetic path. The affirmation of narrative unity in oneself already includes life in common with others, albeit not in their universal otherness. And the command from others already incites something of a social relation, albeit not of a social-systemic kind. In this latter regard, even Levinas speaks, at least in his earlier *Totality and Infinity*, of the larger social "peace" toward which the command from otherness is ultimately, even if impossibly, oriented. But whereas creativity at first belonged to the self as a self *alongside* others, and then was doubled in the self in response to the command created *by* the other, now moral creativity is multiplied even further the point of plurality: to include the self as a participant *with* others in re-creating shared systems of social power. It is still ultimately selves who must create, but now in relation to a situation of even broader moral passivity and alongside the demand for creativity of all.[2]

The new and uniquely social-systemic problem here arises, just as radically and tragically evil as discussed above, out of the self's free participation in the very social conditions by which freedom is historically distorted. Our question is not just how selves can be freed *from* social ideology, but how they can also become liberated, in both its passive and active senses, to create a better and more radically reconciled social history together. The tragic dimension here, as recent feminist readers of the *Antigone* have argued, is the dependency of selves (like Antigone) on larger social systems which, however, deny entire dimensions of who they are as social persons (in this case through the patriarchal oppression of women). Historical finitude can overwhelm social freedom in a wide range of political, economic, cultural, racial, class, gender, and other ways. And yet, as I also insist, and as I think King suggests, no amount of social marginalization obviates the fact that oppression is a dimension of human radical evil and therefore human freedom. Oppressors may find it convenient to attribute inequality to history, but in fact they have the primordial capability to change it. The oppressed may feel hopeless in the face of systemic historical power, and yet their very humanity gives them the capability for renewed social self-empowerment.

Moral creativity in this third sense is as a result "religious" in that it faces humanity with its own unimagined and historically excessive possibilities for radical moral renewal. Its aim is not the elimination of social tension so much as the realization of humanity's created capabilities for a socially tensional new creativity. The term "reconciliation" is understandably suspect in our postmythological and postmodern culture. It is scandalous from a merely historical point of view, in which it could only mean, as in Hegel, the totalization of society, the victory of the strongest historical powers—the victory, in other words, of oppression itself. But in terms of our religious moral poetics, reconciliation may instead symbolize, without being able fully to contain, the human impossible possibility for the total and completely harmonious creative participation of every self in their social world. This is our new figure of radical inclusivity. It is a dimension of ultimate human freedom, a freedom covered over in this world but also primordially presupposed within it. Moral creativity in social life is a searching and restless art. It is not a repetition or realization of what is already known, but an instigation, shock, and summons. It follows the indication of a radical eschatological possibility for a "new creation" on earth that is fully shared in by all.

The seemingly impossible aim of such creativity can be symbolized in the languages of prophecy, promise, resurrection, and the kingdom of God. In the following pages I relate these kinds of language again to the underlying poetic symbolism that we have pursued throughout this book: of humanity as created creative in the image of its Creator. The Creator—in Abrahamic and some non-Abrahamic religions as well—sometimes appears as expansive, embracing, plural, reconciling, harmonizing. Feminist images of the Creator sometimes suggest a divine that gathers humanity up together in encompassing creative renewal. The Creator extends itself through its creativity into the multiplicity, freedom, and heterogeneity of creation itself. Likewise, as made in the image of such a Creator, humanity may be affirmed, like Adam and Eve as they live before the fall in the Garden of Eden, as ultimately capable of making a human society within difference. This new sense of participatory relation is different from the above responsiveness to alterity. Human beings are created also for a kind of creativity in common, a fruitfulness and multiplication on the basis of plurality and heterogeneity itself in which ideology gives way to reconciliation. It is toward this, from a poetic point of view, that we may direct a new kind of morally creative hope.

The Poetics of Ideology

Jürgen Habermas has argued, combining Kantianism with Marxism, that the problem of ethical ideology is not just the forces of history itself but subjects' joint *participation* in such forces. Moral life must face what he calls the "pluralism of ultimate value orientations," the pluralism of the historical aims within which each of us is entrenched.[3] This means that "individuals who have been socialized cannot take a hypothetical attitude toward the form of life and personal life history that have shaped their identity."[4] Rather, in a fundamental hermeneutical sense, each of us is blind to the ways in which we either perpetuate or are victims of our own social distortions. As a result, according to Habermas, only "real argument makes moral insight possible."[5] No self can determine where social discourse should lead, even if each self must be allowed to participate in the conversation. Social discourse is a procedure, not just in Rawls's sense of monologically imagining how others would like to be treated, but in the dialogical sense of differences being negotiated through *actual social participation*. Thus, Habermas's "principle of discourse ethics (D)" states that "only those norms can claim to be valid that meet (or could meet) with the approval of all affected in their capacity as participants in a practical discourse."[6]

Such a view of the moral problem is compelling insofar as it refuses to reduce ideology to history as such. In a more hermeneutically complex way, it insists that however much ideology may blind us to the injustices of power, it is also something in which each of us on some level freely participates. Our moral aim is not, as Marx sometimes implied, simply to wait for (or perhaps to encourage) the dialectics of material history to work itself out. In this Marx remains deeply Hegelian: it is social forces themselves which lead to the desired outcome. In Habermas's view, our aim is instead to actively participate in a different kind of discursive dialogue with one another so that freedom may turn from ideological oppression toward an ever more just intersubjectivity. The moral realm is reducible for Habermas to neither the objective "truth" of history as it really is nor the subjective "expression" of selfhood against history but, rather, the intermediary intersubjective "rightness" that is generated through actual social discourse aimed at the formation of ever greater historical "consensus."[7]

To begin to uncover what may be "poetic" about such a conception of ideology, I want to hold it up to a possible feminist critique that may be made of it from the point of view of moral tragedy. I have been using the notion of tragedy, in various possible meanings, to deepen the poetic moral problem throughout this book. Feminist ethicists interested in social ideology have recently turned for inspiration to new readings of Sophocles' *Antigone*. They have sharply broken from Hegel's reading of the problem as presented in this play, even more sharply than has Nussbaum, as discussed earlier. Tragedy should not be reduced to the historical conflict of moral values or forces. It includes also a fundamental limitation and distortion of moral selfhood. Tragic plays like this one demonstrate the ideological limits placed upon the meaning of social "argumentation" and "participation" in the first place. Social life may not just lack procedures to ensure participation, but tragically distort how it defines (and who is included in) social participation itself.

Luce Irigaray was the first to suggest that the true tragedy of Antigone (whether Sophocles himself intended it this way or not) should be read as the problem of a society with a distorted view of femininity. Antigone and Creon may both have one-sided aims, but Antigone is uniquely disempowered by their shared larger patriarchal culture. "Creon, the king, will, in the end, endure a fate as cruel as Antigone's. But he will be master of that destiny. Antigone is silenced in her action. Locked up—paralyzed, on the edge of the city."[8] Antigone is in fact literally locked alive by Creon in a cave. The reverse would be inconceivable, given the structures of Theban society. Whatever the justice of her claim may be, it does not even receive a hearing.

Antigone's suicide, then, in this prison that becomes her tomb, becomes the only way she can act as female in such a world. She returns herself to the community's hidden feminine "ground" and "blood." Where women can play the role only of bearing and burying, she can at least exercise some power over life and death, even if the death has to be her own. "Femininity [under these circumstances] consists essentially in laying the dead man [Polyneices] back in the womb of the earth, and giving him eternal life.... [Woman] ensures the memory of consciousness of self by forgetting herself."[9] The tragedy of the play is not just that Antigone as an individual is not allowed to participate in social discourse. It is more subtly that the Greek social world defines social discourse itself in an already masculine way. Social participation means having the status of selfhood in the larger *polis*, so that femininity lies beyond argumentation as such.

Pamela Anderson has developed Irigaray's view further to highlight what she calls the "double double-bind" of Antigone in her world. The tragic bind here is that Antigone is marginalized even in the act of resisting marginalization:

> Antigone is, first, marginalized as a woman who remains excluded from the public domain by the ancient *polis*, even when she initiates a political act of dissent; so she would have been marginalized in this sense whether she acted or not. And, second, she is further marginalized from her family and religious community even as a consequence of her religiously motivated duty to bury her brother, since this involves "unwomanly" public dissent from a civil religious duty to follow the king's edicts.[10]

The problem for Antigone is not just that she is the victim of ideological oppression. It is also that this very same patriarchal ideology controls any public dialogical means for overcoming it. It is "unwomanly" for Antigone to defy Creon—not just because her claims themselves are not taken seriously, but more profoundly because her acting to make claims in the first place is not permitted. This is a different reading of the play from Nussbaum's regarding intersubjective moral simplification. It points further to social-systemic moral distortion. The very practice of participating in intersubjective discourse itself is already configured by Antigone's culture along the lines of masculinity. Her only way to make her "argument" at all is secretly, silently, and finally in suicide.

Judith Butler has in a way taken such a reading even further. Butler argues that Antigone is an image for "that political possibility that emerges when the limits to representation and representability are exposed."[11] That is, Antigone exposes and presses at the very limits of moral "language" itself. (Butler does not mean "limits" in the religious sense I will shortly develop). Part of these limits consists in the problematic nature of Antigone's kinship ties themselves. Her father Oedipus is also her brother (since through Oedipus's incest they share the same mother). It remains unclear in the play whether burying her brother Polyneices is not driven by Antigone's unconscious Freudian desire to bury her other "brother" Oedipus, whose previous burial in *Oedipus at Colonus* she had not been able to perform.

But the limits of moral language extend, finally, to what Butler calls language's "performative" force: its function as "not a form of being but a form of doing."[12] Butler is well known for her theory of how language is used to perform social roles. What Antigone "does" or "performs" (and these are particularly conflated, in this case, because Antigone is a character in a staged play) is ultimately to transform the cave in which Creon locks her into what she calls her "bridal chamber" (*numpheion*). By naming it such, she changes it. In this very act of naming her own tomb, "the word [*numpheion*] performs the destruction of the [marriage] institution" as culturally understood. Antigone was to marry Creon's son Haemon, but now cancels that possibility by instead marrying death.[13] Her suicide is then not simply a defeat of her own identity, but also a *reconstruction* of it through the defiant performative act of naming it for herself. Antigone exposes and challenges ideological injustice in the only way she can: by pressing at the limits of the very meanings of marriage, kinship, and brotherhood in her society.

Here also, in Butler, we can detect a certain tragic poetic possibility for response. In exposing the limits of moral language in her culture, Antigone also "performs" new cultural possibilities for defining the meaning of social humanity. "In acting, as one who has no right to act, [Antigone] upsets the vocabulary of kinship that is a precondition of the human, implicitly raising the question for us of what those preconditions must really be."[14] Or, put differently, Antigone represents the force of language "when the less than human speaks as human."[15] Is this "less than human" really in fact *more* than human, more *primordially* human? Butler does not say. But her point is that even when the humanity of a person or group is denied by social discourse, it still retains a capability to attempt to reassert itself, however tragically. Persons can enact a kind of performative speech whose illocutionary force consists in pressing at the limits of already historically established conventions defining "humanity" itself. Social language is at once complicitous in oppression and yet the malleable arena in which we may take up "the possibility of social transformation."[16]

I do not mean to suggest, through these feminist reappropriations of the notion of moral tragedy, that Habermas's conception of intersubjective dialogue is patriarchal. Habermas is right, in the end, that *all* must be able to participate. But it is necessary to understand social participation itself in a more poetically complex way than merely applying universalized discursive procedures. Proceduralism was found to be problematic in Rawls because it omits the otherness of actual substantive values. Here it is not sufficient in the somewhat different sense that it does not address the ways in which substantive social discourse and language themselves may be already socially exclusionary and oppressive. The problem of social exclusion is a problem not of unarticulated social principles but of the poetics of language itself. Principles of discourse cannot be used as a pragmatic antidote to the distortions of ideology because ideology infuses principles of discourse themselves. The very notion of what it means to validate a claim through argumentation can make doing so unwomanly, unblack, unchildlike, unemotional, and so on. The tragedy is that the very discursive means available for addressing social marginalization may themselves be socially marginalizing.

The tragi-poetic moral problem in the end, on the level of social discourse, is at least in part how to transform the very culture by which ideological transformation is prohibited. It is a problem of catharsis rather than application. The above-mentioned feminist readings of moral tragedy show that such a more radicalized social discursive aim is possible. As Anderson puts it, the double bind of women within patriarchy means that "it is left to each of us to attempt the task of narrative refiguration."[17] If we are forced to "perform" certain roles in society, perhaps we can also "perform" in new ways. Such refiguration or social transformation may be tragically bound up with the very languages of oppression it seeks to resist. Certainly in Antigone's case— both in her fictional world and in the fifth century Greek society of her audience—any achieved social transformation remains only slight. But oppressed groups can still, perhaps, somehow transfigure the very moral horizons by which they are bound into new moral horizons with less distorted social possibilities. The tragic problem remains, nonetheless: how the oppressed may speak and act against the language and society which already prevent them from doing so.

Tragedy and Freedom

It is because it is not necessarily the end of the story, however, that we may press the tragic (in this social-systemic sense) to its true "limits" as a figure of human radical evil. There is a kind of moral freedom implied here that remains to be teased out. This figure of a passive-active radical evil is different from a teleological self-enslavement to narrative finitude or a deontological use of justice to instrumentalize the other. But it is also more profound than historical marginalization per se. The question must be asked how it is possible that humanity has the freedom to oppress in the first place. What accounts for the tension between human society as it is actually defined ideologically and human society as it really could be? Without a more primordial sense of human radical evil, we risk merely replacing Hegel's opposition of moral forces with a similarly historically inevitable opposition of oppressors and oppressed. In this case, it becomes difficult to see how the opposition could also serve as a tension that may transform society in the direction of liberation.

On some level, oppressive ideologies are not just historical powers but also humanity's free and inscrutable distortion of its own transcending human possibilities. The *Antigone* itself suggests as much, however implicitly, in the underlying humanity of its characters. Creon is not just a force of oppression but also an at least partially sympathetic character in his misguided desire to do justice. Nor is Antigone a pure victim of her circumstances but also in part (although a smaller part than Creon) a participant in her cultural beliefs and her own tragic end. Most of all, the voice of the chorus constantly reminds us that it is human inventiveness itself that "reaches sometimes evil, and sometimes good." Naming the tragedy as tied to human choice allows it to convict us, its audience, of our own inhumanity as well. Denying this choice, and leaving moral life in the hands of fate alone, robs the audience of its own cathartic possibilities. Our sense of cathartic possibility as spectators rests at least in part on being able to identify with Antigone's failed human attempt to assert herself *and* with Creon's all too human oppressive blindness.

It is here that Ricoeur's poetics of the will becomes once again useful, even if, especially regarding tragedy, it has significant limitations. For Ricoeur suggests a crucial link between moral tragedy and the human responsibility for larger societal failure, between the finitude of oppression and its freedom as a dimension of human radical evil. This link in Ricoeur's writings, however, is not altogether transparent, especially given his tendency to separate philosophy from religion, and so it will have to be carefully reconstructed.

It is in relation to practical discourse, in his later work *Oneself as Another*, that Ricoeur in fact makes his sole, and rather brief, systematic foray into tragedy as a specifically moral term. According to Ricoeur, the tragedy of the *Antigone* (which for Ricoeur, too, is paradigmatic) rests upon the narrowness of human *convictions*. He writes that "the source of the conflict lies not only in the one-sidedness of the characters but also in the one-sidedness of the moral *principles* which themselves are confronted with the complexity of life."[18] By "principles" Ricoeur does not mean Hegelian "moral forces" like family and state. He means the self's interpretation of its larger historicity into its own free convictions or chosen grounds for social action. What is one-sided is that selves' principles or convictions are inevitable formed only in relation to their own narrow worlds, thereby undermining the truly genuine engagement with the convictions of others of which selves are in fact ultimately capable. Antigone exhibits conviction in insisting on burying her brother; Creon does the same in enforcing his own interpretation of the laws of the state. But each also pursues their own apparently (to them) critically justified conviction to its own single-mindedly horrifying end. Thus, Antigone never incorporates her obligations to her state, and Creon, in a more blameworthy way due to his greater moral freedom, never recognizes Antigone's claim to the right of burial (not even, arguably, in his final cathartic self-blaming).

According to Ricoeur, what we spectators of the play, in contrast with the characters, may learn is a certain "tragic wisdom" regarding the inevitably short-sighted nature of all human efforts at living justly in society. We should always be suspicious of our own "narrowness of . . . angle of commitment" or "narrowness of viewpoint."[19] Here, Ricoeur's early career "hermeneutics of suspicion," which he had associated in a fairly direct way with Marx, takes on fuller and more complex ethical dimensions. Creon rightly strives to protect Thebes against future acts of treason, but in the process he is blinded to the effects of this principle upon the claim of Antigone. Antigone rightly pursues ancient family rites and duties that convince her to bury her brother, but in the process she is blinded to the threat her actions pose to the state. Like Hegel[20] and Nussbaum,[21] Ricoeur refuses to let Antigone off the hook: "Her manner of distinguishing between *philos* [friend] and *ekthros* [enemy] is no less rigid than Creon's; for her, the only thing that counts is the family bond."[22] Only Creon finally sees his own narrowness—"Oh, the awful blindness of those plans of mine," he cries (lines 1343–44)—but it is at the end of the play when it is too late, and it leads to no further vision of reconciliation with the family rites that his convictions undermine.

Ricoeur's chief criticism of Hegel, in this regard, is that the conflict of social convictions can lead to no third force of Objective Spirit through which their narrowness is eventually overcome. In Ricoeur's view, the tension between human convictions about justice is "interminable," "unavoidable," "intractable."[23] This is precisely what makes them tragic. And this intractability of convictions underscores Ricoeur's point that social principles are always at bottom interpretations of free selves and not historical forces per se. In this way, Ricoeur could perhaps be said to take a page from Henri Bergson and his French successors in insisting that history, however forcefully it effects consciousness, remains also (and at the very same time) something freely changing, transforming, surprising, and always new.[24] Except that in Ricoeur's case history's changeability is due to the fact that it ultimately belongs to interpreting selves.

It is along similar lines, also, that Ricoeur uses tragedy to critique Habermas. For while he accepts Habermas's view that social discourse requires the participation of all, he refuses to separate the pragmatic procedures by which it may be carried out from the concrete historical convictions which it governs. "Argumentation is not simply . . . the antagonist of tradition and convention, but [is] the critical agency operating *at the heart* of convictions, argumentation assuming the task not of eliminating but of carrying them to the level of 'considered convictions.'"[25] What is tragic is that the needed "dialectic between argumentation and conviction" is never fully complete, each self's convictions always falling short of the "consideration" owed the convictions also of all others.[26] Here is a hermeneutics of suspicion of a concrete and open-ended kind. Critical reflection on one's historical convictions cannot be achieved through pragmatic principles, for principles themselves are also historically constituted convictions. Antigone and Creon are both convinced, not only of the rightness of their actions, but also of the forms of argumentation by which these actions are to be justified. The problem is that these very procedures, especially in the case of the political and rationalistic procedures of Creon, render each blind to the convictions about justice of the other. Only we, the audience, have the perspective required to understand this *radically* suspicious tragic wisdom.

Despite this, however, Ricoeur still does not fully address the trenchant problem with Hegel raised by the feminist critiques above: namely, that any such historical, intersubjective, or convictional dialectics is always already distorted by the limited possibilities available for human representation in social life itself. As Anderson has said of Ricoeur's reading of the *Antigone*, it "does not seem to depend upon reading Antigone as a woman."[27] Indeed, given the wide range of his interests, it is one of the stranger aspects of Ricoeur's ethics that it does not address contemporary feminism in any sustained or systematic way. Here again we encounter Ricoeur's problem appreciating the truly tragic depths of moral history. He does confess that part of the tragedy of the *Antigone* is that Antigone and Creon act "in the service of spiritual powers that not only surpass them but, in turn, open the way for archaic and mythical energies that are also, from time immemorial, sources of misfortune."[28] But these powers are quickly attributed not to a distorted social ideology but to the individual: "The passion that pushes each of these two protagonists to extremes is buried in the mysterious depths of motivations that no analysis of moral intention can plumb: a speculatively unavowable theology of divine blindness is inextricably mixed with the unambiguous claim that each makes to be the sole responsible author of his or her acts."[29] Are there not, however, "spiritual forces" of a larger and cultural kind at work in the tragedy here as well—forces of patriarchal kingship, feminine responsibility for burial, even incestual kinship, that make any kind of public consideration of the convictions at play itself already distorted and marginalizing in a profoundly passive and fateful way?[30]

The Evil of Premature Synthesis

If Ricoeur does not appreciate this historical problem, however, he does better articulate what it means for social tragedy to betray an underlying human radical evil. Because his discussion of tragedy occurs in a deliberately philosophical text, *Oneself as Another*, the connection to evil is obscured. But the above reference to "spiritual powers" provides at least a hint that more is at stake. It is particularly noteworthy that Ricoeur's discussion of tragedy takes place in what he titles an "interlude," deliberately separated from the ordinary course of the philosophical argument of his book, and that this interlude refers constantly to tragedy's "nonphilosophical character." As Ricoeur explains, tragedy involves "aporia-producing limit-experiences"[31]—and limit-experiences, as we know, lie at the heart of Ricoeur's phenomenology of religion and evil. But in what these limit-experiences consist we can only here guess, and must turn to other writings.

It turns out that one does not have to look far to find discussions of radical evil in Ricoeur that could be correlated with this third moment within moral philosophy. What we find is a parallel third moment within Ricoeur's religio-moral "economy of the gift." I am not aware of anywhere where Ricoeur spells out this connection himself. However, if tragedy describes the philosophical problem of ethics in regard to social distortions, then the religious correlate may be found in a failure, not of faith or love as discussed in the previous chapters, but now of Ricoeur's important concept of hope. For hope, in Ricoeur, is precisely a response, in its ethical sense, to social oppression, now understood as a dimension of human fallenness. Its failure is why oppression is inscrutably present in human history at all. Let us therefore try and connect the dots so we can see how social tragedy may begin to relate to a new and still more radicalized figure of the poetics of moral evil.

The ultimately inscrutable problem at the heart of social oppression consists, according to Ricoeur, in what he calls "the lie of premature syntheses." Ricoeur witnessed first hand such a lie on a grand scale in the oppressive regime of the Nazis. He was also an active participant before and after this war in the European Christian Socialist movement, which opposed what it perceived as totalitarianisms of a wide and growing kind: on the one hand the repressive totalitarianisms of fascism and Stalinism, and on the other the oppressive inequalities of unfettered capitalism.

But the problem of oppressive ideology lies not just in particular political systems but in the very grounds of political and social life as such. It lies in the inscrutable human propensity for turning culture into totalizing syntheses. It is, in other words, a problem of human freedom:

The true evil, the evil of evil, shows itself in false syntheses, i.e. in the contemporary falsifications of the great undertakings of totalization of cultural experience, that is, in political and ecclesiastical institutions. In this way, evil shows its true face—the evil of evil is the lie of premature syntheses.[32]

This lie has to do with human life's inherent propensity toward embracing collective blindness. The necessary pursuit of life in common also tends inevitably toward synthesizing difference prematurely, creating social syntheses in which differences of angle of vision have *not yet fully* been taken into account. "It is because man is a goal of totality, a will of total fulfillment, that he plunges himself into totalitarianisms, which really constitute the pathology of hope."[33] Social oppression is chosen by humanity over the longer and more radically human possibility for hope in the reconciliation of all.

Perhaps surprisingly, and certainly not explicitly, Ricoeur resembles in this regard the American theologian Reinhold Niebuhr, who argues that true evil consists in the fact that humanity "pretends that [it] is not limited." For Niebuhr, "moral pride is the pretension of finite man that his highly conditioned virtue is the final righteousness and that his very relative moral standards are absolute."[34] Ricoeur would agree with Niebuhr's claim that human "finitude" as such is not the "cause" but only the "occasion" of sin, the cause being freedom itself in its *relation* to finitude. The difference, at least here, between Ricoeur and Niebuhr consists more in Ricoeur's Continental and Kantian sensibility toward evil's radical "inscrutability," and hence, for Ricoeur, the need to describe it less theologically than mythologically and symbolically. This also leads Ricoeur to the more radical view, shared for example by Moltmann, that the ethics of love, around which Niebuhr's focus lies, must finally be superseded on the societal plane with a liberating ethics of hope. Nevertheless, in each case the problem of social life is a problem neither of freedom alone (as arguably in Kant) nor of finitude alone (as arguably from the point of view of Greek tragedy) but of these two dimensions as they inevitably fall into disproportionality.

It is in this context that Ricoeur argues, from a poetic and symbolic point of view, that ideology is really a debased form of a primordial human capability for what he calls shared "social imagination." Revising the categories of ideology and utopia from Karl Mannheim, Ricoeur claims that ideology emphasizes the passive *conservation* of the social imagination from its given past, while utopia emphasizes the active *subversion* of the social imagination in the direction of its own possible new futures. "Whether it preserves the power of a class, or ensures the duration of a system of authority, or patterns the stable functioning of a community, ideology has a function of conservation in both a good and a bad sense of the word. It preserves, it conserves, in the sense of making firm the human order."[35] By contrast, utopian visions, especially through the distanciating critique of texts, open up the new: "From this 'no place' [u-topia], an exterior glance is cast on our reality, which suddenly looks strange, nothing more being taken for granted. The field of the possible is now opened up beyond that of the actual, a field of alternative ways of living."[36]

In contrast with Habermas and others deeply influenced by Marx, Ricoeur therefore refuses to locate evil in ideology as such. It is true that ideology must be subject to critique and suspicion. But this is only because of its becoming closed off to new innovation. Ideology per se is the inherited stability of shared social imagination that makes social life possible in the first place. It (inevitably) devolves into the evil of oppression insofar as it takes on a life of its own and becomes impervious to ongoing, voluntary, utopian transformation. In this case, ideology (as well also as utopia) becomes (in the Kantian sense of the term) "pathological": "It is as though we have to call upon the 'healthy' function of ideology to cure the madness of utopia and as though the critique of ideologies can only be carried out by a conscience capable of regarding itself from the point of view of 'nowhere.'"[37]

The problem with ideology, in the end, according to Ricoeur, is that it tends to overcome the freely reflexive human capability for imagining new utopias by which society may be submitted to critique. Ideology critique is not performed through pragmatic procedures but through a hermeneutics of suspicion funded by substantively *new* social imaginative possibilities. As Cornelius Castoriadis has said, "Society is creation, and creation of itself: self-creation."[38] But, as Ricoeur would add, it is a creation performed not just by society itself, however open-endedly, but also by selves as free social interpreters called to share in forming their own society reflexively together. Ideology is an expression of radical evil insofar as it distorts the human *capability* for a fully shared social imagination. The answer cannot be only to protect human freedom, for freedom is always situated within a concrete history. Nor, however, can the answer be only to pursue utopian visions, for these too become distorted insofar as they lack a meaningful relation to one's actually inherited ideological world. The distortion of social life in ideology is a failure of the radically primordial, if lost, human capability for collective social imagination at all, for constituting a social world that is both involuntarily (concretely) and voluntarily (freely) participated in by all at once.

The problem of evil as "premature synthesis" can suggest, in the end, that oppression is a problem of tragic finitude and fallen freedom both. Habermas and the feminists discussed above do a better job than Ricoeur of describing oppression's finitude as an already given historical intractability. Patriarchy, racism, poverty, and other social systemic forms of marginalization meet us first of all as the very conditions within which social mores may operate, so that their critique is a matter of radical and "performative" resistance. Ricoeur does not see clearly that some ideologies, in and of themselves, are more distorted than others. However, this does not mean that ideology is not also a problem of the inherent distortedness of human freedom as humanity turns away from its own capabilities for a richer and more inclusive social imagination. The real problem, in the end, is that ideology and capability lie in profound tension. Ideology tragically prevents selves from taking their rightful part in larger social discourse, but selves also, whether oppressors or oppressed, ultimately acquiesce or participate in ideological distortions of their own free will, even if to different degrees.

In this case, the relationship between oppressor and oppressed becomes more complex than described above. It is not just that one group has an active social freedom and the other becomes its passive victim. The more fundamental problem is a narrowing and distortion of the human social imagination. Neither Creon nor Antigone can see their way forward toward a fully just society in which burying one's kin and denying burial to traitors can co-exist. The difference between oppressor and oppressed is in this case a difference between the relative degrees to which a shared imaginative social world permits participation. Some have greater freedom to change their social world than others. Some are excluded from participation to the point of social invisibility. But all persons, as human, are ultimately capable of participating in the formation of a new shared social imagination. Resistance to oppression relies on the free human capability for transforming given historical ideologies in the direction of radical social inclusivity. This capability can be affirmed within each self, whether oppressor or oppressed, even if in each of us it is also fundamentally flawed. Utopia is a *religious* no-place, an impossible possibility, a mythological horizon, an ultimate human limit. It is that toward which historical ideology should be moved. Yet we inevitably fail in one way or another, and to different degrees, to take up this concrete socially transformative task.

Interlude on Two Empty Tombs

If such a relation or tension of freedom and finitude describes the ideological problem, what kind of moral creativity may make a sufficiently radical response? The new dimensions of moral creativity, on this level of social systems, can initially be evoked by the symbolism of two empty tombs. There is the empty tomb of Antigone's dead brother in Thebes, and then there is the empty tomb of the simultaneously dead and living Jesus in Jerusalem. These I propose to read here symbolically: that is, as similar kinds of *imaginations* of the limits of possibility of our own human moral experience. Ricoeur himself does not exploit this symbolic parallel.[39] Nor do I wish to suggest that either empty tomb does not have a range of many other possible meanings or that other symbols could not just as usefully be considered. But a comparison of the two can help to suggest, in an impressionistic way, how the poetics of oppression, as understood above, may itself presuppose the seeds of a still more primordial poetics of social creativity.

Antigone eventually *fills* the empty tomb of her dead brother that had been left empty by the oppressive power of the community of Thebes represented in the kingship of Creon. As Butler above suggests, Antigone may also ultimately desire to fill the longer empty tomb of Oedipus her dead brother/father. The filled tomb should have been a symbol for honoring the singular person within it, but instead it becomes a sign of the tragic distortedness of the Theban community. It is this dark emptiness of Poly-neices' unfilled tomb that drives both Antigone and Creon toward their own tragic choices. And, of course, Antigone's filling of her brother's tomb leads to her filling her own tomb as well.

The empty tomb of Jesus can of course be read in any number of ways. Here I do not read it either literally, historically, moralistically, or as a theo-logical narrative after which to pattern our own lives, but rather poetically, mythologically, symbolically of a radical *human* possibility. This second tomb is also, one could say, "tragically" filled, filled (at least in part) by an op-pressive Roman system of power whose social and political hegemony Jesus threatened. But in precisely the opposite way to Polyneices, Jesus is impos-sibly found to have *emptied* his tomb, and this impossibility becomes a symbol among his followers for the possibility for a new kind of human community. His disciples imagine for themselves a newly liberated society that stands over against Roman (and in part also traditional rabbinic) hegemony under a more powerful experience of God. The empty tomb symbolizes to them, in part, a social resurrection and renewal. The dark empty space is the space, not just of exclusion and lack of power, but also, and at the very same time, of radically new possibility.

Furthermore, if the Theban empty tomb suggests a certain ambiguity in who is to fill it—Antigone's brother Polyneices or, subliminally, her brother/father Oedipus—the Jerusalem empty tomb takes this ambiguity one step further. In Jesus, especially according to the gospel of John, the brother and father motifs are juxtaposed upon one another when he is declared the "Son of God." After rising from the tomb, Jesus tells Mary, "Go to my brothers and say to them, 'I am ascending to my Father and your Father'" (John 20:17). This ambiguous name for the dead leader makes Jesus both a fellow human "child" of God, just like the disciples themselves, and yet also somehow an image of the Father Himself.[40] The Theban tomb is filled with the tragic sense that Antigone's brother may be laid to rest only with dire consequences for Antigone herself. The Jerusalem tomb is both filled by Jesus as a child of God like the disciples themselves, but also emptied by this child as somehow Son and Father at once, a Son who mysteriously *is* the Father, or at least is *like* the Father (a Word become flesh that both is *with* God and *is* God). The first empty tomb is filled by a brother but thereby tragically destroys the social order; the second is not only filled but also impossibly emptied by a brother who as an image of his Father thereby creates hope for the possibility of a new kingdom of God on earth.

While we cannot speak to the many different interpretations given this second empty tomb over the millennia, we can at least make some provisional suggestions about how it may respond, in a poetic way, to our particular concern with the moral evil of social oppression. Of course, the gendered symbolism here must itself be questioned, the story read in part against itself. But we can at least imagine, impressionistically, that the proposed re-sponse to evil is not a set of rules or social procedures, but in fact a dark and empty cavern. It is a site of unknown possibilities, an empty space, indeed an impossibility. This empty tomb opens rather than closes. It suggests a limit-experience opening up the possible empty space that should be kept alive in human society instead of (as in Thebes) leading to suicide. It is a "no-place" by which actual social oppression may undergo the needed transcending critique and transformation. While ideologies "ground" social life, and necessarily so, in the process they are also turned by radical evil into premature social syntheses. An empty tomb is required in order for ideology to be ever more profoundly "unearthed," so that greater and more inclusive social ideals may be brought "back to life" in a more radically reflexive social imagination. What is to be resurrected in history, from a moral point of view, is our own primordial social possibilities for life together, however impossible these may seem. What is to be hoped for is our own enduring promise for human reconciliation as carved out by the empty imaginative space, the no-place, the impossible possibility of death and renewal.

Hope as New Creation

Such a connection of tragedy and renewal can begin take on moral meaning through Ricoeur's reading of the biblical symbolism of hope. For Ricoeur transforms a Kantian view of hope as arising out of human moral freedom alone in a more phenomenologically substantive and tensional direction. For Kant, hope anticipates a reward of happiness given by God in the afterlife for having made oneself morally worthy by acting according to the moral law here on earth. Such is how Kant overcomes his "antinomy" of duty and happiness, in which the former alone perfects freedom and yet the latter would seem to be freedom's highest good.[41] And hope is also a response to Kant's further antinomy in *Religion Within the Limits of Reason Alone* between freedom as the ground of moral perfection and freedom as nevertheless, inscrutably, also the ground of moral imperfection or radical evil.[42] Hope, from this angle, is freedom's possibility for self-renewal. Ricoeur's solution, however, is not to separate freedom on earth from a hoped for reward in the afterlife. Ricoeurian hope is placed instead in the concrete phenomenological human capability for rendering freedom meaningful within its already given world, in the passive-active liberation of the social imagination from selves' participation in premature syntheses of oppression.

To grasp this concretely free kind of hope, it is useful first to take a brief look at Ricoeur's "philosophical" response to tragedy in his highly unique concept of moral judgment in situation that he calls "critical phronesis."[43] We have already examined in some depth, in chapter 2, the concept of "phronesis" itself in relation to the Aristotelian pursuit of the good. And there we discovered that Ricoeur refigures it poetically as not just the ordering of a given traditional history but also the self's creation of new narrative self-coherency. But the notion of *critical* phronesis in Ricoeur takes this discussion to an entirely new level. Here, Ricoeur deliberately moves beyond Aristotle to the question of social ideology. Phronesis here reaches down into what

Ricoeur calls a "wisdom of limits" concerning the use of freedom within the distortions of society.[44]

Critical phronesis is then a capability for "judgment in situation" where the "situation" is constituted by systemic social blindness (as all situations in fact to some degree are). "Practical wisdom [in this sense] consists in inventing conduct that will best satisfy the exception required by solicitude," that is, "the exception on behalf of others."[45] The difference of convictions in a social situation cannot (contra Hegel) be fully resolved, but it can still be placed on a "path of eventual consensus," a path marked by each participant's "mutual recognition" of "proposals of meaning that are at first foreign."[46] Through this *critical* (at once self- and socially critical) phronesis, "recognition [of the claims of others] introduces the dyad and plurality in the very constitution of the self."[47] In other words, critical phronesis is the capability, unrealized especially in Creon but also to some extent in Antigone, for opening oneself to the potentially new social imagination that may arise through substantive dialogue with the social convictions of others.

In a discussion of what he calls "the act of judging," Ricoeur illustrates this critical phronetic social capability through the multivalent meanings of the French word *partager*, or "sharing." Judgment in situation is not just following generalized procedures. It involves at once "taking part in" [*prend part à*] one's constituting social systems and claiming "my share" [*ma part*] of them that is unique or "separate" [*departagé* or *separé*] to me.[48] Again, we see a simultaneous agency and passivity, freedom and finitude, of the will— the notion that even social systems are both exterior powers and yet still belong to me. "The act of judging has as its horizon a fragile equilibrium of these two elements of sharing: that which separates my share or part from yours and that which, on the other hand, means that each of us shares in, takes part in society."[49] In an implicit way we find here again Ricoeur's critique of Habermas. For "participation" in social discourse is not just the freedom to argue for oneself, to "take part"; it is also, and at the very same time, the need to situate oneself as already "being part" of a substantive history that conditions argumentation from the very start. Practical judgment of this kind is concerned with how each self's active "share" in social systems may be related to the way it already passively "shares" such systems in common.

The point, for our purposes, is that the kind of practical wisdom or critical phronesis called for in distorted social systems is not about applying fixed principles to the messy situation but about forming new principles or convictions themselves, what Ricoeur calls (adapting Rawls's term) "considered convictions" that reshape the social imagination itself. What makes a conviction "considered" is not its formation through universally applied procedures but its gradual and difficult movement toward the concreteness of "universals in context" or "potential or inchoate universals."[50] Beyond deontological universality is the potential universality—however little attained— of shared social convictions:

> What makes conviction an escapable party here is the fact that it expresses the positions from which result the meanings, interpretations, and evaluations relating to the multiple goods that occupy the scale of praxis, from practices and their immanent goods, passing by way of life plans, life histories, and including the conceptions humans have, alone or together, of what a complete life would be. For, finally, what do we discuss, even on the level of political practice... if not the best way for each party in the great debate to aim, beyond institutional mediations, at a complete life with and for others in just institutions?[51]

This interlacing of social convictions is a regeneration of selves' already shared teleological social imaginations.[52] But beyond my own good, it pursues the task of forming "a genuine moral invention" that embraces as fully and concretely as possible "the plural character of the debate."[53] The required universalization involves not just participation but also coming to newly shared convictions.

Such a possibility would indeed seem to represent not just an achievable aim but an impossibility for which we can only ultimately hope. The connection between tragically informed conviction and radically embraced hope in Ricoeur is not immediately obvious. The feminist theologian Kathleen Sands has criticized Christian ethics throughout history as generally failing, as Ricoeur does too, to understand hope in its properly tragic dimensions: "The Christian theological tradition, with its severe religious inhibitions about raising fundamental questions regarding elemental power, has been largely unable to grasp the educational and transformative functions of a tragic sensibility."[54] Even Kant, an otherwise as non-otherworldly ethicist as you can get, effaces moral finitude in his hope that moral duty eventually be rewarded in the afterlife. Sands herself is pointing in this regard to the importance of liberation theology, and especially its sense for the tragic tensions of history, which I will look into shortly. Ricoeur, like the large part of the Christian tradition on which he relies, does not clearly relate his religious ethics of hope to tragedy. But he does at least understand hope as a radical poetic response to oppression, and so helps us begin to pave a way toward a notion of hope as practically transformative.

It is, in fact, in his concept of hope that Ricoeur originally intended to develop his never completed "poetics of the will." As Ricoeur's translator Erazim Kohák somewhat freely interprets Ricoeur's early notion of hope (in Kohák's introduction to the book in which Ricoeur anticipates his poetics of the will, *Freedom and Nature*): "The term poetics [in Ricoeur indicates]...the vision of a reconciled humanity...[and] poetry in its broadest sense is the evocation of that vision."[55] As Ricoeur's career unfolds, hope comes to be developed more concretely, not only as the evocation of a vision, but also ethically as the ultimate response to the above lie of premature synthesis. Hope becomes a sense of vision lived out in historical practice and pressing at the limits of engrained worldly distortion. In its capability for hope lies humanity's opening, beyond its actual participation in oppression, toward the impossible possibility for reconciliation in this world.

Many readers of Ricoeur have in fact taken hope to be his central and most abiding moral theme.[56] It is much debated in this literature to what extent Ricoeur's vision of hope is Kantian in the above sense. My view is that while hope does share in Ricoeur a certain Kantian nature as a limiting presupposition of ordinary moral life, it differs from Kant in not being oriented around freedom alone. Rather, it liberates freedom to realize itself within a renewed phenomenological social history. Hope is a response not so much to the imperfection of freedom itself as to the imperfect relation or tension of freedom to its already given finitude. This means that hope cannot be conceptualized "within the limits of reason alone," as governed by autonomy, but ultimately transgresses even autonomy itself in the "limit-experience" of the impossible possibility for shared human participation in this world. This is why hope in Ricoeur is not just a philosophical presupposition but also a symbolic dimension of a larger religious "economy of the gift," a gift that disorients an already fallen moral world in order to reorient it around its own most radically primordial social possibilities. The renewal is not just of freedom but also of humanity's moral history.

Hope is summarized for Ricoeur by what he calls "the creative imagination of the possible."[57] It is a "gift" in the same sense as are faith and love: an opening of selves to their own primordial moral capabilities. But in this case, the gift opens selves not just to their created goodness or their potential for loving others but, in the broadest possible sense, to the future they might share with others collectively. Hope in its moral sense reveals the human possibility for society's "new being" or "new creation."[58] Ricoeur plays on this classic symbolism of Paul and Augustine to suggest that "the God of hope and the God of creation are one and the same God at two extremes of the economy of the gift."[59] The God of hope reveals humanity's lost original capability, not just for goodness, but now for goodness shared universally in common: for a goodness in which social synthesis is no longer premature but fully and totally realized. This new creation must appear impossible to us limited and self-limiting creatures, something achieved only by postponement and delay, and yet it remains that which through hope becomes our own ultimate moral capability.

This means that what hope "gives" is neither an actual plan or narrative for this world nor a transcending vision beyond it. What it gives is an ongoingly renewed capability for new historical direction. Although Ricoeur does not point out the parallel himself, just as phronesis "repeats" in a critical way the human capability for the teleological good, so also hope "repeats," now in a way directed toward the future, the affirmation of the human capability for goodness made by faith:

> [A]t the extremity of the symbolic keyboard is found the eschatolog-
> ical symbol that gives rise to the representation of God as the source
> of unknown possibilities. The symbol of the creator is "repeated," but

from the angle of anticipation and not just from that of rememoration. The God of beginnings is the God of hope. And because God is the God of hope, the goodness of creation becomes the sense of a direction.[60]

This "sense of a direction" is just as hyperbolic and scandalous as the notion of my own originally created goodness or the possibility that I may truly love my enemies. But it is turned toward, not the primordial past or the other immediately before me, but what may be imaginatively anticipated as a yet unknown future of human capability for society. History as we presently know it is imbued with a capability for still more radically primordial directionality, however little this may actually be realized.

Hope, then, is not just a vision but also a task. "Our vision is turned toward the future, by the idea of a *task* to be accomplished, which corresponds to that of an origin to be discovered."[61] Such a "vision" cannot be contained within only sacred or any other kind of texts, but must also be interpreted and appropriated into selves' own renewed practices. Human primordial creativity is to be renewed in a "regeneration of freedom" toward an "anticipation of a liberated and revived humanity."[62] Freedom must be liberated not just from irrational principles but from its own participation in ideological alienation. It can be regenerated in the face of its own participation—whether as instigator or as victim—in the distortions of social oppression. Thus, "hope makes of freedom *the passion for the possible* against the sad meditation on the irrevocable."[63]

It is in this light that Ricoeur reads the symbolism arising out of the life and death of Jesus. He places Christology at the end, not the beginning, of his three-part economy of the gift, not because it is some kind of fulfillment of the moral law, but because it takes to their broadest social limits what faith and love already suggest: the promise of a new human community. In this regard, Ricoeur agrees with Johannes Weiss, Albert Schweitzer, and Jürgen Moltmann that "the preaching of Jesus was concerned essentially with the Kingdom of God...[an] eschatological perspective [from which] we should rethink all of theology."[64] Such a view sets Ricoeur in his sharpest opposition to Barth and contemporary Barthians like Hauerwas, for whom Christology is the beginning of moral life and the witness to a revelation that has come about *already*. In Ricoeur's view, Jesus introduces into the world a possible new opening, and an opening not just for so-called believers but for human capability as such. Nor, as a result, is it the only such possible symbolism. It is an opening that directs us toward what has not yet been imagined and what can still yet come.

The kingdom of God symbolized in Jesus is, for Ricoeur, a form of religious mythology that repeats the mythology of human creation, except now with hyperbolically universalized ambitions: "Freedom in the light of hope has a personal expression, certainly, but, even more, a communitarian, historical, and political expression in the dimension of the expectation of *universal* resurrection."[65] The kingdom of God signifies that "the God of the promise, the God of Abraham, Isaac, and Jacob, has approached, has been revealed as He who is coming for all."[66] Hope is not tied to any particular enclave of humanity—whether it is the saved, the elect, or a particular historical community—but is *radical* or *religious* precisely in the sense that it is for a new kingdom of the entire diversity of humanity. It is humanity that, through Adam, is to be affirmed as given to itself as primordially created good. And so it is humanity as such, and not just some members of it, who should be affirmed as capable of sharing—and taking a share—in the hoped for social reconciliation.

Hope contains this universalizing dimension, however, because it is not only grounded in Adam's originary teleological affirmation, but also passes through the deontological moment of love toward the other. Hope is faith that has passed through the ever disorienting test of love. Jesus' love command as a "logic of superabundance" is now turned toward a further "absurd logic of hope" in which love becomes realized for and between others universally. Hope includes not just the particular other before me but all possible others universally. It thus "repeats" faith's primordial affirmation of human goodness on the higher level of an affirmation of the ultimate goodness of all, and precisely in all others' absolutely singular otherness. This does not mean that all are to be embraced in their actual historical ends. It means that hope resists the lie of premature synthesis in which the task of an ultimate, even if unfathomable, reconciliation of all with all is cut short. Echoing Paul's Letter to the Romans, Ricoeur says that hope introduces a new kind of logic of superabundance: "The logic of crime and punishment was a logic of equivalence ('the wages of sin is death'); the logic of hope is a logic of increase and superabundance ('When sin increased, grace abounded all the more' [Romans 5:20])."[67] Hope is the superabundance of the goodness of Creation now extended toward all.

But the unique possibility for hope, beyond faith and love both, is most fully symbolized for Ricoeur in Jesus' resurrection. This brings us back to our second empty tomb. What is important here is not whether Jesus actually came back to life in a biological sense or whether there may not also be other meanings of this resurrection or other resurrection symbolisms elsewhere in the Bible and in other religions. What is important is how this strange and paradoxical symbolism may "give rise to thought" for our own radically distorted humanity today. Indeed, according to Ricoeur, "it may even be that Jesus himself does not know he was the Christ. And it is the community that recognizes this and states it, established as it is on this nonknowledge."[68] It at least seems to have been the case that Jesus' first disciples were indeed moved to interpret the resurrection as a call to a new and hopeful community, for according to Acts they evidently formed new kinds of life in common where the attempt was made to share all with all. But two thousand years later, the question for us, at least from a poetic moral point of view, is what this resurrection may open up to thought in terms of the impossible possibilities for human community as such.

What the resurrection symbolizes for Ricoeur is the poetic possibility for renewing a primordially universal human bond. It suggests the possibility for "a partnership between God and God's people and the rest of humanity."[69] This originary "partnership"—that is, both being part and taking part—would overcome all actual historical partiality and apartness. "The resurrection may be understood only through the memory of God's liberating acts [such as of the Israelites from slavery in Egypt] and in anticipation of the resurrection of every human being."[70] The resurrection is not accomplished in the rebirth of just one individual two thousand years ago but in the realization of such a possibility among humanity overall, a realization evidently not yet fulfilled. Hope is the point at which human primordiality most universally meets human historicity.

This means, in the end, that hope is not for merely personal redemption, as suggested even in Kant, but for a total end to human oppression in society. Hope is lived out in both the cross each of us carries and the cross we take up for others. "As the Reformers used to say, the resurrection is hidden under its contrary, the cross."[71] That is, the resurrection arises out of and in response to the suffering of this world. But this resurrection is globalized, in Ricoeur, as the full and universal liberation of humanity as such from the death symbolized in Adam's fall. The cross of human suffering may be said to reveal the more primordial cross of hope for universal human renewal. "Theology understands hope as the anticipation through history of the resurrection of all from among the dead."[72] Hope is for an end not just to self-enslavement but to the enslavement of humanity collectively in systems of injustice and oppression.

We can now invest our above rather impressionistic symbolism of the empty tomb in Jerusalem with a more concrete ethical meaning. Beneath the actual grounds of social life in which we bury and murder those who are oppressed is an empty space of impossible new possibility for a still more radically shared community of all. This is the always future and humanistic end which Ricoeur thinks should be the business of "the church" broadly understood: "Does not the empty tomb signify the gap between the death of Jesus as elevation and his effective resurrection as the Christ in the community?"[73] In its widest moral sense, however, the empty tomb of Jesus may be taken to symbolize the task of overcoming social marginalization everywhere. "Hope is recaptured reflectively in the very *delay* of all syntheses, in the *postponement* of the solution to all dialectics."[74] Hope is the task of the ever more primordial reconciliation of humanity from within the inevitable premature syntheses of humanity in this world.

What exactly such a poetic vision of hope says to human moral tragedy is still not clear. We can at least at this point say, however, that hope reaches beyond a merely Hegelian or idealist response. It refuses the narrowness of social convictions, not through the reconciliation of history as it can actually be known, but through the renewal of history at its own very limits, through the negative imaginative space opened up by history's own new impossible possibilities. Social transformation is not an inevitable dialectical process, or even the result of applying rational procedures to concrete situations. Rather, it is an interruption of the convictions of history and meaning themselves from their own silent and dark margins, an interruption by which history may be "resurrected" in the direction of a universal, if unknown, human reconciliation.

Ricoeurian hope is therefore "poetic" in its profoundest sense, not only in that it arises out of symbolism and myth, but also in that it affirms a human capability for its own practical liberating self-transformation. This poetic capability is a radical response to humanity's incessant lies of premature synthesis, lies that infect our very deepest principles and convictions. Hope replies that humanity is always capable of social syntheses of a still more excessively universal kind. Such total synthesis none of us can possibly imagine in historical actuality, for each of us is already enslaved to radical evil and its narrowing of social horizons. So far as any of us can tell, it may never actually come about. But this should not tempt us to an ethical otherworldliness (as has so often been the case in Christianity) in which all we can hope for is God's own intervention or reward. Nor, however, should it tempt us to give up on our own primordial possibilities. Rather, hope can be placed in a resurrection and renewal of our own very human capabilities. Arguably, hope of this practical kind represents a needed radicalization of a kind of critical phronetic capability for participating or sharing in our social world together.

Hope Within History

This poetics of social transformation takes us a long way toward developing a third dimension of radical moral creativity. Shortly, I want to exploit the notion even further than does Ricoeur of hope as "new creation." But before I do this, I want to return to the kinds of critiques of social transformation offered by the feminist readings of tragedy discussed above and ask whether Ricoeur has sufficiently accounted for the oppressive nature of the very *languages* and *discursive means* available for participating in social transformation in the first place. I think Ricoeur has admirably articulated moral hope's mythological end: humanity's universal reconciliation against its own free self-captivity to oppression. But an adequate account of moral creativity must explain further what this transformative possibility means within the concreteness of an already radically distorted history. This means we must consider perhaps the most trenchant problem facing social creativity of all— namely, the marginalization from participation in social transformation of those groups for whom social transformation is most required. The problem in the end with a purely symbolic reading of hope is that it conflates into a single definition of "humanity" the very real difference between oppressor and oppressed. It is this difference that most intractably confronts us if we want to know how to create ever more radical social reconciliation in our systematically distorted social world itself.

The historical dimensions of social transformation have been nowhere more forcefully articulated than in the broad late-twentieth-century movement of liberation (and "political") theology, out of which much feminist and other theological ethical discourse arises, including King with whom this chapter began. Ricoeur himself admits a profound debt to the European political theologian Jürgen Moltmann.[75] In fact, it is to liberationism, whatever else one may think of it, that should be attributed the contemporary rebirth of *hope* as a central moral category. We cannot expect here to do justice to the many differences among the various forms of liberation theology: South American liberationists like Gustavo Gutiérrez, Juan-Luis Segundo, and Leonardo Boff; their European counterparts in political theology like Jürgen Moltmann, Johann Baptist Metz, and Dorothee Sölle; North American appropriations in figures like James Cone, Rosemary Radford Ruether, and Elizabeth Johnson; and worldwide liberation practitioners like Mohandas Gandhi, Martin Luther King Jr., Oscar Romero, and Bishop Desmund Tutu. But through select illustrations, it is possible to deepen Ricoeur's notion of hope for human renewal and begin to identify more concretely how hope may function to "re-create" the actual historical situation.

Gutiérrez's groundbreaking 1971 *A Theology of Liberation* is not only a classic text in this movement but also especially useful for our purposes because it makes contact with the notion of creative ethical transformation. As Gutiérrez puts it:

> [Liberationism] is a theology which does not stop with reflecting on the world, but rather tries to be part of the process through which the world is transformed. It is a theology which is open—in the protest against trampled human dignity, in the struggle against the plunder of the vast majority of humankind, in liberating love, and in the building of a new, just, and comradely society—to the gift of the Kingdom of God.[76]

As in our own account so far, Gutiérrez holds out the possibility for building a new society in common, a possibility which, moreover, is given as a divine gift. But this newness is precisely a transformation of the oppressions that are supported by entrenched distortions of power. For Gutiérrez, the great classic themes of Christian theology all point to this hope for a less oppressive society in practice: the crucifixion of Christ that makes him the champion of sufferers and particularly the poor; faith that "proclaims that the fellowship which is sought through the abolition of exploitation is something possible"; love as modeled on "the fullness with which Christ loved us" in his renewing of humanity's "communion."[77] The hoped-for kingdom of God is the prophesied transformation of the conditions of the socially oppressed, just as the Israelite slaves were freed as the people of God from Egypt.

Similarly, Moltmann describes this concreteness of historical transformation in his vision of the Christian eschatological "mission." Moltmann sharply separates the meaning of Christ's resurrection from any abstract neoplatonic epiphany of eternity (Christ as *logos* alone). Hope must be placed instead, he argues in his classic 1965 *Theology of Hope*, in the paradox of the mission of historical liberation through sacrifice:

The world is not yet finished, but is understood as engaged in a
history. It is therefore the world of possibilities, the world in which
we can serve the future, promised truth and righteousness and peace.
This is an age of diaspora, of sowing in hope, of self-surrender
and sacrifice, for it is an age which stands within the horizon of a new
future.[78]

God's "promise" is realized in no suprahistorical ideal but in the practical
theological "mission" of transforming history itself: "The *pro-missio* of the
kingdom is the ground of the *missio* of love to the world."[79] As in Gutiérrez,
hope cannot be separated from social praxis. It takes its bearings from a world
of possibilities. But in Moltmann this hope realizes itself through what he
calls "creative discipleship": "In practical opposition to things as they are, and
in creative reshaping of them, Christian hope calls them in question and thus
serves the things that are to come."[80]

But it is perhaps in feminist liberationism that we find most profoundly
articulated the concrete historical problem of the opposition between oppressor and oppressed. For here marginalization is explored in moral life
and hope's very symbolic languages, languages that for millennia have been
shaped and formed principally by men. Here we move even further inside the
kind of distorted world experienced by Antigone, a world not just bound by
suffering but also double-bound (as Anderson puts it above) by suffering
compounded by marginalization from the very processes in society by which
suffering may be redressed.

A good example of such a vision of hope, for our purposes, lies in the
work of the American liberationist Sallie McFague, for McFague not only
articulates this deeper problem but also meets it with a kind of feminist
theological poetics. In her 1982 *Metaphorical Theology*, McFague argues that
"feminists generally agree that whoever names the world owns the world."[81]
The same is true, she claims, for religious symbolism. In Christianity in
particular, "the model of 'God the father' has become an idol" to such an
extent that " 'patriarchy' then is not just that most of the images of the deity
in Western religion are masculine—king, father, husband, lord, master—but
it is the Western way of life: it describes patterns of governance at national,
ecclesiastical, business, and family levels."[82] If, as she explicitly agrees with
Ricoeur, religious language "names God," it is vital, she suggests beyond
Ricoeur, also to question those names themselves used for God and their
usefulness for overcoming cultural and historical distortions.

McFague believes that religious language can become socially liberating
only insofar as it takes on transformative, reformative, and as she says "tensional" or "metaphorical" proportions. The problem with Western religious
symbols is not their religiousness as such but their idolatrous fixation into
merely historical terms dominated by men and masculinity. Religion itself
demands new language that can witness to a more authentic divine-human
relation. This language, McFague argues, should be precisely not hierarchical

but relational, for what God holds out as the world's ultimate possibility is not dominance but love and hope. "Christian liberation at its most profound level must address human bondage to the conventions and expectations of the ways of the world in contrast to the freedom of life according to the way of God's new rule. This is the heart of Jesus' announcement."[83] The very message of hope can be heard only through new metaphors in which the languages of actual worldly domination are placed in tension with the greater possibility of freedom for all.

McFague herself suggests, in this book, that one such liberating metaphor for hope is that of God as "friend." Elsewhere she explores metaphors of God as Mother and Lover.[84] "The model of God as friend...supports an 'adult' view of shared responsibility with God as friend [as opposed to a childlike submission to a father], identifying with us in our suffering and working with us toward overcoming the oppression brought about in large part by our own perversity and selfishness."[85] Such a religious metaphor is transformative of our distorted moral languages because it not only claims humanity is sinful and suffering but also affirms humanity as primordially capable, against oppression, of developing new languages and practices of relationality and shared responsibility. We transform the world that marginalizes us by challenging traditionally patterned symbols for God. Through new symbols like friend and mother, we may discover senses in which, however much we suffer, we can count on a God of everlasting and steadfast inclusiveness. To hope to change the world, we have first to change the languages through which we understand the human relation to God.

These and other broadly liberationist accounts of hope allow us distinguish, with and beyond Ricoeur, not just between the actuality and the primordial possibilities of social life but also, in terms of the actuality itself, between oppressor and oppressed. We can state this more complex picture of the poetics of hope by revising the symbolism of the cross. A *vertical* tension between humanity and the kingdom of God involves also a *horizontal* tension between the powerful and the powerless. This "crossing" of polarities describes moral life as involving a fuller tensionality than in Ricoeur that is both radical and concrete at once. Social transformation originates in this double meeting of freedom and finitude. The imperfect freedom of oppressors leads to the doubly distorted freedom of the oppressed: distorted by human sin but then distorted again by cultural and historical marginalization. This situation lends to oppression, as the above-mentioned feminist accounts attest, an aura of tragic fatedness. I participate in a self-defeat that also seems written into the fabric of my world and meaning itself. But in this case, the impossible possibility for a vertical relation with God opens up a deeper hope: not only for human freedom's historical renewal, but also, and at the very same time, for humanity's capability for transforming the radically distorted horizontal realm of history itself. Hope cuts like Alexander's knife through the Gordian Knot of social intractability, opening those marginalized from historical participation itself to their own primordial historically transformative capabilities.

We need not replace Ricoeur's poetics of the will in order to deepen it into such a more tragically and historically situated hope for renewing the very conditions that support historical oppression. The human self can ultimately be affirmed as capable of re-creating its distorted social world in such a way as to overcome its own marginalization within the very processes and possibilities available for doing so. Imagining God as Friend instead of Father is a good example of this practice. It not only changes our vision of the possibilities of human freedom but also empowers this freedom to challenge its own distorted parameters as set by this world. Such a radically concrete poetics of hope contains what Butler calls the "performative" power of language to change the very dynamics itself of oppressor and oppressed. Indeed, "performance" is itself poetic insofar as it suggests this world's literally being "formed through" language. Or, as I have been putting it, hope can be "transformative" to the extent that our accepted social imagination is "formed beyond" its own entrenched historical limits. Moral poetics must simultaneously deconstruct the hegemony of a historically assumed (often patriarchal) social imagination and reconstruct in its place the impossible possibility for a new social imagination inclusive of even those marginalized by it. Humanity can hope to transform the historical relation between the powerful and the disempowered only by practicing, through new relations to God, its own ever more primordially shared humanity.

The Poetics of Reconciliation

This discussion leaves us, however, with the question of the precise sense in which hope in the face of ideological oppression is finally socially "creative." Although McFague's metaphor of humanity's "friendship" with God is a powerful one, it does not fully articulate the sense in which human beings can ultimately participate in primordial social creativity itself. Rather, I want to conclude by arguing that a more apt symbolism for the human possibility for concrete social liberation lies in a further dimension of what it means for humanity to be created creative in the image of its Creator. This symbolism reveals the fight against oppression as a poetic one. The prophecy of the coming kingdom of God, in a similar way to the command from Sinai, rests on a prior mythology of Creation. It is humanity's God-given and God-like creativity that is ultimately the grounds, at least in part, for the possibility for the radical re-creation of social languages and systems. McFague herself, and liberationism generally, both exemplify and presuppose—without, however, clearly articulating—this radical creative capability.

The difference in this social dimension from creativity in the previous chapters is not its radicality. The difference is that moral creativity is now directed primarily toward a "new creation" in the direction of a socio-historical new future. It is true that the human capability for narrative unity implies a future for the self in relation to others, but this future falls short of the "final" hoped for end of reconciliation *for all*. Narrative unity is "repeated" here at a higher level that has now passed through the critique of love for others *qua* other and arrived at its most universalistic possible expression. It is also true that love for others implies a possible future of nonviolent peace. But its eschatological implications are fully realized only in a more positive hope, not just for the undoing of violence, but for the reconciliation of all others together. Hope is positive and negative at once, an aim combined with a prohibition, a sense of direction constrained by responsibility to alterity. The "new creation" transforms the relations between selves and others in the universalizing direction of an eventual, if to each of us ultimately unimaginable, shared humanity to come.

Liberationism is sometimes critiqued, if a critique can be made of such a broad movement, for lacking a substantive sense for what the liberation should be aimed *toward*. It is frequently clearer describing the evil of oppression than what a nonoppressive society would actually look like. The very term "liberation" implies this critical but not so substantive intention, since liberation suggests (generally) movement *from* more than movement toward. As we have seen in the case of Antigone, however, opposing oppression does not necessarily mean one has a fully adequate vision of human peace. The tragic dimension of this evil is that in fact no one can. Even more or less successful liberationist movements like that in South Africa against Apartheid have struggled afterward to shift toward more constructive visions of a good society itself. Bishop Desmund Tutu had to form a "Truth and Reconciliation Commission" to work out what a "reconciled" post-Apartheid society might begin to look like. It is not that liberationism could not take up this more substantively positive task, only that its center of gravity as a fight against oppression has typically lain in undoing history rather than in imagining its impossibly new possibilities.

The problem, of course, is that any substantive vision of a reconciled human history is fraught with the likelihood, perhaps even the inevitability, of replacing one narrow ideology with another. Perhaps the very greatest sufferings of humankind have been perpetrated by those who felt they were creating a more harmonious society: Roman imperialists, Medieval Christian crusaders, Protestant missionaries and colonialists, Stalinist communists, fervent nationalists, globalizing capitalists, and the like. These large worldviews frequently produce forms of tragic social blindness and premature synthesis far beyond the comparatively smaller world of the *Antigone*. Indeed, in our present technologically sophisticated, highly interdependent, and increasingly global social environment, the threat of systematic oppression in the name of social freedom is only likely to increase.

A vision of socially transformative hope that is both radical and substantive at once can be aided by further developing our poetics of human moral creativity. I believe King begins to suggest a more substantive direction to social creativity in particular when he sees that the great urgency of "the promised land of racial justice" involves a profound sense for historical *tension*:

> I must confess that I am not afraid of the word "tension." I have
> earnestly opposed violent tension, but there is a kind of constructive,
> nonviolent tension which is necessary for growth. Just as Socrates felt
> that it was necessary to create a tension in the mind so that indivi-
> duals could rise from the bondage of myths and half-truths to the
> unfettered realm of creative analysis and objective appraisal, so must
> we see the need for nonviolent gadflies to create the kind of tension
> in society that will help men rise from the dark depths of prejudice
> and racism to the majestic heights of understanding and brother-
> hood.[86]

What King sees is that social tension can be turned around so as to put history
on a transcendingly creative path. As he puts it, "Christ...was an extremist
for love, truth, and goodness, and thereby rose above his environment. Perhaps the South, the nation and the world are in dire need of creative ex-
tremists."[87] This kind of constructive and radical creative tension refuses to
cover over ideological difference and instead insists on pressing it to its most
extreme limits, not just to deconstruct history but to bring oppressor and
oppressed together into an entirely new relation as fellow human beings.

Hope is socially creative because it opens up new vistas for the shared
social imagination that, rather than simply applying already formulated social
convictions, which is inherently tragically flawed, but rather also than getting
lost in symbolic transcendance, include the fullest possible range of humanity
in the socially creative task itself. The hoped-for new creation could never be
reduced to the particular vision for social transformation of any single person
or group. Nor, however, need it remain utterly unimaginable and abstract. For
the substance of the hoped-for "new creation" consists at least in part in a
new kind of social creativity that is participated in by all. Social peace in this
sense does not mean the end of historical transformation but its ever new
beginning, its ever more radical realization in the total participation of those
who have been excluded. This kind of ethical "participation" is more radically
poetic than in Habermas. Each of us always fails to act in the image of the
Creator who created the possibility for human society in the first place. But
each of us is called nonetheless from the mysterious depths of our own
humanity toward the realization of a renewing creativity in common.

Such socially inclusive creativity turns what King identifies as the *tensions*
causing social oppression toward a more radically *extended* "stretching out" of
society to include ever wider groups within the formation of society itself. If
we can speak of a poetic teleological "intentionality" or "stretching toward"
one's own narrative unity, as well as a poetic deontological "distentionality" or
"stretching apart" in response to the other, now we may speak in this third
dimension of moral life of a poetic social "extentionality" or "stretching out"
to include the radical participation of all. Rather than merely *reforming* existing social structures, a hopeful social creativity *transforms* them in systematically new directions. Just as a potter begins with clay, water, tools, ideas,
and traditions of craftsmanship and taste, so also the great social dialogue of

which each of us is in some way a part begins from histories, stories, mores, convictions, relationships, precedents, and social traditions, but also makes of them something inclusive and absolutely new. This something new is not Hegel's triumphalist "Eternal Justice" or "true ethical Idea,"[88] but a form of social reconciliation that is created ever more radically and plurally by all. We can imagine such a possibility only mythologically because none of us could alone foresee what an undistorted society created by all would actually look like. The kingdom of God is not an "Idea" but an impossible possibility, symbolizing a profound tensional possibility at the heart of the mystery of human creativity itself.

One thing that is striking when Ricoeur and the above liberationists are placed side by side is that, for all their differences, each defines hope in terms of the formation of ever greater social *inclusivity*. For Ricoeur inclusivity is of all selves, for liberationists of the historically oppressed. But what they share is a sense for the complex possibilities for open-ended social discourse that may create an ever more inclusively shared future in common. Selves are parts of distorted social systems; at the same time, these systems belong ultimately to selves. A reconciled social world would be one that is created by all those who participate in it at once, as opposed to one where the creative participation of some is practiced at the expense of that of others. It would consist in a kind of narrative unity of narrative unities, a story of human life together that included the stories of life together told by all. Such an impossible possibility arises only insofar as selves can have faith that as human beings they are ultimately capable of socially transformative creativity with one another.

Such a hope can in fact be symbolized, at least in part, from still a third reading of the Creation mythology of Genesis. Here it becomes significant in a new way that there is more than one human being created in God's image: Adam and Eve as also, from the point of view of Genesis 1:27, "male and female" (*zakar* and *neqebah*) broadly. The myth imagines not just individuals before God but also different individuals in Creation and in the Garden of Eden *together* in a kind of primordial human community. It is true that this myth is itself distorted in Genesis 2 by Adam being said to have been created first and then Eve as his helper. But at the same time, and prior to this distortion, male and female also symbolize a still more primordial human life in common that is "very good" even in difference. Herein lies, indeed, an innocent community in which, as we may interpret it, "it is not good that humankind [*adam*] should be alone" (Genesis 2:18). In other religions, it is not just two ancestors but sometimes an entire host of ancestors who stand at this mythological origin. Mythology from this angle has the poetic power to open our imaginations up to the possibility that not only are selves or others *singularly* created like God—as I argue in the previous chapters—but so also, ultimately, *in social relations*.

These first persons are created both primordially different and primordially in common. Prior to the second story of creation and fall, they are affirmed to have been originally other yet in Created harmony. The fall itself, into history as we know it, subsequently raises the question of "shame" about difference and its need to cover over difference itself. The same difference of maleness and femaleness remains, but it is now experienced as divisive and alienating. Why such a fall should have taken place is just as inscrutable as why we fail to be happy or to love one another fully. It is equally a defeat of our own primordial human capabilities. But its result, from this new angle of social relations in common, is not just personal failure or disobedience of the other's command but humanity's *joint* guilt in community. "They hid themselves from the presence of the LORD God among the trees of the garden" (Genesis 3:8). This form of radical evil is not individual but collective, the sign of a fallen human community, of the loss of a primordial capability for participating in life in common in and through difference itself.

In hiding themselves from each other, in fact, the male and the female paradoxically find a new commonality with each other precisely in hiding themselves from their Creator. This fallen shared humanity emerges from at once having become more like God through a found knowledge of good and evil and having separated themselves from God in their joint shame. Human society before such a fall is a commonality *inclusive* of difference, afterward a commonality *merely* of difference. What humanity is left with in common in actual fallen history is difference itself: difference from each other experienced as difference from God. If all people share anything with each other in fallen history, from this mythological point of view, it is their common self-enslavement to separation. We know this in part because we can also stretch our imaginations, through such mythologies of created origins, in the direction of humanity's still more primordial *difference in harmony*. We can still imagine, however imperfectly, a primordial community created in common through the dark glass of our very fall. We sense that oppression is not our ultimate reality because we can begin to imagine, through the translucent veil of symbolism, what it is distorted *from*.

The story of Adam and Eve has of course been used for millennia, in all three of the Abrahamic religions grounded in it, for upholding patriarchal oppression itself. The interpretation goes that Eve was created second and sinned first, so woman must be the weaker and less God-like vessel. Christian theologians all the way from Augustine through Calvin and beyond have been guilty of this pre-feminist reading of the text, and we would be deceiving ourselves if we did not see the original symbolism itself as also expressing fundamental patriarchal beliefs. Of course, the problem we are seeking to address of the ideological use of moral language cannot help but infect mythological language as well, for myths are still human creations. But at least by reading the text as a myth, instead of merely a historical narrative (or, worse, an empirical truth), we can stretch our imaginations past its own gendered essentialism. I will make no effort to suggest, for example, that herein lies evidence for different gendered forms of social creativity—a male productive creativity through work, and a female reproductive creativity through child-bearing. For the text, like the larger myth of Creation in which it is embedded, is first of all about our primordially shared *humanity*.

An alternative reading can be made, from a poetic perspective, in what the text has to suggest about social creativity. On this account, gender is an apt symbol, although not the only one possible, for the creativity of human difference generally. For it is in the meeting of the genders that (cloning aside) humanity both pro-creates and, as a result, re-creates the very conditions for the possibility of historical human community. If our interest is in the kind of mysterious creativity that may take place between persons in common, then reproductive sexuality and the formation of the next generation may be its profoundest symbol. It is in the formation of new generations that humanity also faces perhaps its most challenging social task, for children are the most socially vulnerable of us all. But most importantly, such social creativity is the task, precisely, not of individuals but of social relations. And it is a task of radical and original social transformation and renewal.

What male and female specifically symbolize, on this reading, is the seemingly impossible human possibility for creating life in common *within* difference, indeed *on the very basis* of difference itself. Even the profoundly embedded historical oppression of women can ultimately be critiqued from the mythological point of view of a still more profoundly inclusive human community in common, however actually hidden in this world. A human capability for life in common amidst difference can be represented symbolically, in a glass darkly, as a dim reflection of still more primordial human possibilities. What has been lost through the fall is not the absence of difference, for female and male are different from the very beginning, but a still more radical possibility for difference existing together in creative social harmony. Human beings are different but they are also, paradoxically it must seem, at the very same time "one flesh."

But in the end, following the trajectory of our larger poetic account of moral life, what is opened up here is the impossible possibility that humanity remains capable, "in the image of" its Creator, of still a third kind of radical moral creativity. The Creator itself makes its "very good" creation out of oppositions every bit as trenchant as male and female (or black and white, young and old, rich and poor). God's creativity harmonizes a succession of profound separations: heaven and earth, night and day, water and land, plants and animals, humanity itself and its world. These are not just binary oppositions but irreducible differences placed into creative tension with one another. Separation is not destroyed but *inaugurates* the very substance and goodness of Creation. The culminating Sabbath of Creation is not the annihilation of difference but its vital, complex, concrete, and plural harmony.

In *this* Creator's image, humanity may hope to make its own social differences—whether of gender, race, wealth, age, values, culture, nationality, or traditions—also ultimately creative of difference in harmony. It can hope to transform its actual social history of premature syntheses of difference in the direction of syntheses that are ever more radically all-inclusive. This would not mean the acceptance of social differences as they actually happen to exist. Nor would it mean acceptance of the inherited languages by which such differences are named and codified. Neither selves generally nor social ethicists in particular should rest content with accepted practices or thought. Social creativity involves existing historical differences' ongoing systemic transformation into a new social imagination in which even our understandings of difference itself are utterly reconfigured. My own relations to the starving child would be systematically restructured so that the child creates the relation as much as do I. In light of the primordial origins of human history, each of us may affirm our own impossible human possibility for participating in the creation of society alongside different selves all at once. If humanity is created ultimately in the image of its Creator, it is not simply *created* harmonious but, in the face of its own radical evil, created *to create* social harmony ever anew.

Moral creativity therefore has to do, once again, not just with what can be presently imagined but also with an endless and unimaginable excess. The difference between human and divine social creativity is that the former is mired in evil, the evil in this case that each of us has already freely chosen to perpetuate or acquiesce in social marginalization. Those who enjoy the benefits of social distortions have betrayed their own more primordial possibility for using their creative power to form a better world *with* others in common. They use their God-given freedom, meant to create social harmony amidst difference, directed toward a human Sabbath, to create instead mere social difference itself. Those who are victims of historical marginalization are doubly restrained: by their own failure of primordial social creativity and by the effects of their oppressors' as well. This is not to blame the victims but to acknowledge the original sinfulness of human social creativity overall, its always falling short of what it could possibly become. Justice makes correspondingly different demands: a positive demand upon those oppressed to work toward creating a better world; a simultaneously positive *and* negative demand upon oppressors to create such a world and to cease destroying it. But in each case, the failure or suffering can be overturned only to the extent that each self's participation in the historical present is creatively exceeded in the direction of a new and more radically inclusive historical future. To create harmony amidst the concreteness of oppression is to realize an always still more primordial human capability for creating its shared social world anew.

The above liberationists are therefore right to argue that the kingdom of God is to be sought after, not in ultimate ideals alone, but through the actual struggles of social history in response to human suffering and ideology. But this struggle has its substantive end and purpose, not just in the negative goal of ending existing oppression, but also in the positive activity of universal participation in the creation of a more inclusive society. The reconciliation is not just of aims, goods, or rights but also, and underlying these, of humanity's different socially creative capabilities. In a way what is required is a radicalized and poetic Habermasian discursive situation in which all selves actually participate in forming their social world together. But because this social world is already tragically deformed, and because even the principles by which we would reform it are finally mired in the self-defeat of radical evil, such participation is always the excessive creation of history itself anew, a creation driven by the impossible possibility for substantive social reconciliation. What social participation ultimately means is radically all-inclusive social creativity.

What is truly excessive about liberating social discourse is not just its stand against oppression but also its implicit aim of creating a transformed social world. Such a future is inherently mysterious and elusive—not only because we are too narrow to see beyond our own current ideologies (the tragic problem), but also because our poetic freedom to do so inscrutably turns against itself to begin with (the problem of radical evil). We cling to our own merely limited worlds, however profoundly distorted, because we refuse the uncomfortable and hyperbolic task of re-creating it together with one another. A new moral extentionality or stretching out of society to include difference is painful, cathartic, plural, unending. Even social ethicists and liberationists are captive to distorted ideals and imaginations which they must constantly strive to re-create. And yet the poetic task of social reconciliation lies, as it were, in our blood. Every failure to live inclusively within the complex plurality of others witnesses to that which it is a failure from: our human capability for joint participation in the creation of community. Antigone is forced to spill her own blood, her own life, because shared life in common appears tragically no longer possible. Jesus' blood may be interpreted poetically as spilled in witness to the still more primordial possibility for a kingdom of God on earth. Empty tombs symbolize both despair and hope at once. We too are called by these and other cathartic symbols of oppression and resurrection to participate in the ever more radical creation of a reconciled human society, however impossible the task must seem.

Conclusion

The Poetics of Moral Life

At the end of this multidimensional investigation into moral creativity—at each level passing through the limits of radical evil and on toward the possibility for a still more primordially transformative renewal—the question remains whether, after all, moral creativity is *necessary*. It may be granted that there are certain discrete poetic dimensions to moral life, but *must* we create?

There are good reasons to be suspicious of any such overarching poetic imperative. As the Greek tragedians knew, human creativity is a strange and ambiguous force. It reaches sometimes evil and sometimes good, often blind to its own meaning and consequences. On this, the ancient poets and philosophers apparently agree. In addition, biblical writers and prophets dramatically condemn our peculiar ability to close our ears to genuine goodness by creating what is good into false images and idols. Art is all too easily bent to our fallen appetites. And from a more contemporary angle, moral creativity not only empowers the oppressed but also gives power to the ruling classes to manipulate the social imagination to its own ends. One need only mention the counterexample of the enormous creative energy of the Nazis. Is moral creativity not in the end, after all, a dangerous pursuit, to be kept secondary to the act of choosing what is right to begin with?

I argue in conclusion that the reason we must create has to do with the inescapable reality of human moral tension. The word "tension" has pervaded our discussion throughout, but it is now time to lift it up in its own right and examine its underlying function as a transitional concept between the poetics of evil and the poetics of good. It is tension that lies at the heart of the moral poetic problem, but tension also that makes possible moral poetic renewal.

The word itself has a varied history from its Latin roots as "stretching," as I have discussed, to artistic senses of relations between colors and spaces, chemical and biological senses of pressure and growth, musical juxtaposition of notes and movements, and, most recently, psychological meanings as in Freud of anxiety and need for inner catharsis. But the word "tension" has not traditionally taken an important place in moral thought, and so here we must justify its use and examine its moral importance.

In each of the ways that I have argued for tension as a dimension of moral life—in the world of the self, in response to others, and within social systems—it has always meant more than just differences in moral subjectivity. Tension arises out of the more profound human moral condition of simultaneous finitude and freedom, involuntariness and voluntariness, passivity and agency—in all their moral complexity and variation. (I have used these pairings more or less interchangeably.) This means that moral tension as understood here remains by definition obscured to any form of moral thought that emphasizes one of these poles to the exclusion of the other, as I have argued is the case on one side in Kantianism and its contemporary expressions and on the other in historicism, communitarianism, and certain kinds of postmodernism. The Cartesian dualism of finitude and freedom has to be more decisively overcome. There is no moral agency without it being realized in a particular and already given historicity, and there is no moral passivity that we are not still responsible for interpreting freely for ourselves. The two are inextricably related to one another.

The term "tension" helps to focus the larger significance of this investigation because it describes the central pivot around which have operated my two major theses. The first of these is that moral evil is poetic in being simultaneously free and tragic, and the second is that moral creativity exceeds moral evil through humanity's radical capability for the transformation of its world. The absolute necessity of exercising moral creativity lies in the requirement for making the transition from the former to the latter. Moral tension in its "evil" sense cries out for becoming rendered productive of "good." This requirement is not imposed on creativity from without, not even from any discernible will of God, but arises out of the seemingly impossible yet implicitly possible realization of human creativity itself. If a Creator made this creative capability, it is nevertheless the creative capability itself that makes it ethically imperative. Our poetics of moral life represents in this sense a perfection of freedom within finitude, the perfection of a primordial capability for forming meaning with and in response to others in the world. It calls human beings to render productive the tensions of their moral lives in their own ever more radically realized humanity.

The Tension of Moral Evil

Reflection on the relation of moral agency and passivity, freedom and finitude, has of course a long history. I have been able to touch on some of this history in the pages above. At the risk of gross oversimplification, I hazard the claim that the Jewish-Christian worldview has consistently emphasized agency over passivity, the Greek worldview the reverse. From Adam's fall to the denunciations of the prophets, from Jesus' "be perfect, therefore, as your heavenly Father is perfect" (Matthew 5:48) to Paul's theology of freedom from sin, from Augustine's turning of the heart to Kierkegaard's existentialism, the biblically based traditions have largely attributed evil to human freedom, however much they have also to varying degrees acknowledged human finitude. This is part of the biblical traditions' genius. The Christian ethicist Reinhold Niebuhr is well known for relating freedom to finitude, but even he insists that "human evil, primarily expressed in undue self-concern, is a corruption of its essential freedom and grows with its freedom."[1]

But Sands was right, as discussed above, that in its anxiety to proclaim human culpability, the Christian tradition, at least, has generally obscured the tragic depths of human moral passivity. This is where the Greeks, as well as their various recent descendents, become useful by consistently emphasizing the foundations of moral life in history, tradition, community, power, sexuality, biology, and other powerful human conditions. Throughout this discussion, I have suggested roots of this sensibility in ancient Greek tragedy and its attribution of the choices we make in moral life ultimately to fates, spiritual powers, and blind forces not quite within our control. But Plato and Aristotle, too, never lost sight of the situatedness of moral decisions within the *polis* and its larger social history, and Aristotle in particular, as Nussbaum has shown, situates virtue within goodness's sheer fragility, first of all in that one must already have been raised well to be truly good, and secondly in that goodness also depends on fortune and makes one vulnerable. The recovery of Greek tragedy in Continental thinkers from Hegel and Nietzsche up to Freud and Irigaray is in this regard to be welcomed, and again helps overcome any straightforward Cartesian dualism of freedom and finitude.

But of course any such biblical-Greek dichotomy is far too simple, to say the least. It has constantly been traversed. This is no less true today than in the past. Thus, Levinas, for example, can ground his entire ethics of the face, despite its deep roots in Judaism, in a sense for pure moral passivity. Hauerwas can blend Christianity and communitarianism to situate freedom and sin within already given historical narratives. From the other side, as it were, feminists like Butler can use Greek tragedy to articulate not only human moral vulnerability but also a sense for liberating performative freedom. An essentially Hegelian thinker like Charles Taylor can argue for a historically conditioned ethics involving the authenticity of selves. And Nussbaum can call tragic wisdom a vital moral capability.

The contribution our discussion now stands in a position to make to this great historical conversation is not just to affirm once again that moral agency and passivity are related, which only a few ethicists have ultimately denied, but more specifically to characterize this relation as involving (even if not exhausted by) an implicit radical poetic tension. This tension pervades moral meaninglessness, suffering, violence, and oppression. Were human beings perfectly capable of realizing their freedom to create their world alongside one another, they would experience moral tension only as the pure possibility for complete harmony and meaning in time, perhaps the way God may be imagined mythologically to have experienced the world's Creation itself. But in fact such an experience is for us impossible. Perhaps we reach closer than usual to it in liminal events—like weddings, rites of passage, births of children, shared laughter, artistic concentration, reaching out to others in need, and making a real social difference—where our lives are newly infused with meaning or newly joined with others. But these are only partial and fleeting, and their very partiality and fleetingness attest to humanity's more primordial creative failure. There is no apparent end to what we must "make" of our lives together. In fact, the more we try to make meaningful narratives of our lives in this world, the more we seek to become accountable to others, and the more we work to remedy the injustices of society, the more aware we surely become of the depths of the moral tension between our actual moral situation and what it may become.

Let us take our previous example of the thousands of perfectly innocent children around the world who die every day from malnutrition and easily preventable diseases. The extremity of this situation reveals the fault lines within moral life in a particularly stark way. I argue above that part of the truly perverse character of this moral evil lies in the inscrutable disproportion between the needs and rights of such children themselves and the larger social systemic structures on which these needs and rights implicitly depend. This example magnifies humanity's sheer tragic passivity before its social world, while at the same time demonstrating that, even here, the very least powerful among us still make an active demand, however inarticulately and weakly, however much it may be ignored. But the larger problem raised by this situation is of course what those with more resources in the world should do about it. This problem is larger because herein lies the more profound culpability. Why do such children, however difficult and dispiriting to face, make a claim upon *us*, whoever we are and whatever particular traditions or histories we happen to inhabit?

The answer, or at least part of the answer, is that they make a claim because they introduce into our lives a real moral tension and crisis. On the one hand, each of us is ultimately free to act, to do something to help such children out, whether it is as little as donating to charities or voting for politicians who will do more, or as much as getting involved in advocacy or making the cause our profession. This freedom makes us culpable; it comes with an implicit moral responsibility. I *can* do something. But, on the other hand, none of us is altogether free from the larger social and historical conditions that underlie the problem in the first place. Each of us is in fact constrained to greater or lesser degrees by unjust global economies, harsh political realities, distorted histories and traditions, and our own narrow families and needs. And each of us is also prey to sheer incapacity of will.

The radical evil is not just, therefore, that such innocent suffering exists—although this is surely tragic enough—but also that none of us ever fully realizes our capability in the world to address it, our freedom to transform the situation. We are aware of needing to act, but we allow ourselves to be overwhelmed by radial evil and by the passivity of the situation. This is true whether we fail colossally by not even seeing the problem, or whether we fail in lesser ways by not doing enough. Failure is not absolutely necessary, but it appears, at least in the here and now, more or less inevitable. It is possible to act, but at the very same time seemingly impossible. A fundamental moral tension exists in our placing our very own moral freedom in disproportion with the finite conditions within which it may be realized. We are constrained and culpable at once.

Such a tension or problem infects all three levels of moral life that we have examined. The above example, despite primarily highlighting the level of social practice, illustrates this. A tension exists here in the teleological realm in the narrative incoherency of the life of such a child herself, at once having very basic needs to be met and yet belonging to communities and histories which do not provide for them. Such a child has among other things a greatly reduced possibility for narrative wholeness. There is also the tension introduced into our own more privileged narrative aims between our freedom to live coherently in the world and the larger realities of living in a world that is already economically and politically distorted. Whether I personally know any such children or simply live on the same planet with them, my story is bound up with theirs implicitly, in the vast range of social, cultural, economic, and political conditions and contexts that we share. Part of my story, whether I admit it or not, is that I take part in a world in which children do not have enough to eat, and this fact, insofar as it remains unredressed, leaves my own narrative identity—albeit not as much as the child's—greatly lacking in meaning and wholeness.

But of course an even sharper tension is also present insofar as such children command deontologically as others: that is, as absolutely irreducible to any such shared narrative at all. Levinas is right that others reduce me to a pure passivity in the face of their overwhelming alterity, but it is also the case that I am required to make others some sort of response and, hence, to exercise my own free moral capabilities in hearing and being disoriented by their otherness. The tension here between passivity and agency is sharper than that involved in my own, or even the child's, narrative incoherency. It is a more complex tension initiated by human alterity or nonsubstitutability. I am called to give others a response of which, however, I inevitably fall short—to the extent that I fail not to do others the violence of reducing them to sameness. The tension in this case, as opposed to above, is negative. I am commanded *not* to violate the face of alterity as such. And yet, my response to this command violates otherness inevitably, insofar as the other is entrapped, in any effort I make to respond, within my own too narrow moral horizons. Rather than saying that moral agency itself should therefore be knocked out of orbit, it is more accurate—even if more paradoxical—to say that the required moral passivity is never fully, never responsibly, enacted.

But even more profoundly, at least in this case, a third, social-practical level of moral tension arises between my freedom to make a difference in the world and the passivity of both these children's and my own shared social systems. Passivity here has to do neither with narrative inheritances nor with alterity as such, but with the intractable structures of power embedded within language, culture, family, economics, politics, and other social institutions. These structures are not necessarily, as some claim, antithetical to freedom itself. My conclusion is not that freedom is socially constructed through and through. Rather, social systems are ultimately human efforts to express and realize, through social participation, moral freedom in common. The tension or disproportion here is not between power and power but, rather, between power and freedom. It arises in the way that social systems degrade into premature syntheses, ideological forces under which freedom is tragically constrained. Poor children do not become invisible in a vacuum but through the very social, economic, and political conditions they share with us. Those of us with any power to transform the situation, however small, are therefore faced with our own attachment to these very same marginalizing forces, an attachment that we at once actively participate in and passively accept.

It is in this sense of tension, and this sense alone, that it becomes helpful to speak of radical evil as *qualified*, albeit not entirely constituted, by a sense of moral tragedy. Tragedy is an incomplete but nevertheless important dimension of the poetic tension of moral evil. If I have not proposed a unified theory of moral tragedy in this book—a much more complicated historical and constructive task than could be accomplished here—I have nevertheless traced certain tragic themes from ancient Greece and up into modernity and postmodernity that illustrate how moral freedom is *conditioned* by the forces of finitude in a more profound way than Western religious traditions of evil generally acknowledge. Tragedy allows us to press a longstanding sense for moral evil as primarily the choice of freedom against itself toward a further sense for its profound cathartic tension with the unforgiving conditions of history.

This approach to the poetics of evil is fairly novel. From Augustine and Aquinas we have models of how to mediate biblical and Greek ethical worldviews around conceptions, chiefly, of the good. But neither pursues the possibility of a corresponding connection of original sin with the deeper tradition of Greek mytho-poetic tragedy. As I have shown, both worldviews came to adopt a Greek philosophical assertion of the separation of ethics from tragic poetics, and both, if anything, deepen it. Indeed, largely following Plato's censure of the poets, tragedy was hardly considered central to Greek moral thought until relatively recently, beginning with nineteenth-century German Idealism and Romanticism. But here, of course, we have witnessed precisely a waning of the influence of biblical conceptions of radical evil, since the goal is either to affirm the philosophical rationality of history as such (Hegel), to lift up the goodness of the natural human spirit (Hölderlin), or, alternatively, to transvalue moral values under a tragipoetic nihilism (Nietzsche). If anything, the ascendancy of tragedy as a moral category seems precisely to have *replaced* radical evil as a less guilty, resentful, or mythologically mysterious description of the moral problem. Tragedy and sin have mutually agreed on only one thing: not to cross paths.

Kant is again a more ambiguous figure in this history in that his other-wise rationalistic moral philosophy does admit a figure of "radical evil" as the paradox of perfect and imperfect moral freedom. Kant's resolution of his antinomies attests to his implicit rejection of evil as tragic by his insistence that freedom alone—and not fate, fortune, or even, ultimately, desire—is responsible for the human moral problem. Freedom is finally culpable over against all human finitude. Yet even Kant suggests, as I have argued, that perfect freedom is corrupted also in a sense by its relation to finite heteron-omous desire, implying at least an inchoate tension between the two. It is partly the existence of a finite world that allows for (even if it does not finally cause) moral wrong. But in the end, the larger tension could be admitted here only if the moral problem goes beyond freedom and its self-defeat as such. Only then would we be able truly to overcome Kant's antinomy of perfect and imperfect freedom by opposing the freedom of radical evil *in* history with a still more primordial freedom *to create* history.

It becomes possible to wager that there may be a connection between radical evil and tragedy only after the latter has been stripped of the idealist pretensions given it by Hegel and grasped in its utter paradoxicality. Such has been the case in certain elements within postmodernism. Here, however, if tragedy is viewed in a more complex way, it is still not tied to radical evil explicitly. Thus Nussbaum, for example, highlights the tragedy of our own particular finite moral imaginations, yet she does not press this toward any basis in a primordial human freedom. She appears more concerned, as I have shown, with vulnerability than with culpability. Irigaray and Anderson explore through their readings of the *Antigone* the tragic double-bind placed on wo-men by patriarchy, and Butler considers the sense in which tragedy presses performatively at the moral limits of oppressive language. But, as shown in chapter 4, while each thereby rejects rationalistic accounts of tragedy as in Hegel, none quite fully connects tragedy to the radically evil conditions for the possibility for humanity, primordially and mythically, to choose and to ac-quiesce in the tragedy of oppression in the first place.

The closest any contemporary ethicist that I know of comes to making such a link between evil and tragedy is Ricoeur. As I argue throughout these pages, Ricoeur insists that the freedom to choose evil is conditioned by selves' already existing historical finitude, and, from the opposite perspective, trag-edy's finite fatedness is still on some primordial level chosen by free indi-viduals. Such, indeed, is required by his poetics of the will, in which the involuntary and voluntary dimensions of the self are each absolutely incon-ceivable without the other. But Ricoeur in fact nowhere makes the connection between radical evil and tragedy more than indirectly or inchoately, opening the way but not going there himself. In his early work on the symbolism of evil, Greek conceptions of tragedy are in fact viewed as insufficient for moral reflection because of their ultimate subordination of freedom. And while later he revises this view and incorporates tragedy into his philosophical ethics, the connection with religion then goes unexplored. This reflects the larger problem again of Ricoeur's too sharp separation of philosophical from religious ethics. This distinction, while perhaps serving pragmatic interests, is, as I have shown, utterly artificial, even from the point of view of Ricoeur's own hermeneutics. For philosophical accounts of moral tragedy are ultimately faced with their own symbolic origins and limits, and biblical accounts of free radical evil must finally be related to their tragic obstacles and effects in the passivity of this world.

Tragedy provides a useful qualification on biblically grounded conceptions of evil because it highlights the awful tensionality introduced by evil *as it appears in actuality in finitude*. Aristotle is in a way right that tragedy is the height of poetics. It drives us through pity and fear toward the possibility for concrete moral catharsis. But tragedy is not just a literary genre (as Aristotle largely assumed) but also (as Hegel was among the first more recently to recognize) a dimension of the human moral condition itself. Tragic plays and novels speak to us because there is something tragic in human historical existence itself. But tragedy is always also something chosen by humanity, an expression of human original sin or radical evil. What is tragic is not just that we become overwhelmed by larger historical powers, but also that we enslave ourselves to this overwhelmingness ourselves: that we participate in our own distorted social passivity. A new sense of evil qualified by tragedy can lift up how humanity ultimately chooses its own moral blindness, however much this blindness, paradoxically, hides its act of making this choice.

This means that human moral tension, poetically understood, is doubled—a tension stretched from both poles of finite freedom at once. Freedom at once chooses against itself and in the process chooses an already constrained and distorted finitude. It always already defeats itself both from within and in relation to its world without. This doubling of moral evil is no mere accident but follows from each self's ontological condition of being double to begin with: finite and free, involuntary and voluntary, passive and active at once. This doubleness needs to be taken seriously from both sides simultaneously: not as a duality in which one side might claim a final victory, but as a relation or tension constitutive of human moral selfhood as such. Although no philosophical explanation could be offered for why this disproportionality comes about—it remains, as Kant says, utterly inscrutable—we can infer from the sadness, violence, and oppression of this world that what should ultimately be realized in the world has not come about, and that this lack of realization in turn propels our own incapability for addressing it.

Evil is in this sense a vicious hermeneutical circle. The breakdown and self-defeat of freedom distorts the finite world in which it is expressed, which in turn makes finitude itself an arena for the further distortion of freedom. We are caught up in a cycle of moral meaninglessness and violence which we are ultimately responsible for perpetuating. Any kind of meaningful relation between agency and passivity is experienced as the crisis of freedom failing to be at home in its world. Like Adam, our possibility for naming and living in creation falls into toil, pain, and death, lost to its own actual primordial possibilities. It is the whole hermeneutical circle that is broken and distorted, a house lying in ruins that remains nevertheless the only house in which we can live.

The concept of tension allows us, therefore, to mediate between a long-standing Western religious sense for the primordiality of free sin and certain both Greek and postmodernistic sensibilities concerning moral limits and historicity. The Greek sense of tension *within* history implies also, and is in turn implied by, a biblical sense of tension *between* history and freedom. This makes radical evil in its poetic sense here even more radical than in Kant. It acknowledges also the kind of tragic finitude to human moral existence portrayed by masters of suspicion like Marx, Nietzsche, and Freud. Poetic evil describes the profoundly inscrutable fact of freedom not only relinquishing itself but also enslaving itself to a history that is already distorted. In this, we might say in a symbolic sense, is our poetic moral "cross": a horizontal tension within historicity perpetuated by a vertical tension between history and freedom. It is in this crossing itself that we may locate the truly radical depths of poetic moral evil. Evil is poetic in the sense that it is a failure to create the world itself anew, a failure to render productive through meaningful life in common the two-way human tensionality of passivity and agency together.

The Creative Capability

A response to such poetic radical evil rests first of all on an anthropological affirmation of the human self's still more radical creative capability, its capability for working through and rendering productive such moral tension itself. The evil of moral tension is a covering over of a capability for tension that is still more primordially good. The "cross" of tension is not just a burden but also a hidden possibility. Tension can reveal moral life's cathartic impossible possibility for renewal. Prior to any actual creation in the moral world is an absolutely primitive capability to create. It is this capability or possibility that is the central focus of this book.

The language of "creativity" today has largely been reduced to subjective dimensions of artistic genius, skill in scientific inquiry or technological innovation, or, more generally, having a unique and interesting view on the world: "What a creative mind!" It is possible that this deep subjectivism is a reaction in art in particular to its becoming aware of its potential for worldly commodification—its awareness, in other words, of all the ways identified in postmodernity that inner expressivity can be marginalized. There is also a certain poetic subjectivism implied in what Philip Rieff has called the "triumph of the therapeutic" in postindustrialized cultures in which our major task in life becomes merely to remake our own inner person.[2] In any case, we do not generally think of creativity as fundamental to moral relations with one another.

If there is a sense of "creativity" in moral life at all, it can best be detected in such intersubjective activities as striving for larger narrative meaning, responding to the alterity of others, and fighting for social justice. It can also be seen when ethicists and students of ethics understand themselves as not just recovering past values or repeating generalizable ones but instigating and innovating the social imagination by pressing at the limits of accepted moral wisdom. If freedom and finitude comprise an intractable tension, they also open up impossible possibilities for infusing moral relations with radically new meaning and direction. And if moral tension is a function of an ultimately inexplicable evil, then any such creative capability must exceed evil itself as more primordially inexplicable still, as a matter of a mythological rather then merely historical faith in humanity. It is in this that creativity's true excess lies: beyond the merely subjective excesses of aestheticism and nihilism, beyond the evolving self-creativity of the course of history itself, and beyond also freedom's inscrutable lack of realization in the world.

This strange language of moral creativity has found various historical traces throughout this inquiry. Aristotle may distinguish *phronêsis* from *poiêsis*, but, as Nussbaum shows, his *Nicomachean Ethics* is from a certain angle also a book in moral education, in the sense of a creative transformation of human natural potentialities into socially meaningful practices. In a different sense, while Kant constricts poetics to the narrow realm of subjective taste (developing the concept of aesthetic "genius" that will later inform the Romantics), he also insists that the moral will must *make itself* worthy and good, must *form* its own imperfect freedom in the direction of its own greater perfection. And Hegel, in a different light again, although he ends up absolutizing history itself, views the rise of individual freedom into universal Spirit as a kind of moral formation or cultivation (*Bildung*). This Hegelian view of the possibilities of human historical formation is further shared, as Gadamer shows, by Herder, Vico, and the larger German humanist tradition.[3]

I also found inchoate traces of the moral creative capability in contemporary anti- and postmodernity. Aristotelian communitarians believe that although moral individuals are utterly conditioned by their received moral communities, it is still possible to refashion in a more epistemologically justifiable way those historical traditions and narratives themselves upon which such communities rely. Poststructuralists, alternatively, are not necessarily above suggesting that although "the other" disrupts selfhood altogether, there is still a certain deconstructive inventiveness and free play of signifiers involved in how this disruption is carried out. And, most explicitly of all, liberationists like King and Gutiérrez often speak of the creative power of the marginalized for radically transforming the larger social systems by which they are oppressed. Although I argue that none of these perspectives fully articulates the morally creative capability they presuppose, even within their own dimensions of moral discourse, each nevertheless touches upon a certain sense in which the tensions of moral life can be rendered still more radically transformative. Each attests implicitly to a primordially human creative capability.

It is here again that I find uniquely powerful assistance from Ricoeur. In fact, the central contribution of Ricoeur to this project—and, indeed, in my view the central contribution of Ricoeur to moral thought as such—lies in his notion of human moral capability as rooted in the poetics of the will. Ricoeur's central moral claim, it seems to me, is that the radical disproportions infecting moral life from within demand an esteem and affirmation of selves as such as capable of a still more radical social transformation. Such is the underlying meaning of Ricoeur's three-part economy of the gift, calling selves to faith in their own original human goodness, love toward irreducible others, and hope for an eventual universal human reconciliation. These are neither realizable actualities nor abstract ideals but, rather, calls to wager the self's own possibility for making this a better world. And, I would claim, this essentially dynamic and transformative view of ethics places Ricoeur's writings in moral philosophy ultimately on religious grounds, both in patterning its three-part movement from teleological self-esteem to deontological respect to practical wisdom, and, even more importantly, in placing the sine qua non of moral life in a primary affirmation of human capability. Moral life is the endless facing of normative disproportionality through the self's primordial and finally inexplicable passive-active capability for making moral meaning.

My difficulty with Ricoeur does not lie in whether such a primordial human moral capability exists, for in this I think he is absolutely right. My difficulty lies in its nature as morally creative. For one thing, as I have repeatedly indicated, Ricoeur ultimately does himself a disservice by separating the moral self's philosophical from its religious dimensions. As I have shown, this separation reflects Ricoeur's nervousness about the charge of cryptotheology, or the subordination of philosophy under a hidden theological agenda. This nervousness is understandable given the deep suspicions about religion pervading the academy, especially among phenomenologists in Europe who are so deeply influenced by the antireligious suspicions of Marx, Nietzsche, and Freud. It is also understandable from the point of view of the need to critique "theology," if this is understood as the "rational" explanation of God. But as Ricoeur's own hermeneutics suggests, and as Continental thought has come increasingly to accept in figures like Levinas, Marion, Kearney, and even Derrida and Caputo, such a boundary can be productively traversed. A firewall between generalizable ethics and particular religion now appears as something of a residue of modernity, something phenomenology and hermeneutics are well suited to help us surpass. If Ricoeur himself contributes to this breaking down of the boundaries, he does not explore the fuller possibilities thereby opened up for a poetics of moral life in its simultaneously historical and radical complexity.

More substantively, Ricoeur's moral poetics finally stops short of grasping the full depths of the tension of freedom and finitude. In this respect, Ricoeur's Kantianism, while an advance over Kant himself, makes him still insufficiently appreciative of the senses developed in postmodernity for moral life's absolute finitude. This primordial moral finitude has come to light in our discussion in several ways: the prior historical meaning that tragically conditions even freedom's interpretation of narrative goods; the original otherness of other persons before freedom can make them a response; and the already distorted nature of social language and ideology before freedom takes up its resistance to it. Ricoeur lacks a sense for these ultimately finite moral conditions, not because he sees no relation between freedom and finitude, but because he locates *primordial* humanity in freedom alone rather than in finitely free creativity. In this respect, I do not think Ricoeur appreciates the full force of postmodernity's multiple regraspings of moral finitude and tragedy. It is for this reason, also, that Ricoeur interprets God as an origin *to be named* rather than also, and at the same time, the original name—as Creator—for *naming* as such.

Our task has been to see how humanity's moral creative capability does not lie in freedom or finitude alone but in their tension being rendered radically productive. This productive possibility of the tension, this making or forming something new of it, can only be an object of primordial attestation. The disproportion of human radical evil is too profound to be overcome by humanity itself as we actually know it, either in its existing moral freedom or in the movement of the historical processes constituting its moral finitude. In the end we cannot accept Kant's faith that freedom overcomes its own imperfection, for doing so would have to imply a still more radical human freedom beyond our ultimately unreliable capabilities as such. It is in this way that I have sought to overcome Kant's antinomy of freedom being perfect and imperfect at once, by positing perfect freedom as an object of a primordial rather than merely historical or rationalized faith. Nor can a resolution be found in a contemporary Aristotelian faith in the possible coherency of history itself, for not only did no such coherency ever exist, but it *could* not exist, as far as any of us can tell, because history is also a problem of the self-enslavement of human freedom. If we are capable of moral creativity in the face of moral tension, it is a capability we can grasp only "religiously" through symbolisms and mythologies of humanity's always still more primordial possibilities, at the limits of how humanity itself can in fact historically be explained.

The central symbolism I have taken up in this regard in this book (and by definition not the only possible symbolism) is that of humanity as created creative "in the image" of its Creator. The advantage of this symbolism is that it suggests all at once human life's passivity (as created), agency (as creative), and radicality (as in the image of its Creator). That is, it affirms that these dimensions of human capability are primordially united, that their experienced disproportionality in this world is not their original possibility. Symbolically prior to our fall into history, where we experience freedom as self-defeating and finitude as constraint, can be imagined a primordial human capability for inhabiting this tension productively, for the tension itself to generate meaning rather than alienation. What is imagined here is what humanity has fallen *from*. And what it has fallen from is not just God's created order, much less some actual historical Golden Age of virtue, but *its own* original human capabilities. The fall into history as we know it is a fall from humanity as such, in its created capability for creating meaning within its world.

It is not particularly novel to use this symbolism to argue for a still more primordial moral depth than that which is experienced in history itself. John Calvin classically claims that in God's grace the "sole end is to restore in us the image of God that has been disfigured and all but obliterated through Adam's transgression."[4] Reinhold Niebuhr interprets the image of God as pointing to a *justitia originalis* in which "the perfect harmony of the soul with itself [in spite of its actual sinfulness] is ... a derivative of its perfect communion with, and love of, God."[5] But it is less frequently noted how, as I suggest in the opening discussion of Michelangelo's Creation of Adam, this original moral createdness, prior to evil, may itself involve a certain primordial human creativity. On the one hand our created goodness is simply given to us as its passive recipients, but on the other hand it uniquely implies, perhaps in contrast with all other creatures, a certain likeness to God the Creator having to do with creatively going forth and multiplying actively for ourselves. The generosity of the Creator carries over into the generosity possible in human practice in this world, a generosity that, like the Creation itself, continually renews and exceeds itself. Or, as one might say adapting another classic formulation, the original agency of the Creator of history is in a sense also a *testimony* to our own ultimate continuing possibility, as the Creator's image, for historical creativity ourselves, however much we inevitably fall short.

It is noteworthy in this regard that the creation mythology in Genesis, as in other creation mythologies, is a narrative: that is, a mythology in the sense of a symbolism played out over a course of time (seven days). For what is being symbolized is not just the act of creativity itself, but this act as instantiated within a certain primordial history. It is indeed time (day and night) that God is said to have created first, and Creation then takes place in a time of its own. As images of this Creator, we can be affirmed as ultimately capable of creativity not just *within* history but also *of* history. That which is a "likeness" in us to God is not of a wholly transcendental order. Rather, it is a mysterious and covered over capability for making this temporal world a better place. Just as the Creator on the sixth day finally creates us as images of Itself, so also ultimately may we be capable of creating more perfect images of our own humanity in the narrative fullness of historical time.

This means that my account must be carefully distinguished from present-day "narrative theology" in the form proposed by ethicists like Hauerwas, for whom the image of God is something we receive passively through grace. For Hauerwas, "I need to learn how to make my own the peace that comes from the knowledge that I am a creature of the gracious God."[6] Such historical narratives, such "knowledge," cannot address the radically evil tension of our own free enslavement to history as such. Indeed, narrative per se may only deepen it. Moral creativity neither rests upon nor advances toward any preconceived "grand narrative" of history itself. It is inherently open rather than closed. As Calvin and Niebuhr both suggest, the image of God should be revived only as a primordial renewal of human freedom. What is required, from a poetic point of view, is a *mythological* narrative of the very limits of history itself, a narrative that does not establish a pattern for historical virtues but portrays in symbolic form the primordial origins of the human moral capability for *narrating* itself. This capability is of necessity more primordial than any actual narrative of which we may be able to conceive.

While it is time to which we enslave ourselves as we disinherit our creative freedom, it is also time that forms the axis of our human possibility for creativity in the historical world. I have examined three dimensions of this temporal axis: the narrating of goods received from the past, the responsiveness to others in the immediacy of the present, and the hope for transforming history in the direction of a reconciled future. But underlying all of these (and no doubt other dimensions of moral creativity as well) is the mythological time of human creativity as such. If there is a primordial human creative capability in the image of a Creator, it is a capability to refigure time itself, in all its past, present, and future temporal thickness. Time is not abolished in this process but taken up into history's ever more radically transformed meaning. We can only imagine what God's creativity in time might look like, but we cannot imagine our own creativity *without* time, for time in the form of historicity is a condition for its very possibility. This is why the creative capability involves neither merely repeating history nor simply overcoming it, but always transforming it anew.

Why, then, is such a morally creative capability in the end absolutely necessary? It is because only in this way can we imagine ourselves as exceeding history's actual moral limits. Even in art and science, what is already historically given, in the form of materials, ideas, sensibilities, traditions, understandings, and so forth, is constantly "exceeded" in the search for the expression and realization of something new and more meaningful. Nothing has really been "created" if it does not surpass all that has gone before, even if only in the most minimal way, and even if always also on its predecessors' bases. Such excess does not destroy history but renders its own inner tensions of meaning and understanding into some "product" that takes history in a new direction. History's actual meaninglessness and disproportionality demands its constant creative renewal.

Such is only even more radically the case with morality. In moral life, creative excess is superabundance of narrative unity, responsibility to otherness, and participation in social systems. An argument can be made for morality exceeding even the creative excesses possible in art. For moral freedom is to be extended beyond itself not only into the expression of personal insight but also into relation with the multiple and irreducible persons of others and, ultimately, of all of humanity, including even the poorest and most distant infant. The loci of moral capability are by definition multiple and other. Art *can* be created by others together, but morality is so created *necessarily*. What is more, moral finitude is constituted not only by actual historical materials and objects at one's disposal, like the potter's clay or the scientist's observations, but also by the tragic situation of the historical limits to which we have already made ourselves and others enslaved. This tragically blind attachment infecting moral relations from the very start must also somehow be exceeded. Art and science may be useful for moral life insofar as they *help* us exceed our assumed moral limits, but they cannot finally substitute for the profoundly creative element within moral practice itself. Here, human relations must be exceeded beyond all that any one of us alone could ever possibly imagine.

But this does not mean that the kind of "excess" required by moral creativity moves us merely "beyond" history. Such transcendentalism has characterized neo-Platonic and Stoic conceptions of moral life as rising above worldly existence per se, whether to a pure equanimity of the soul, a mystical union with Being, or some other "transcendence" beyond historical change and materiality. It also characterizes some Romantic and existentialist views of gaining moral authenticity through an "aesthetic" freedom beyond actual social mores, obligations, and constraints. And as Marx, the high priest of historical materialism, reminds us, it is a distortion of actual moral practice to seek one's reward for goodness beyond this world in some kind of postponed moral heaven.

The kind of excess required by moral creativity is the excess *of* history itself, excess in the sense of realizing history's own impossible possibilities. Gutiérrez rightly describes the *imago Dei* in historical terms when he says that "humankind is created in the image and likeness of God and is destined to... come to a full consciousness of [itself] as subjects of creative freedom which is realized through work."[7] Only by a radical creativity of this world as such can we respond to the poetic tensionality of freedom *within* finitude, agency *within* passivity. Only in this way can moral freedom be realized in the concrete excesses of narrative unity, love for otherness, and hope for actual social reconciliation. The Creator in the image of which we may affirm our own moral creativity is the Creator, after all, of this world.

Language falls short of describing this creative capability because language itself is caught up in the historical tensions needing to be remade. This is why moral language must finally give way to its own paradoxical limits as expressed in symbols and myths. Symbols and myths are themselves language, of course, but they are language that radically breaks language's own transparency and meaning, language that points to the limits and origins of language itself in mystery. This limit and origin lies, ultimately, in a mysterious and primordial human capability for the creation of language as such. We can use language creatively. It can playfully exceed itself from within itself. It contains its own inner possibility for new superabundances of meaning. Each time we use language we invent something new—however insignificantly, and indeed however wrongly—in forming it into meaning for ourselves.

Levinas says that the other appears in the world as an infinite "saying" and thus, beyond all that is actually "said," as the face of a Wholly Other. As he puts it in his closest analogy to our image of God, "The 'here I am' signifies me *in the name of* God."[8] I have suggested that this "saying" has its ethical roots not only in the call to Abraham and the Judge at Mount Sinai, but ultimately in the Creator who creates through divine speech: "And God said...." The human creative capability calls us to a "saying" of our own, a saying in God's image that can respond creatively to the saying of others and that can also say *with* others in the formation of new moral worlds. The limits of language are also pressed in tragedy, insofar as it leads us to the breakdown of ordinary conceptions of rightness and hence to our own silent catharsis as spectators. But the mythology of human Creation goes even further and gives voice to this cathartic possibility itself, this capability in the image of God for "saying" our own lives anew. It says that the impossible disproportions of this world are betrayals of a still more radical human possibility for creating its own moral world anew.

In the end, there would be no possibility for responding to the poetic depths of human evil—indeed, we would not be aware of its evilness as such—were we not able to affirm the still more primordial human capability for rendering productive moral tension. I have used this notion of poetic "capability" to adapt the classic, if here undefended, view of the human being as primordially free. The passivity of our tragic bindedness to history *can* submit to our own new historical transformation. The radical evil of freedom defeating itself *can* give way to freedom's own realization in history. The tension of the self's passivity and agency, in all areas of moral life, can be reclaimed from its actually experienced disproportionality in the self's formation of new meaning and possibility. Such becomes possible insofar as we can have a poetic faith in a human capability for creating history anew by exceeding our own historical self-limitations, however impossible and endless such a task must seem and however much the reality of history itself might lead on the contrary toward inertia or despair. We are capable of creating again the life we share together, however little this possibility may in fact find evidence in this world.

Creating Inclusivity

If such a creative capability is necessary for persons to respond to the inherent limits and tensions of moral life, the question remains what it should produce, what sense of historical direction or meaningful purpose it may concretely give rise to. This book, as I say in the beginning, is not a complete ethics. It does not provide substantive guidelines for moral action. Nevertheless, its meta-ethical conclusions do at least suggest inchoate directions for moral creativity's inner perfection. To recall the ode from the *Antigone*, it is impossible in the end to avoid the problem of how to distinguish human inventiveness that reaches good from that which reaches evil. It is natural to point out that a creatively storied life can also be an unhappy and socially alienated one; that we are capable of enormous imagination in reducing the stranger and the poor to our own reductive fantasies about them; and that great evils like colonialism, racism, and totalitarianism are monumental social creations of a sort. Moral creativity may not dictate any particular historical pattern, but it should at least open up our fallen historical existences to their own more radically excessive possibilities. If moral creativity is a response to the disproportion of freedom within history, it would not mean very much in the end if it remained *merely* mythological and had nothing to say about history itself. Let me propose, then, not conclusive normative guidelines, but at least directions for thought—directions that should be developed much further than they can be here.

The way in which the creative capability gains meaning in history lies in its inner normative perfection. Such perfection inherently exceeds history as we can actually know it, but it also performs the transformative function of opening history up toward its own inherent radical possibilities. Kant sees moral life similarly as the effort to perfect in humanity what otherwise remains inscrutably imperfect. The difference here is that a poetic account admits the fully mythological, paradoxical, and tensional dynamics of this task. The perfection of the human moral creative capability—which is free and finite at once—is a perfection which, to us fallen creatures, remains an impossible possibility. It is impossible because of human radical evil but possible because of humanity's still more primordial creative capability. Without this mythological "still more," moral creative perfection would remain *merely* paradoxical, instead of holding out before us our own paradoxical possibilities. I have been calling this perfection or realization moral creativity's *possible* impossible possibility.

Throughout the previous chapters I use the term "inclusivity," at some risk, to indicate something of the common element underlying the various teleological, deontological, and practical forms of perfection of moral creativity developed therein. If understood not as a historical totality but as a religious limit of historical possibility, "inclusivity" can be used to suggest what moral tension rendered perfectly productive might begin to look like. In this we might find a sense, in both moral practice and moral reflection, of greater historical direction. A narrative unity of life, an adequate response to otherness, a reconciled humanity—these are all forms of the kind of inclusivity I am speaking of. They are not historical *totalities*, of which postmodernity makes us rightly critical, but symbolically attestable *possibilities* that convict history of its own fallenness and call it to its own ever more radically creative renewal.

What ties these dimensions of moral inclusivity together, and hence what determines any realization of moral creativity as such, is their affirmation of the ultimate harmony of finitude and freedom. The human creative capability actualizes itself in moral life insofar as it renders meaning out of its vast and ultimately unfathomable diversity of passive moral conditions. Inclusivity here is not the mere collection together of already existing goods and responsibilities, much less the imposition of a preconceived hegemony upon them. Rather, it is something still yet—and, as far as we can see, never in this world fully able—to be formed. It stands out as the excessive possibility calling us always at the horizons of our actual moral worlds. It stands out as opposed to all actual moral *exclusivity*: in which goods remain incoherent, others are done violence, and entire social groups are oppressed. In each of these ways, freedom and finitude exhibit an irrelationality that betrays their more perfect possible relationality. It is this irrelationality or disproportionality that ethical selves and ethical thinkers must allow themselves to inhabit and plumb to the greatest possible depths. They are then in a position to begin to turn meaninglessness, violence, and oppression around. Ever at the limits of the historical situation lies the still more perfect possibility, not for negating moral tension or destroying it altogether, but for rendering it newly productive of a more rather than less radically reconciled world.

Take again the example of the cancer patient whose health insurance does not cover a promising but expensive new treatment. Among other things, she faces a seemingly intractable tension between her desire for a longer life and her wish not to leave her family in poverty if she has to pay for the new treatment herself. Let us say she chooses to prioritize absolutely the former of these goods, longer life for herself, over the latter, and so puts her family hundreds of thousands of dollars in debt for an uncertain outcome over the course of the next few months. Such a decision might be understandable given that life is obviously in general more valuable than money, and her family might very well support it. It would be the only kind of choice available, a tragic choice, were such goods inherently determined and fixed. But is there not a sense in this case (barring exceptional circumstances) that her longer life is gained at the expense of the even more perfect possibility that she may create her own still more inclusive narrative unity of life? Part of the story she has told about herself so far in her life is that she is a spouse and parent who contributes financially, practically, and emotionally toward her household. Insofar as this dimension of her own past is tossed aside at the moment of crisis, is this not likely to be a narrowing and distortion of her life's larger temporal narrative wholeness?

The issue in this case is not just how to weigh different goods over against one another (such as life versus money). Nor is it only a question of finding some larger historical story within which this tension of goods may be decided (although such a story might help). The issue is at least in part, and necessarily so, what *new* kind of story this singular person is called to create in order to work as far as possible through the very real tensions with which her life is now faced. The problem is that existing narratives, which may have served very well in past situations and other contexts, simply no longer suffice; they leave a situation of tragic alternatives. While the tensions between life and family, health and money, and so forth, may never be resolvable completely, the moral demand here places them in crisis and hence requires rendering them as productive of new directions of narrative wholeness as possible. She might, for example, try to come up with alternative funding sources outside those she would normally be able to rely upon, campaign for changes in insurance and hospital rules, or perhaps face her own death in a new way by opting for a peaceful end at home with her loved ones. There is no absolutely perfect solution, and certainly none we could determine here in the abstract. But her choice is "good"—at least in part—to the extent that she can render existing teleological tensions productive of *new* teleological possibilities for a more rather than less unified narrative of her life.

The kind of inclusivity demanded here is "radical" in the sense that it is a historical perfection of freedom that must appear finally impossible. No one ever achieves complete narrative unity, not even in death. Our lives are far too socially and historically complex, and we inevitably fail to use our freedom in ways that do not even further deepen their incoherency. This kind of inclusivity is always a matter of religious excess. Against the disordered historical narratives that we inherit, the poor choices we inevitably have to live with, and the tragic disproportions with which we are constantly faced, a certain kind of poetic moral faith is required that, nevertheless, as a human being, one is still capable of *creating* some greater narrative harmony of one's life. Apart from any kind of heavenly other world one might find comfort in imagining, and apart from despair at the incongruity of this world as it is, is the more productive and meaningful realization of a radically creative freedom within finitude, a creative agency capable of hyperbolically exceeding its given tragic conditions in the direction of greater narrative inclusivity.

The aim here is not, therefore, a preconceived narrative of history but, rather, an ever more primordially perfect realization of one's own human narrative intentionality. Narrative tensions can be "stretched toward"—*intensio*—an ever more whole and coherent narrative unity, even if this narrative unity constantly disappears over the horizons of how we actually conceive of it. The aim of this tensional capability can be conceived of only mythologically, as a kind of inclusivity of the elements within our own histories always calling us from beyond the limits of actual history itself. Religious faith functions here neither to explain the world as it is nor to leave the world behind, but to open up the impossible possibility for creating it anew. Just as the world's original Creator may be claimed to have created the world whole and good, so also may humanity in its image likewise be able to create a greater inclusivity of goods within it. The *possible* impossible possibility here is that each of us may continually renarrate our world, in the face of its hidden exclusions of meaning, into a new world of ever more radically inclusive direction.

A different dimension of creative inclusivity can be illustrated by again returning to the example of Auschwitz. The cancer patient discussed above also faces questions of "otherness"—those in particular of her family members, as well as of herself—but in the anti-Semitism of the death camps this question is posed in its extreme. This place, this event, this symbol, this question is one of the sharpest ways of pointing to a human violence that is arguably present in all human relations to one degree or another. It is true that the death camps were products of the vast social creativity of the Nazis, an effort to forge an overarching social narrative through a highly ordered final solution. It is also true that they mark a victory of presence over absence: the presence of history over the absence that is the commanding face of the Wholly Other. But from a poetic point of view, Auschwitz also defeated a profound moral tension, the tension of absolute otherness and the historical world called to give it a response. The "faces" of its victims were not only done violence, they were also refused the commanded formation of a more radically inclusive world.[9]

The deontological tension here is not just that those done violence were irreducible to any narrative framework at all, true though this is. It is also that, as images of their Creator, such "others" demand, and still demand even from us after their deaths, a hyperbolically creative response in which their singular alterity transforms our social imaginations. Such a disruption is not only of action but also of expectation and memory. It not only stops short action and thought but also demands its radically new formation. Nazi violence in this case was, in part, a profound and enormous failure of the human moral imagination, a failure of the capability for risking a new response to those who appear different and strange. Any social creativity here was attached only to social duties that were rigidly preconceived, lacking all human responsibility for facing tensions with others and creating the world anew. Failures of this magnitude are rare in human history, but this *kind* of failure pervades human history throughout to greater or lesser degrees.

Inclusivity here has a more complex meaning than in relation to narrative unity above. Each self is called not to a renewed intentionality but, rather, to an ever more radically excessive distensionality or "stretching apart" of their own preconceived world. In the face of actual violence in the world, human beings are capable of a poetic *distentio* in which they transform their own existing moral horizons in the negative sense of undoing their implicit violence. The great danger of the word "inclusivity" is that it may suggest quite the opposite: the folding or closing of otherness into my own perspective and plans. But understood as a dimension of religious hyperbole, a moral limit-expression, inclusivity here has the meaning of the ultimate human possibility for perfect love. In this case, the tension of other and self, passivity and agency, is not stopped short but rather rendered productive of an absolutely singular and particular self-creative response.

Such a poetic imperative is finally necessary because it is selves, in the end, who both do violence to the other and are ultimately capable of undoing it. Violence cannot be met through pure transcendence of the being of the world as such. Rather, it demands of humanity a radically more inclusive history, a history in which I cease doing the violence I already do, a history that "includes" alterity in my own impossibly transformed historical world. Creativity becomes necessary in responding to the face of the other because the other's passively received claim on me, however prior and primordial, also demands my own active new use of freedom in ever more excessively nonviolent ways. This command is ultimately for the self's own ever greater perfection of its capability for creative distention, for undoing itself in response to the tension introduced by the other. This poetic possibility not only exceeds the world as any of us actually knows it, but is more precisely for my own ever more other-inclusive re-creation of it.

Finally, the aim or perfection of moral creativity can be illustrated in a third and social systemic dimension by the still more complex kind of moral "inclusivity" demanded by our above-mentioned poverty-stricken infant. Although our other examples also contain elements of larger social-systemic tension—the cancer patient facing distortions in medical insurance coverage, the victim of Auschwitz oppressions of culture and political power—the thousands of young children around the world who have been dying for decades every day from preventable causes face systemic marginalization of a peculiarly intractable kind. This routine slaughter of vast populations of innocents is not just a failure of intersubjective responsibility, but in certain respects also built into the very economic structure of global capitalism that is now increasingly dominating the world.

Here, what demands being created is not just narrative wholeness (whether in such children or in myself), or even just a response to each such child's singular otherness, but also, and in an even more complex way, entire new systems of social order. History does not undertake such creativity alone. Those with the power to perform it have entrenched interests in the status quo. Those victimized by it are systematically disempowered. And all of us to one degree or another participate in the inherited social presuppositions that support such injustices in the first place. Nor, however, is the tension here addressed merely through a transcending promise offered by God, as if each of us were not somehow also transcendingly responsible. What demands creative transformation are the very systems of social power in which all of us participate.

Moral creativity is realized on this level only to the degree that such marginalized groups are "included" in humanity's shared formation of its social world. Moral creativity is perfected here, not in the intentionality of narrative unity or in the distentionality of other-responsiveness, but in what I have been calling the ex-tensionality of "stretching out" of social participation to include all. Such children must somehow be placed meaningfully within our midst.

The poetically tragic tension of oppression is a social systemic tension between oppressor and oppressed, and so its radical possibility involves the transformation of how social systems as such are to be shared in. Creativity does not here mean the making of a world where all tensions are overcome, where we can finally wipe our hands together and consider the social task complete. Freedom could never be so realized within a radical social end that is to be formed simultaneously by all humanity together in its full diversity. Creativity means here the making of an ever more fully *humanized* social world in which social tensions come fully to life, so that social differences are not obliterated but liberated for their perfect mutual participation in the social order. This inclusive social creativity, I argue in chapter 4, can be symbolized in one way in the procreativity of the male and the female before the fall, a symbol which, beyond the actual sexism of the text itself, also imagines an impossible human possibility for ongoing social harmony through difference. A positive aim of human community is united with a negative protection of alterity in the possibility for including all in their plurality.

A poetics of the social order ultimately suggests that humanity can hope, not just for a better world at the end of time, nor even simply to overcome oppression, but to realize its distinctively human capability for participating inclusively in the formation of society. Poetic hope is neither for an other-worldly realm nor for history as it has ever actually been known, but for an ongoingly new world of ever more radically universal human involvement in forming history together. In this case, human creativity anticipates not its end but rather its coming fully and totally to life. Inclusivity in this dimension is the scandalous aim of the reconciliation of all human beings—from the most powerful world leader to the poorest infant—in their shared primordial capability for creating society as one flesh. It means the participation of all humanity in the creation of their shared world as ultimately images of the one Creator of all.

As I state at the beginning of this book, these three dimensions of moral creativity are illustrative rather than exhaustive. They provide diverse angles from which to describe a complex and mysterious phenomenon, like different views of the inner beauty of a statue. A further possibility would be to test this notion of created inclusivity against the still broader tension of humanity with "creation" in the sense of the natural environment. If we were to inquire along such lines—which I have not here done—we might perhaps say that human creativity and natural creation do in fact exist in a seemingly endless active-passive tension, and that the solution would not consist merely in the pure human passivity of our living "according to" nature. This would deny our own nature as creatively free beings. The kind of inclusivity we might hope for, instead, is one where our freedom to transform the earth is directed away from its all too frequent destructiveness and toward deeper creative tensionality with the conditions the earth itself sets around our strivings. Moral creativity might be directed in such a way as to more fully account for the tragic dimensions of being earth-bound creatures, so that it may transform this relationship in ever more nature-inclusive ways, including among other things the nature of our own bodies.

A useful concept here might be Elizabeth Johnson's "Creator Spirit" as a certain originary intentionality of the natural creation itself within which human life may find greater purpose and meaning. As Johnson puts it, "Human spirit expressed in self-consciousness and freedom is not something new added to the universe from outside. Rather, it is a sophisticated evolutionary expression of the capacity for self-organization and creativity inherent in the universe itself." [10] A similar image of the relation of human freedom to natural evolution is made by Henri Bergson in his widely influential 1907 book *Creative Evolution*, indeed in great detail and in relation to a Creator God in ways that would be well worth renewed (if critical) exploration today.[11] And one could turn, too, to Philip Hefner's image of humanity as God's created co-creator, touched upon here in chapter 1. While there was never a Golden Age in which persons and their natural environment existed in perfect harmony—except in mythological images like the Garden of Eden—today the threat of disharmony and destruction is potentially catastrophic. This question, of course, tests humanism at its limits—but not, I would argue, to the point of destroying humanity's primordial creative responsibility. A poetic solution would lie in understanding what it means to create new ways of living, new technologies, and new social orders in which the tensions of freedom and nature reveal to us our own untold possibilities for humanity within the earth or *humus* from which we arise.

Overall, the term "inclusivity" does not provide, in any of these ways, a ready historical blueprint. And it would have to be worked out in greater depth if it were to offer practically useful norms for moral choices. But it does describe some of the inner possibilities of the human capability for moral creativity. It opens up directions along which to imagine, at the limits of our actual historical existences, the radical meaning of creative moral perfection. This perfection consists in rendering one's tensions with human moral passivity—narrative, other-originating, social-systemic, even natural—productive of one's own ever more inclusive being in the world. To reduce inclusivity to anything less is a failure of the human creative capability itself—a failure in which each of us is in fact embroiled, yet to which each of us can also give a response.

It is finally impossible to imagine what such perfect moral creativity would look like except in clearly mythological terms. Mythology becomes necessary for moral poetics, not just because it is itself poetically formed, but because it holds out before us our own ultimate poetic possibilities. The creative capability is defeated by its own radical evil through the slackening or fixation of its implicit moral tensions. Yet humanity can still ultimately be affirmed as creative in the image of its own original Creator. Just as this Creator, which religions have symbolized in any number of ways throughout human history, is the Creator of all that the world includes, so also is each of us ultimately called to create our world in ever more radically inclusive ways. Only humanity appears capable of imagining and receiving this moral demand. In this lie both its depths and its heights. Let us therefore risk the affirmation of being created alike in such a way so that we may hold ourselves capable of creating together a better moral world.

The Poetics of Moral Life

Allow me to hazard, in conclusion, a hypothesis as to why the term "creativity" has been so difficult in at least Western ethical traditions to apply to moral life. I have already argued that major ethicists from Aristotle to Augustine and Kant have in different ways suspected human creativity of irrationality, hubris, subjectivism, and other sins. Probably the strongest influence over how Europeans and North Americans think about creativity today has been the more recent tradition of Romanticism, which, while embracing the value of human creativity itself, generally opposes it to morality as an aesthetic sensibility grounded in subjective expression. This, combined with a sense from the twentieth century for humanity's capabilities for massive horror, has made our own times perhaps singularly wary of creative activity when it comes to human relations and society.

But the more profound difficulty in exploring the possibly creative dimensions of moral life lies in the nature of moral creativity itself. Creativity with, for, and among others is difficult, tragic, and fraught with peril. It is an inherently endless, decentering, and open-ended task. It is in the end even more mysterious than creativity of an artistic or scientific kind, because it necessarily involves multiple poetic capabilities at once: whether in forming social narratives, in responding to each other, or in participating together in the renewal of society. *Moral* creativity must be practiced at the same time by all of us and none of us alone. And it must embrace the unknown, the imaginative, the mythological, and the new in an ethically self-transforming way that challenges the self's very deepest assumptions and practices.

What is more, such is the case not only for the practice of an ethical life in the world but also for the study of ethics and for "ethicists." An artist challenges conventional assumptions, and a scientist presses at the limits of accumulated knowledge. How much more, then, should those whose professional lives are dedicated to ethical reflection be willing to challenge, instigate, transform, even shock and scandalize? In this they would be following the ancient example of the prophets, Socrates, the tragic poets, and Jesus, as well as recent examples like Gandhi, King, feminists, and many others. In all these cases, moral life is not pinned down into a formula only needing application, or already represented in a golden past, but rather is issued as a challenge for radical self- and social transformation. Ethicists should immerse themselves in the wisdom of the ages in order, finally, to stimulate and transfigure current ethical wisdom in the direction of still unknown meaning and inclusiveness. Not to take up this inherently transformative task is not to appreciate the tragic depths of radical evil infecting human moral life at its core. The study of ethics should be just as creative as the practice of moral creativity itself.

In our postmodern world, the mystery of moral creation can be grasped only in the end insofar as we are able to find new ways to think about ethics symbolically and mythologically, and this means we must find new ways to link ordinary moral practice and thought to their religious ethical limits. Religious ethics goes astray, from this angle, when it becomes either a merely subjective expression of private beliefs or, by contrast, the embodiment of an authoritative community that imposes social norms from above. These twin temptations arise out of the false alternative that moral life is grounded in *either* freedom or finitude, agency or passivity, selfhood or historicity—and not their inherent tensionality with one another. From a poetic point of view, ethical subjectivity and ethical objectivity are both ultimately antihumanistic. True ethical wisdom lies in the endless tension between them that calls humanity toward its own ongoing creative self-renewal. In regrasping moral life's more primordial creative dimensions, religion may overcome its contemporary marginalization in social discourse and take on a more meaningful socially transformative role.

Religion functions in moral life finally, however, to call us to the originally and necessarily "creative" nature of moral life as such. It should convict humanity of its own radically evil choice to enslave itself to narrow, violent, and distorted worlds. But it should also hold up the still more primordial human possibility for transformative self-renewal. The function of religion in moral life, from a poetic point of view, is then to remind us of moral life's own radically poetic nature as such, its origins in Creativity itself. Religion should point to moral excess because morality itself should be creatively excessive. In this way, as in Michelangelo's painting, we may come to see ourselves, as through a glass darkly, as mirror images in this world of an original world Creator. It is toward creativity that our own humanity primordially calls us.

And so, paradoxically, we are called constantly to exceed ourselves, in order to become ever more fully human.

Let us therefore (creatively!) revise the slogan of the Enlightenment, taken not insignificantly from a letter of advice on poetry by the great classical poet Horace, that reads "*Sapere aude!*"—literally "Dare to be wise!" or "Dare to taste!" This slogan was rendered by Kant as "Have the courage to use your own reason!" ("*Habe Muth dich deines eigenen Verstandes zu bedienen!*").[12] Let us say instead, with even greater radicality, "Dare to create!"

Notes

INTRODUCTION

1. All translations of the Bible are from the New Revised Standard Version.

2. Friedrich Nietzsche, *Ecce Homo* [German original 1898] in *The Geneology of Morals and Ecce Homo*, trans. Walter Kauffmann (New York: Random House, 1967), 304; see also 309.

3. Jean-Luc Marion, *God Without Being* [French original 1982], trans. Thomas A. Carlson (Chicago: University of Chicago Press, 1991).

4. Richard Kearney, *Strangers, Gods and Monsters: Interpreting Otherness* (New York: Routledge, 2003), 11.

5. Hannah Arendt, *Eichmann in Jerusalem: A Report on the Banality of Evil*, revised and enlarged edition (New York: Penguin, 1994).

CHAPTER I

1. See the Selected Bibliography.

2. Don Ihde, *Hermeneutic Phenomenology: The Philosophy of Paul Ricoeur* (Evanston, IL: Northwestern University Press, 1971), 7 and 98.

3. Domenico Jervolino, *The Cogito and Hermeneutics: The Question of the Subject in Paul Ricoeur* (Boston: Kluwer Academic, 1990).

4. See Gabriel Marcel, *Being and Having* [French original 1935], trans. Katherine Farrer (Philadelphia: Westminster, 1949); and Marcel, *The Mystery of Being*, trans. G. S. Fraser (Chicago: Henry Regnery, 1950).

5. Paul Ricoeur, *Freedom and Nature: The Voluntary and the Involuntary* [French original 1950], trans. Erazim V. Kohák (Evanston, IL: Northwestern University Press 1966), 12.

6. Ibid., 10.

7. Interestingly, the body is so central to willing for Ricoeur that he goes so far as to make the rather strange claim in *Freedom and Nature* that "the acid test of a philosophy of the will is indisputably the problem of

muscular effort" (308). His explanation is as follows: "There is, to be sure, also intellectual effort, as the effort of recalling memories, etc., but in the last instance *the terminus of willing is in the muscles*. All other effort is finally effort in virtue of its muscular components, of its mastery over a body" (308; my emphasis). This claim is tempered in Ricoeur's subsequent thought, which pays significantly greater attention to the involuntary contexts of language, history, tradition, and society. But it does demonstrate his commitment to thinking freedom in relation to its world.

8. Ricoeur, *Freedom and Nature*, 484.

9. Paul Ricoeur, "The Problem of the Foundation of Moral Philosophy" [French original 1975], *Philosophy Today* 22.3–4 (1978): 175–92, 176.

10. See, respectively, Ricoeur, *Freedom and Nature*, 312–14; Ricoeur, *Freud and Philosophy: An Essay on Interpretation* [French original 1965], trans. Denis Savage (New Haven, CT: Yale University Press, 1970); Ricoeur, *The Symbolism of Evil* [French original 1960], trans. Emerson Buchanan (Boston: Beacon Press, 1967); Ricoeur, *The Rule of Metaphor: Multidisciplinary Studies of the Creation of Meaning in Language* [French original 1975], trans. Robert Czerny (Toronto: University of Toronto Press, 1977); and Ricoeur, *Time and Narrative*, Vol. 3 [French original 1985], trans. Kathleen Blamey and David Pellauer (Chicago: University of Chicago Press, 1988).

11. Ricoeur, *Freedom and Nature*, 482.

12. Ricoeur, *The Symbolism of Evil*. The exact titles in French are *Philosophie de la volonté. Finitude et Culpabilité. I. L'homme faillible* and *Philosophie de la volonté. Finitude et Culpabilité. II. La symbolique du mal*. These refer back to the "philosophy of the will" begun in *Freedom and Nature*, whose French title is *Philosophie de la volonté. I. Le volontaire et l'involontaire*.

13. David Rasmussen, *Mythic-Symbolic Language and Philosophical Anthropology: A Constructive Interpretation of the Thought of Paul Ricoeur* (The Hague: Martinus Nijhoff, 1971).

14. Paul Ricoeur, *Fallible Man* [French original 1960], trans. Charles A. Kelbley (New York: Fordham University Press, 1986), 19; my emphasis.

15. Ibid., 140.

16. Ibid., 69–70.

17. I will not enter here into Ricoeur's extensive discussion in *Fallible Man* of what this disproportionality means specifically for ethics. This discussion is significantly extended and improved in later writings that I examine in depth in the next chapters. Suffice it to say that the *moral* self is even here considered a passive-active relation. On the one hand, it contains an already given "character," understood as "the zero origin of my total field of motivation," "the radically non-chosen origin of all my choices" (62), indicating a vast range of cultural, social, habitual, psychological, and biological conditions. On the other hand, it projects before itself its own freely chosen ideals of "happiness," understood as a "horizon" of meaning—close to "what Aristotle called the human *ergon*, that is, man's existential project considered as an indivisible whole" (65)—against which "the partial aims and disconnected desires of our life stand out" (66).

18. Ricoeur, *Freedom and Nature*, 3–4.

19. Paul Ricoeur, "Intellectual Autobiography," in Lewis Edwin Hahn, ed., *The Philosophy of Paul Ricoeur* (Chicago: Open Court, 1995), 2–53, 13.

20. Ricoeur, *Freedom and Nature*, 30.

21. Ibid.

22. Ibid., 191.

23. Ibid., 468.

24. Ricoeur, *The Symbolism of Evil*, 348.

25. Ibid., 355.

26. Ricoeur, "Intellectual Autobiography," 14.

27. Paul Ricoeur, *Time and Narrative*, Vol. 1 [French original 1983], trans. Kathleen McLaughlin and David Pellauer (Chicago: University of Chicago Press, 1984), ix.

28. Ibid., 27.

29. Ricoeur, *The Rule of Metaphor*, 303.

30. Ricoeur, "Intellectual Autobiography," 47.

31. Ricoeur, *The Rule of Metaphor*, 7. See also Ricoeur, *Time and Narrative*, Vol. 1, 31–51. Interestingly, *muthos* in these works is given no specifically religious valence, as Ricoeur's originally anticipated poetics would have suggested. Indeed, it is remarkable in his exceedingly long and detailed three-volume *Time and Narrative* that Ricoeur manages to use Augustine's *Confessions* to elucidate the meaning of "time" without exploiting in any depth the evident possibilities for viewing life's story religiously, as Augustine himself clearly intends. See Augustine, *Confessions*, trans. R. S. Pine-Coffin (New York: Penguin, 1961), Books I, VIII, X, and XIII.

32. Richard Kearney, "Paul Ricoeur and the Hermeneutic Imagination," in T. Peter Kemp and David Rasmussen, eds., *The Narrative Path: The Later Works of Paul Ricoeur* (Cambridge, MA: MIT Press, 1989), 1–31, 2.

33. Ricoeur, interview in *Le Monde*, February 7, 1986, 2; quoted and translated by Kearney, "Paul Ricoeur and the Hermeneutic Imagination," 24.

34. I am not alone in this assessment. Domenico Jervolino calls Ricoeur's theory of narrative identity the "poetic . . . culmination of [Ricoeur's] philosophical discourse on the will" (Jervolino, *The Cogito and Hermeneutics*, 135). Hans Kellner similarly calls it "the quintessence of Ricoeur's vision of humanity" (Kellner, "As Real as It Gets: Ricoeur and Narrativity," in David Klemm and William Schweiker, eds., *Meanings in Texts and Actions: Questioning Paul Ricoeur* [Charlottesville: University Press of Virginia, 1993], 55).

35. Ricoeur, *Time and Narrative*, Vol. 3, 248.

36. Paul Ricoeur, "Self as *Ipse*," in Barbara Johnson, ed., *Freedom and Interpretation: The Oxford Amnesty Lectures 1992* (New York: Basic Books, 1993), 103–19, 105.

37. Paul Ricoeur, *Oneself as Another* [French original 1990], trans. Kathleen Blamey (Chicago: University of Chicago Press, 1992), 148–51; Ricoeur, "Self as *Ipse*," 106; Ricoeur, "Narrative Identity" in David Wood, ed., *On Paul Ricoeur: Narrative and Interpretation* (New York: Routledge, 1991), 189–99.

38. Ricoeur, "Self as *Ipse*," 108.

39. Johannes van der Ven, *Formation of the Moral Self* (Grand Rapids, MI: William B. Eerdmans, 1998), 40–41.

40. In this vein, Ricoeur tellingly critiques Derek Parfit's empiricist thesis that, when it comes to personhood, "identity is not what matters" (Parfit, *Reasons and Persons* [Oxford: Oxford University Press, 1986]). Parfit's fictional thought-experiments (for example, imagining the creation of two "selves" out of one through teletransporting one self into its exact replica) only show that empiricism cannot grasp this phemonenon of "mineness" central to human experience. As Ricoeur argues: "As much as I am willing to admit that imaginative variations on personal identity lead to a crisis of selfhood . . . I still do not see how the question "who?" can disappear in the extreme cases in which it remains without an answer. For really, how can we ask ourselves about *what* matters if we could not ask *to whom* the thing mattered or not? Does not the questioning about what matters or not depend upon

self-concern, which indeed seems to be constitutive of selfhood?" (*Oneself as Another*, 137).

41. Here it is interesting to note the ambiguous influence on Ricoeur of the highly influential but now largely forgotten early-twentieth-century French thinker Henri Bergson. Ricoeur cites Bergson frequently in his early texts, both to reject what he calls Bergson's "irrationalism" and to build upon his idea of time as an unfolding and creative "duration" rather than merely a sequence of predictable empirical events (see, for example, Ricoeur, *Freedom and Nature*, 160). Ricoeur also comes back to Bergson at some length in his latest book, *Memory, History, Forgetting* [French original 2000], trans. Kathleen Blamey and David Pellauer (Chicago: University of Chicago Press, 2004), which, as in part touching on moral themes, would be well worth further consideration regarding its passive-active exploration of "the past." Bergson is suggestive for our own enterprise because he links free human selfhood to a larger creative life and to an *élan vital*. For example: "For a conscious being, to exist is to change, to change is to mature, and to mature is to go on creating oneself endlessly" (Bergson, *Creative Evolution* [French original 1907], trans. Arthur Mitchell [Westport, CT: Greenwood Press, 1944], 10). Or: "That action increases as it goes on, that it creates in the measure of its advance, is what each of us finds when he watches himself act" (ibid., 271–72). Ricoeur is significantly more hermeneutically and ethically sophisticated than Bergson. But perhaps in Bergson we find some of Ricoeur's initial inspiration around the relation of human creativity to the ceaseless duration of time in the world.

42. Ricoeur, *Time and Narrative*, Vol. 3, 248–49.

43. Ibid., 246.

44. Ibid., 247.

45. Hans-Georg Gadamer, *Truth and Method* [German original 1960], 2nd rev. ed., trans. Joel Weinsheimer and Donald G. Marshall (New York: Crossroad, 1989), 270.

46. Alasdair MacIntyre, *Whose Justice? Which Rationality?* (Notre Dame, IN: University of Notre Dame Press, 1988), 350.

47. Gadamer, *Truth and Method*, 301.

48. Ibid., 290.

49. Paul Ricoeur, "Hermeneutics and the Critique of Ideology" [French original 1973], in Ricoeur, *Hermeneutics and the Human Sciences: Essays on Language, Action, and Interpretation* (New York: Cambridge University Press, 1981), 63–100, 68.

50. Gadamer, *Truth and Method*, 361.

51. Paul Ricoeur, "Phenomenology and Hermeneutics" [French original 1975], in Ricoeur, *Hermeneutics and the Human Sciences*, 101–28, 117–18; see also Ricoeur, "Temporal Distance and Death in History," in Jeff Malpas, ed., *Gadamer's Century: Essays in Honor of Hans-Georg Gadamer* (Cambridge, MA: MIT Press, 2002), 239–55.

52. Ricoeur, "Hermeneutics and the Critique of Ideology," 100.

53. Ricoeur, "Phenomenology and Hermeneutics," 115.

54. See Ihde, *Hermeneutic Phenomenology*, 6–7; and Domenico Jervolino, "The Depth and Breadth of Paul Ricoeur's Philosophy," in Lewis Edwin Hahn, ed., *The Philosophy of Paul Ricoeur* (Chicago: Open Court, 1995), 538.

55. Ricoeur, "Phenomenology and Hermeneutics," 108–9.

56. Ibid., 112.

57. Ricoeur, *Time and Narrative*, Vol. 3, 219–27.

58. Ibid., 220–21; my emphasis.

59. Ricoeur, *Time and Narrative*, Vol. 1, 68.

60. Ricoeur, *Time and Narrative*, Vol. 3, 220–21.

61. Ricoeur does not himself make this connection of traditionality to symbols, but in *The Symbolism of Evil* he does suggest the following: "There is no philosophy without presuppositions. A meditation on symbols starts from speech that has already taken place, and in which everything has already been said in some fashion; it wishes to be thought with its presuppositions. For it, the first task is not to begin but, from the midst of speech, to remember; to remember with a view to beginning" (348–49).

62. Ricoeur, *Time and Narrative*, Vol. 1, 69–70.

63. David Pellauer, "The Significance of the Text in Paul Ricoeur's Herme-neutical Theory," in Charles Reagan, *Studies in the Philosophy of Paul Ricoeur* (Athens: Ohio University Press, 1979), 97–114, 109.

64. Ricoeur, "The Hermeneutical Function of Distanciation" [French original 1975], in Ricoeur, *Hermeneutics and the Human Sciences*, 131–44, 136–38.

65. See, respectively, Ricoeur, *Freud and Philosophy*, 5–6; Ricoeur, "The Her-meneutical Function of Distanciation," 136–38; and Ricoeur, "The Model of the Text: Meaningful Action Considered as a Text" [French original 1970], in Ricoeur, *Her-meneutics and the Human Sciences*, 197–221, 203–9.

66. Ricoeur, "The Hermeneutical Function of Distanciation," 135–38.

67. See Ricoeur, "Hermeneutics and the Critique of Ideology," 91; Ricoeur, "The Hermeneutical Function of Distanciation," 132–38.

68. Ricoeur, "Hermeneutics and the Critique of Ideology," 91.

69. Ricoeur, "The Hermeneutical Function of Distanciation," 140–42; see also Ricoeur, "Hermeneutics and the Critique of Ideology," 93.

70. Jean Ladriere, "Herméneutique et épistemologie," in Jean Greisch and Richard Kearney, eds., *Paul Ricoeur: Les métamorphoses de la raison herméneutique* (Paris: Les Editions du Cerf, 1991), 107–25.

71. Paul Ricoeur, "The Task of Hermeneutics" [French original 1975], in Ricoeur, *Hermeneutics and the Human Sciences*, 43–62, 45–48 and 50–52. We need not enter here into the complex relation in Ricoeur between the "understanding" of language and the "explanation" of texts (a distinction adapted from Dilthey). Suffice it to say that this relation mirrors what we have been exploring between immersion in traditionality (and its Gadamerian *Verstehen*) and the structural explication of the world of meaning of traditional texts. See Ricoeur, "What Is a Text? Explanation and Understanding" [French original 1970], in Ricoeur, *Hermeneutics and the Human Sciences*, 145–64, 145–57; and various essays in Ricoeur, *The Conflict of Interpretations* [French original 1969], ed. Don Ihde (Evanston, IL: Northwestern University Press, 1974). Authors who have explored this aspect of Ricoeur's thought in depth include Theodore Marius Van Leeuwen, *The Surplus of Meaning: Ontology and Eschatology in the Philosophy of Paul Ricoeur* (Amsterdam: Rodopi, 1981), 4–5, 16–18; Patrick L. Bourgeois and Frank Schalow, *Traces of Understanding: A Profile of Heidegger's and Ricoeur's Hermeneutics* (Amsterdam: Rodopi, 1990), iii–iv; David Carr, "Épistemologie et ontology du récit" in Jean Greisch and Richard Kearney, eds., *Paul Ricoeur: Les métamorphoses de la raison herméneutique* (Paris: Les Editions du Cerf, 1991), 205–14; Mary Schaldenbrand, "Metaphoric Imagination: Kinship Through Conflict," in Charles Reagan, *Studies in the Philosophy of Paul Ricoeur* (Athens: Ohio University Press, 1979), 57–81; and Leonard Lawlor, *Imagination and Chance: The Difference Be-tween the Thought of Ricoeur and Derrida* (Albany: State University of New York Press, 1992).

72. Ricoeur, *Time and Narrative*, Vol. 3, 205–6; my emphasis.

73. David Klemm, *The Hermeneutical Theory of Paul Ricoeur* (East Brunswick, NJ: Associated University Presses, 1983), 140.

74. Paul Ricoeur, "Life in Quest of a Narrative," in David Wood, ed., *On Paul Ricoeur: Narrative and Interpretation* (New York: Routledge, 1991), 20–33, 26.

75. Ricoeur, *Time and Narrative*, Vol. 3, 222–27; Ricoeur, "The Hermeneutical Function of Distanciation," 143.

76. Ricoeur, "What Is a Text? Explanation and Understanding," 159.

77. Paul Ricoeur, "Metaphor and the Central Problem of Hermeneutics" [French original 1972], in Ricoeur, *Hermeneutics and the Human Sciences*, 165–81, 174.

78. Ricoeur, "Phenomenology and Hermeneutics," 111.

79. Van Leeuwen, *The Surplus of Meaning*. We should also note that the French term *"réflexive"* makes this passive-active hermeneutics more available than the more distant English "reflective," for it includes both English meanings of "reflective" *on* an object and "reflexive" *within* oneself. As Ricoeur says, "the interpretation of a text culminates in the self-interpretation of a subject who thenceforth understands himself better, understands himself differently, or simply begins to understand himself. This culmination of the understanding of a text in self-understanding is characteristic of the kind of reflective [*réflexive*] philosophy which, on various occasions, I have called 'concrete reflection.' Here hermeneutics and reflective philosophy are correlative and reciprocal. On the one hand, self-understanding passes through the detour of understanding the cultural signs [i.e., texts] in which the self documents and forms itself. On the other hand, understanding the text is not an end in itself; it mediates the relation to himself of a subject who, in the short circuit of immediate reflection, does not find the meaning of his own life" ("What Is a Text? Explanation and Understanding," 158).

80. Ricoeur, *Oneself as Another*, 355.

81. David Tracy, *Blessed Rage for Order: The New Pluralism in Theology* (Minneapolis, MN: Winston Seabury Press, 1975), 32–33.

82. Sallie McFague, *Metaphorical Theology: Models of God in Religious Language* (Philadelphia: Fortress Press, 1982), 29.

83. Richard Kearney, *Strangers, Gods and Monsters: Interpreting Otherness* (New York: Routledge, 2003), 230; see also Kearney, *The God Who May Be: A Hermeneutics of Religion* (Bloomington: Indiana University Press, 2001).

84. The most important of these efforts to show how Ricoeur is located between Tillich and Barth are made in Peter Joseph Albano, *Freedom, Truth, and Hope: The Relationship of Philosophy and Religion in the Thought of Paul Ricoeur* (Lanham, MD: University Press of America, 1987); David Stewart, "Ricoeur on Religious Language," in Lewis Edwin Hahn, ed., *The Philosophy of Paul Ricoeur* (Chicago: Open Court, 1995); Mark Wallace, *The Second Naiveté: Barth, Ricoeur, and the New Yale Theology* [1st ed. 1990], 2nd ed. (Macon, GA: Mercer University Press, 1995); and Dan R. Stiver, *Theology After Ricoeur: New Directions in Hermeneutical Theology* (Louisville, KY: Westminster John Knox Press, 2001). My own discussion borrows heavily from these deeper investigations.

85. Paul Ricoeur, "Evil, a Challenge to Philosophy and Theology" [English original 1985], in Ricoeur, *Figuring the Sacred: Religion, Narrative, and Imagination*, ed. Mark I. Wallace (Minneapolis, MN: Fortress Press, 1995), 249–61, 256.

86. Ricoeur, *Freud and Philosophy*, 531.

87. Jean-Luc Marion, *God Without Being* [French original 1982], trans. Thomas A. Carlson (Chicago: University of Chicago Press, 1991), 22 and 24.

88. Paul Ricoeur, "Manifestation and Proclamation" [French original 1974], in Ricoeur, *Figuring the Sacred*, 48–67, 60–61.

89. Ibid., 60.

90. Paul Ricoeur, "Naming God" [French original 1977], in Ricoeur, *Figuring the Sacred*, 217–35, 229.

91. Ricoeur, "Manifestation and Proclamation," 60.

92. Paul Ricoeur, "The Logic of Jesus, the Logic of God" [English original 1979], in Ricoeur, *Figuring the Sacred*, 279–83, 281; Ricoeur, "Love and Justice" [French original 1990], in Ricoeur, *Figuring the Sacred*, 315–29, 329.

93. Wallace, *The Second Naiveté*, 30.

94. Ibid., 50.

95. Paul Tillich, *Systematic Theology*, Vol. 1 (Chicago: University of Chicago Press, 1951).

96. Paul Tillich, *Theology of Culture* (New York: Oxford University Press, 1959).

97. Ricoeur, "Evil, a Challenge to Philosophy and Theology," 257.

98. Ricoeur, "Naming God," 223.

99. Ibid., 224.

100. Ibid., 234.

101. Paul Ricoeur, "The Summoned Subject in the School of the Narratives of the Prophetic Vocation" [French original 1988], in Ricoeur, *Figuring the Sacred*, 262–75, 262.

102. Paul Ricoeur, *What Makes Us Think? A Neuroscientist and a Philosopher Argue about Ethics, Human Nature, and the Brain*, with Jean-Pierre Changeux [French original 1998], trans. M. B. DeBevoise (Princeton, NJ: Princeton University Press, 2000), 291.

103. Langdon Gilkey, *Naming the Whirlwind: The Renewal of God-Language* (New York: Bobbs-Merrill, 1969).

104. Paul Ricoeur, *History and Truth* [French originals 1955 and revised 1964], trans. Charles Kelbley and others (Evanston, IL: Northwestern University Press, 1965), 110.

105. Ibid., 486.

106. Ricoeur, *Oneself as Another*, 24.

107. Ibid.

108. Kearney, *The God Who May Be*, 108.

109. Philip Hefner, *The Human Factor: Evolution, Culture, and Religion* (Minneapolis, MN: Fortress Press, 1993), 239.

110. Ibid., 253.

111. Homer, *The Odyssey*, 2 vols., Loeb Classical Library, trans. A. T. Murray (Cambridge, MA: Harvard University Press, 1919), Book 1, lines 1 and 21.

112. Ibid., Book 2, lines 98–110.

113. Sophocles, *Antigone*, in *Sophocles I*, 2nd ed., trans. David Grene (Chicago: University of Chicago Press, 1991), lines 369–74.

114. Martin Buber, *On the Bible: Eighteen Studies by Martin Buber* (New York: Schocken Books, 1968), 72 and 87.

115. Mathetes (anonymous "disciple"), *Epistle of Mathetes to Diogenes* in *The Apostolic Fathers* (Grand Rapids, MI: Eerdmans, 1975), chap. 10.

116. Clement of Alexandria, *Stromateis* (Washington, DC: Catholic University of America Press, 1991), Book II, chap. 19.

117. Origen, *Contra Celsum* [*Against Celsus*], trans. Henry Chadwick (New York: Cambridge University Press, 1953), Book VIII, chap. 18.

118. Pseudo-Clementine, *Recognitions*, in *The Apostolic Fathers* (Grand Rapids, MI: Eerdmans, 1975), Book V, chap. 14.

119. Moses Maimonides, *A guide for the Perplexed*, trans. Michael Friedländer (New York: E.P. Dutton, 1904), chapter 54.

120. Although it is beyond my expertise, I suspect it may be possible to expand such symbolisms beyond the Western traditions. Victor Turner, for example, speaks of Ndembu rites of passage as transformative experiences of "liminality," transformation taking place ritually and symbolically in both the individual and their community (Turner, *The Forest of Symbols: Aspects of Ndembu Ritual* [Ithaca, NY: Cornell University Press, 1967], 93–111). Gananeth Obeyesekere has written, partly influenced by Ricoeur, on what he calls the "transformative" power of the use of symbols in the human "work of culture" (Obeyesekere, *The Work of Culture: Symbolic Transformation in Psychoanalysis and Anthropology* [Chicago: University of Chicago Press, 1990]). Generally, world religions frequently direct their practitioners to questions of human and worldly Creation, and frequently at the same time ask for the ongoing re-creation of self and society.

121. Kearney, *The God Who May Be*, 1.

CHAPTER 2

1. I do not follow Ricoeur and others in identifying teleology with the Greek term "ethics" and deontology with its Latin equivalent "morality"; instead, I use these terms interchangeably.

2. Charles Taylor, *Sources of the Self: The Making of the Modern Identity* (Cambridge, MA: Harvard University Press, 1989), 35.

3. Aristotle, *Nicomachean Ethics*, trans. Martin Ostwald (Englewood Cliffs, NJ: Prentice Hall, 1962), Book VI, 1140b, lines 5–6. The Greek is as follows: "*tês men gar poiêseôs heteron to telos, tês de praxeôs ouk an eiê: esti gar autê hê eupraxia telos.*" I discuss this distinction in Aristotle and contemporary Aristotelianism also in John Wall, "Phronesis, Poetics, and Moral Creativity," *Ethical Theory and Moral Practice* 6.3 (September 2003): 317–41, on which much of the following section is based.

4. See, for example, Gaëlle Fiasse, "Aristotle's Phronèsis: A True Grasp of Ends as Well as Means?" *Review of Metaphysics* 55 (December 2001): 323–37.

5. Aristotle, *Nicomachean Ethics*, Book VI, chap. 5, 1140a, lines 26–28.

6. Ibid., Book VI, chap. 12, 1144a, line 8.

7. Ibid., Book VI, chap. 13, 1144b, lines 31–32.

8. Aristotle, *Poetics*, trans. I. Bywater, in *Introduction to Aristotle*, 2nd ed., rev. and enl., ed. Richard McKeon (Chicago: University of Chicago Press, 1947), chap. IX, 1451b, lines 28–29.

9. Joseph Dunne, *Back to the Rough Ground: "Phronesis" and "Techne" in Modern Philosophy and in Aristotle* (Notre Dame, IN: University of Notre Dame Press, 1993), 381.

10. Ibid.

11. Alasdair MacIntyre, *Whose Justice? Which Rationality?* (Notre Dame, IN: University of Notre Dame Press, 1988), 350.

12. Ibid., 115–16; my emphasis.

13. Alasdair MacIntyre, *After Virtue*, 2nd ed. (Notre Dame, IN: University of Notre Dame Press, 1984), 222.

14. MacIntyre, *Whose Justice? Which Rationality?* 362; my emphasis.

15. MacIntyre, *After Virtue*, 204–221.

16. Ibid., 219.

17. Ibid., 216.

18. Ibid., 220.

19. Ibid., 194–95; my emphasis.

20. Ibid., 2.

21. Stanley Hauerwas, *A Community of Character: Toward a Constructive Christian Social Ethic* (Notre Dame, IN: University of Notre Dame Press, 1981), 1.

22. Ibid., 148–49.

23. Ibid., 149 and 151.

24. Ibid., 37; my emphasis.

25. Ibid., 150.

26. Ibid.

27. Stanley Hauerwas, *The Peaceable Kingdom: A Primer in Christian Ethics* (Notre Dame, IN: University of Notre Dame Press, 1983), 48.

28. Ibid., 47.

29. Martha Nussbaum, *The Fragility of Goodness: Luck and Ethics in Greek Tragedy and Philosophy* [first published 1986], updated ed. (New York: Cambridge University Press, 2001), 5, 138.

30. Martha Nussbaum, *Love's Knowledge: Essays on Philosophy and Literature* (New York: Oxford University Press, 1990), 162.

31. Ibid., 154, 164, and 183–85; see also Martha Nussbaum, *Poetic Justice: The Literary Imagination and Public Life* (Boston: Beacon Press, 1995).

32. Nussbaum, *Love's Knowledge*, 184.

33. Aristotle, *Nicomachean Ethics*, Book I, chap. 10, 1101a, lines 6–8.

34. For this argument about German thought on tragedy, see Dennis J. Schmidt, *On Germans and Other Greeks: Tragedy and Ethical Life* (Bloomington: Indiana University Press, 2001); and Peter Szondi, *An Essay on the Tragic* [German original 1978], trans. P. Fleming (Stanford, CA: Stanford University Press, 2002).

35. Nussbaum, *The Fragility of Goodness*, 7.

36. Ibid., 5.

37. Sophocles, *Antigone*, lines 1343–44.

38. Ibid., lines 1413–19.

39. Nussbaum, *The Fragility of Goodness*, 66.

40. Georg Wilhelm Hegel, *Hegel on Tragedy*, 2nd ed., ed. Anne and Henry Paolucci (Smyrna, DE: Griffon House, 2001), 49, 51, 237, 281, and 325.

41. Ibid., 325.

42. Nussbaum, *The Fragility of Goodness*, 72, 78.

43. Sophocles, *Antigone*, lines 368–74 and 393–403.

44. Hans Jonas, *The Imperative of Responsibility: In Search of an Ethics for the Technological Age* [German original 1979], trans. Hans Jonas (Chicago: University of Chicago Press, 1984), 2–3.

45. Nussbaum, *The Fragility of Goodness*, 52–53.

46. Ibid.

47. Ibid., 52; the line is Sophocles, *Antigone*, 1348–49.

48. Arthur Schopenhauer, *The World as Will and Representation*, trans. E. J. Payne (New York: Dover, 1958), 252.

49. Friedrich Nietzsche, *The Birth of Tragedy* [German original 1872], in *The Birth of Tragedy and The Case of Wagner*, trans. Walter Kauffmann (New York: Random House, 1967).

50. See Schmidt, *On Germans and Other Greeks*, 258–59.

51. Sigmund Freud, *The Ego and the Id* [German original 1923], trans. Joan Riviere (New York: W. W. Norton, 1960).

52. Bernard Knox, *The Heroic Temper: Studies in Sophoclean Tragedy* (Berkeley: University of California Press, 1964), 107.

53. Terry Eagleton, *Sweet Violence: A Study of the Tragic* (Malden, MA: Blackwell, 2003), 3.

54. Paul Ricoeur, "The Problem of the Foundation of Moral Philosophy" [French original 1975], in *Philosophy Today* 22.3–4 (1978): 175–92, 177.

55. Ibid.

56. Paul Ricoeur, *Freedom and Nature: The Voluntary and the Involuntary* [French original 1950], trans. Erazim V. Kohák (Evanston, IL: Northwestern University Press 1966), 75; my emphasis.

57. Paul Ricoeur, *Freud and Philosophy: An Essay on Interpretation* [French original 1965], trans. Denis Savage (New Haven, CT: Yale University Press, 1970), 407–30, 462–68, and 514–24.

58. Paul Ricoeur, *Fallible Man* [French original 1960], trans. Charles A. Kelbley (New York: Fordham University Press, 1986), 68.

59. Paul Ricoeur, *Oneself as Another* [French original 1990], trans. Kathleen Blamey (Chicago: University of Chicago Press, 1992), 172 and 239.

60. Ibid., 176.

61. Ibid.

62. Ibid., 163. Ricoeur adds later: "For MacIntyre, the difficulties tied to the idea of a refiguration of life by fiction do not arise. . . . [H]e does not draw any benefit, as I try to do, from the double fact that it is in literary fiction that the connection between an action and its agent is easiest to perceive and that fiction proves to be an immense laboratory for thought experiments in which this connection is submitted to an endless number of imaginative variations. . . . [H]ere a difficulty unknown to MacIntyre arises, namely: how do the thought experiments occasioned by fiction . . . contribute to self-examination in a real life?" (ibid., 159). Ricoeur also makes similar critiques of MacIntyre in *Time and Narrative*, Vol. 3 [French original 1985], trans. Kathleen Blamey and David Pellauer (Chicago: University of Chicago Press, 1988), 248–49; and in "Narrative Identity," in David Wood, ed., *On Paul Ricoeur: Narrative and Interpretation* (New York: Routledge, 1991), 195–99.

63. Ricoeur, *Oneself as Another*, 177.

64. I leave Ricoeur's own discussion of "critical phronesis" in *Oneself as Another* to chapter 4, for Ricoeur's point in that discussion has to do less with teleological goods than with systemic social practice.

65. Ricoeur, *Oneself as Another*, 177.

66. Ibid.

67. Ibid., 175.

68. Ibid., 178.

69. Paul Ricoeur, "The Teleological and Deontological Structures of Action: Aristotle and/or Kant?" in A. Phillips Griffiths, ed. *Contemporary French Philosophy* (New York: Cambridge University Press, 1987), 104.

70. Ricoeur, *Oneself as Another*, 180.

71. Ibid.

72. Peter Kemp, "Toward a Narrative Ethics: A Bridge Between Ethics and the Narrative Reflection of Ricoeur," in Peter Kemp and David Rasmussen, *The Narrative Path: The Later Works of Paul Ricoeur* (Cambridge, MA: MIT Press, 1989), 66.

73. Ricoeur, *Oneself as Another*, 192.

74. Ibid., 193.

75. Ibid., 194–202.

76. Ibid., 202.

77. Don Browning, "Ricoeur and Practical Theology," in John Wall, William Schweiker, and David Hall, eds., *Paul Ricoeur and Contemporary Moral Thought* (New York: Routledge, 2002), 251–63, 260.

78. Helen Buss, "Antigone, Psyche, and the Ethics of Female Selfhood: A Feminist Conversation with Paul Ricoeur's Theories of Self-Making in *Oneself as Another*," in John Wall, William Schweiker, and David Hall, eds., *Paul Ricoeur and Contemporary Moral Thought* (New York: Routledge, 2002), 64–79, 72.

79. Immanuel Kant, *Religion Within the Limits of Reason Alone*, trans. Theodore M. Greene and Hoyt H. Hudson (New York: Harper Torchbooks, 1960), 38.

80. Ibid., 32.

81. Ibid., 38.

82. St. Augustine, *The City of God*, trans. Henry Bettenson (New York: Penguin, 1972), 481.

83. Kant, *Religion Within the Limits of Reason Alone*, 38.

84. Ibid., 107–8.

85. Ibid., 108.

86. Ibid., 107.

87. Paul Ricoeur "A Philosophical Hermeneutics of Religion: Kant" [French original 1992], in Ricoeur, *Figuring the Sacred: Religion, Narrative, and Imagination*, ed. Mark I. Wallace (Minneapolis, MN: Fortress Press, 1995), 75–92, 81.

88. Paul Ricoeur, "Reply to Patrick L. Bourgeois" in Lewis Edwin Hahn, ed., *The Philosophy of Paul Ricoeur* (Chicago: Open Court, 1995), 569; my emphasis.

89. Paul Ricoeur, "Hope and the Structure of Philosophical Systems" [English original 1970], in Ricoeur, *Figuring the Sacred*, 203–16, 211.

90. Charles Mathewes, *Evil and the Augustinian Tradition* (New York: Cambridge University Press, 2001), 101. In fact, Mathewes compares Augustine extensively with Ricoeur, arguing that they share the view that "we must find a way to affirm both our realization of the disparity, perhaps even incommensurability, between our experience of inexplicable suffering and tragic conflict in the world, and our tradition's insistence (and indeed the attestation of our lives) that God is supremely good and supremely powerful" (ibid., 98). Oddly, however, Mathewes faults Ricoeur for being too pessimistic about evil and failing to grasp the alternative possibility of "hope"—a claim that neglects the fact (as discussed here in chapter 4) that hope is Ricoeur's culminating, and for many of Ricoeur's readers his central, reply to evil.

91. Paul Ricoeur, *Thinking Biblically: Exegetical and Hermeneutical Essays*, with André LaCocque, trans. David Pellauer (Chicago: University of Chicago Press, 1998), 135.

92. Paul Ricoeur, *The Symbolism of Evil* [French original 1960], trans. Emerson Buchanan (Boston: Beacon Press, 1967), 154.

93. Ibid., 156–57.

94. Ibid., 103 and 107.

95. Ibid., 233.

96. Ibid., 255.

97. Ibid., 247.

98. Ibid., 257.

99. Ibid., 259.

100. Ricoeur, "The Problem of the Foundation of Moral Philosophy," 178 and elsewhere.

101. Ibid.

102. Van Leeuwen, *The Surplus of Meaning*, 1.

103. William Schweiker, *Responsibility and Christian Ethics* (New York: Cambridge University Press, 1995), 227.

104. Paul Ricoeur, "Love and Justice" [French original 1990], in Ricoeur, *Figuring the Sacred*, 315–29, 325.

105. Ricoeur, "The Problem of the Foundation of Moral Philosophy," 189.

106. Ibid., 189–90.

107. Ricoeur, *The Symbolism of Evil*, 250–51.

108. Ibid., 251–52.

109. Ricoeur, *Thinking Biblically*, 40–43.

110. Ibid., 43.

111. Stanley Hauerwas, *The Peaceable Kingdom: A Primer in Christian Ethics* (Notre Dame, IN: University of Notre Dame Press, 1983), 27.

112. Stanley Hauerwas, *Character and the Christian Life: A Study in Christian Ethics* [first published 1975] (Notre Dame, IN: University of Notre Dame Press, 1985), 211.

113. Marcel Mauss, *The Gift: The Form and Reason for Exchange in Archaic Societies* [French original 1950], trans. W. D. Halls (New York: W.W. Norton, 1990), 18.

114. Jacques Derrida, in Derrida and Jean-Luc Marion, "On the Gift: A Discussion between Jacques Derrida and Jean-Luc Marion," in John D. Caputo and Michael J. Scanlon, eds., *God, the Gift, and Postmodernism* (Bloomington: Indiana University Press, 1999), 54–78, 59.

115. Dominique Janicaud, "The Theological Turn of French Phenomenology," in Dominique Janicaud, Jean-François Courtine, Jean-Louis Chrétien, Michel Henry, and Jean-Luc Marion, *Phenomenology and the "Theological Turn": The French Debate* [French original 1991], trans. Bernard G. Prusak (New York: Fordham University Press, 2000), 3–103, 62–68.

116. John D. Caputo and Michael L. Scanlon, eds., *God, the Gift, and Postmodernism* (Bloomington: Indiana University Press, 1999), 4.

117. Jean-Luc Marion, in Jacques Derrida and Jean-Luc Marion, "On the Gift: A Discussion between Jacques Derrida and Jean-Luc Marion," in John D. Caputo and Michael J. Scanlon, eds., *God, the Gift, and Postmodernism* (Bloomington: Indiana University Press, 1999), 54–78, 70. A similar critique is made, incidentally, of the anthropology of Mauss by Maurice Godelier in *The Enigma of the Gift* [French original 1996], trans. Nora Scott (Chicago: University of Chicago Press, 1999). See also Marion, *Being Given: Toward a Phenomenology of Givenness* [French original 1997], trans. Jeffrey L. Kosky (Stanford, CA: Stanford University Press, 2002).

118. Jean-Luc Marion, *God Without Being* [French original 1982], trans. Thomas A. Carlson (Chicago: University of Chicago Press, 1991), 75.

119. Marion, "On the Gift: A Discussion between Jacques Derrida and Jean-Luc Marion," 74–75.

120. For example, in his discussion of biblical moral poetics in the article "Naming God," Ricoeur proposes a "poetics of politics" by which "the naming of God at the heart of the biblical poem" would provide "models [which] can nourish an ethical and political reflection inasmuch as they govern the anticipation of a liberated and revived humanity" (Paul Ricoeur, "Naming God" [French original 1977], in Ricoeur, *Figuring the Sacred*, 217–35, 234–35). "Poetics" here refers to the radically

transformative power of the biblical text (albeit within its reader's life) rather than to a radically transformative capability within selves as such. Of course, this does not make Ricoeur's a merely "formal" biblical poetics, for the text still has meaning only for the world of its reader; but it does not take the further step of applying the poetics of Creation to human creativity itself.

121. David Tracy, *Blessed Rage for Order: The New Pluralism in Theology* (Minneapolis, MN: Winston Seabury Press, 1975), 249.

122. Luc Ferry, *Man Made God: The Meaning of Life* [French original 1996], trans. David Pellauer (Chicago: University of Chicago Press, 2002), 139.

123. Ricoeur, *The Symbolism of Evil*, 251.

CHAPTER 3

1. Immanuel Kant, *Critique of the Power of Judgment*, trans. Paul Guyer and Eric Matthews (New York: Cambridge University Press, 2000), 166.

2. David Guyer, *Kant and the Experience of Freedom: Essays on Aesthetics and Morality* (New York: Cambridge University Press, 1993), 335.

3. Ibid., 3.

4. Immanuel Kant, *Groundwork of the Metaphysics of Morals*, trans. J. J. Paton (New York: Harper and Row, 1964), 88.

5. Ibid., 96.

6. Ibid., 61.

7. Paul Ricoeur, *Oneself as Another* [French original 1990], trans. Kathleen Blamey (Chicago: University of Chicago Press, 1992), 217; see Kant, *Groundwork of the Metaphysics of Morals*, 111–12.

8. Ricoeur, *Oneself as Another*, 215. Pamela Anderson has claimed that "Ricoeur's reclamation of autonomy exhibits a deeper debt to, and insight into, Kantian philosophy than his explicit rejection of a formalized Kant would suggest," since Ricoeur conceptualizes "exceptions made on behalf of other persons" along the lines of a Kantian "architectonic" of unity, plurality, and totality (Anderson, "Ricoeur's Reclamation of Autonomy: Unity, Plurality, and Totality," in John Wall, William Schweiker, and David Hall, eds., *Paul Ricoeur and Contemporary Moral Thought* [New York: Routledge, 2002], 15–31, 23 and 26). While this is true, it must also be said that Ricoeur places the notion of "autonomy" itself into profound question, since autonomy is always relative from the very start, in his poetics of the will, to the passivity of the world around it in which alone it may be constituted into meaning.

9. John Rawls, *A Theory of Justice* (Cambridge, MA: Harvard University Press, 1971), 60.

10. Ricoeur, *Oneself as Another*, 233.

11. Paul Ricoeur, "Is a Purely Procedural Theory of Justice Possible? John Rawls's *Theory of Justice*" [French original 1990], in Ricoeur, *The Just* [French original 1995], trans. David Pellauer (Chicago: University of Chicago Press, 2000), 36–57, 57.

12. Ibid., 50.

13. Ricoeur elsewhere argues that Rawls's "original position" is a culturally constructed "fiction" without realizing this to be the case: "[T]he social contract [of Rawls] appears to be capable only of drawing its legitimacy from a *fiction*—a founding fiction, to be sure, but a fiction nonetheless. Why is this so? Is this because the self-foundation of the political body lacks the basic attestation from which good will and the person as end in himself draw their legitimacy? Is it because peoples, enslaved for millennia to a principle of domination transcending their will to live together, do not

know that they are sovereign, not by reason of an imaginary contract, but by virtue of the will to live together that they have *forgotten*?" (Ricoeur, *Oneself as Another*, 239).

14. Martha Nussbaum, *Love's Knowledge: Essays on Philosophy and Literature* (New York: Oxford University Press, 1990), 182.

15. Ibid., 186.

16. Martha Nussbaum, *The Fragility of Goodness: Luck and Ethics in Greek Tragedy and Philosophy* [first published 1986], updated ed. (New York: Cambridge University Press, 2001), 353.

17. Nussbaum *Love's Knowledge*, 162.

18. See Alain Badiou, *Ethics: An Essay on the Understanding of Evil* [French original 1998], trans. Peter Hallward (London: Verso, 2001).

19. John Caputo, *Against Ethics: Contributions to a Poetics of Obligation with Constant Reference to Deconstruction* (Indianapolis: Indiana University Press, 1993), 8.

20. Simon Critchley, *The Ethics of Deconstruction: Derrida and Levinas*, 2nd ed. (West Lafayette, IN: Purdue University Press, 1999), 4.

21. Alphonso Lingis, *The Community of Those Who Have Nothing in Common* (Bloomington: Indiana University Press, 1994), 10.

22. Richard Kearney, *Strangers, Gods and Monsters: Interpreting Otherness* (New York: Routledge, 2003), 79.

23. Ricoeur, *Oneself as Another*, 220.

24. Ibid.

25. Paul Ricoeur, "The Human Being as the Subject Matter of Philosophy," in *Philosophy and Social Criticism* 14.2 (1988): 203–15, 213.

26. Richard Kearney, "Narrative Imagination: Between Ethics and Politics," in Kearney, ed., *Paul Ricoeur: The Hermeneutics of Action* (London: Sage, 1996), 186; my emphasis.

27. Paul Ricoeur, "Ethical and Theological Considerations on the Golden Rule" [French original 1989], in Ricoeur, *Figuring the Sacred: Religion, Narrative, and Imagination*, ed. Mark I. Wallace (Minneapolis, MN: Fortress Press, 1995), 293–302.

28. Ibid., 300.

29. Paul Ricoeur, "The Teleological and Deontological Structures of Action: Aristotle and/or Kant?" in A. Phillips Griffiths, ed., *Contemporary French Philosophy* (New York: Cambridge University Press, 1987), 107. See also Ricoeur, "L'ethique, la morale, et la règle," in *Autre temps, Les cahiers du Christianisme social*, no. 24 (fevrier 1990), 55; and Ricoeur, *Oneself as Another*, 222–27. On this interpretation, I assume (although Ricoeur does not make this clear) that we are supposed to read the word "as" in the golden rule—do to others *as* you would have them do to you—not ma-terially but formally: not "do to others *what* you would (actually) have them do to you," but "do to others *in the same manner as* you would have them do to you."

30. Ricoeur, *Oneself as Another*, 219.

31. Paul Ricoeur, "The Logic of Jesus, the Logic of God" [English original 1979], in Ricoeur, *Figuring the Sacred*, 279–83, 283.

32. Paul Ricoeur, "The Memory of Suffering" [English original 1989], in Ricoeur, *Figuring the Sacred*, 289–92, 290.

33. Ibid., 291.

34. Paul Ricoeur, "Love and Justice" [French original 1990], in Ricoeur, *Figuring the Sacred*, 315–29, 329.

35. Paul Ricoeur, *Thinking Biblically: Exegetical and Hermeneutical Essays*, with André LaCocque, trans. David Pellauer (Chicago: University of Chicago Press, 1998), 129.

36. Emmanuel Levinas, *Otherwise than Being, or Beyond Essence* [French original 1974], trans. Alphonso Lingis (Boston: Kluwer, 1981), 4.

37. Ricoeur, *Oneself as Another*, 204.

38. Paul Ricoeur, "Ethical and Theological Considerations on the Golden Rule," 300; see also Ricoeur, "Love and Justice," 325.

39. Jean-Luc Marion, *God Without Being* [French original 1982], trans. Thomas A. Carlson (Chicago: University of Chicago Press, 1991), 107.

40. Ricoeur, "Ethical and Theological Considerations on the Golden Rule," 300.

41. Ibid., 298.

42. Ricoeur, "The Logic of Jesus, the Logic of God," 281.

43. Ricoeur, "Love and Justice," 324; and Ricoeur, "Ethical and Theological Considerations on the Golden Rule," 300.

44. Ricoeur, "Love and Justice," 324; see also Ricoeur, *Thinking Biblically*, 129.

45. Paul Ricoeur, "Manifestation and Proclamation" [French original 1974], in Ricoeur, *Figuring the Sacred*, 48–67, 57; Ricoeur, "The Summoned Subject in the School of the Narratives of the Prophetic Vocation" [French original 1988], in Ricoeur, *Figuring the Sacred*, 262–75, 263–67; Ricoeur, "The Logic of Jesus, the Logic of God," 280; Ricoeur, "Ethical and Theological Considerations on the Golden Rule," 301; and Ricoeur, *Thinking Biblically*, 282.

46. Ricoeur, "Love and Justice," 324.

47. Ricoeur, *Thinking Biblically*, 128.

48. Ricoeur, "Ethical and Theological Considerations on the Golden Rule," 300.

49. Ricoeur, *Thinking Biblically*, 131; Ricoeur, "Love and Justice," 319; Ricoeur, "The Logic of Jesus, the Logic of God," 281.

50. Ricoeur, *Thinking Biblically*, 131.

51. Ibid., 127; see also Ricoeur's larger discussion of "forgiveness" (*le pardon*) in *Memory, History, Forgetting* [French original 2000], trans. Kathleen Blamey and David Pellauer (Chicago: University of Chicago Press, 2004), 457–506.

52. Ricoeur, "Love and Justice," 329; see also Ricoeur, "Ethical and Theological Considerations on the Golden Rule," 301.

53. Ricoeur, "The Logic of Jesus, the Logic of God," 283.

54. See, respectively, Ricoeur, "Love and Justice," 324, and Ricoeur, *Oneself as Another*, 25.

55. Cohen misreads Ricoeur's claim that Levinas's ethics is "scandalous" to mean that Ricoeur finds it morally repugnant, whereas in fact Ricoeur and Levinas share the category of "scandal" as an element within religious moral excess itself. For example, Ricoeur calls the love command "scandalous" in its disruption of ordinary justice (Ricoeur, "Love and Justice," 315–29), and he says the same thing of moral faith and hope. Cohen says: "It seems that Ricoeur agrees, contra his own criticism of Levinas, that rhetorical exaggeration is neither camouflage nor adornment, but required by 'moral reflection' and 'philosophical reflection in general.' So be it" (Richard Cohen, *Ethics, Exegesis, and Philosophy: Interpretation After Levinas* [New York: Cambridge University Press, 2001], 317). Yet this hyperbolic requirement is precisely, as we have seen, what Ricoeur thinks religious ethics is all about. All this would be clearer, however, if Ricoeur did not repeatedly separate his philosophical from his religious writings.

56. Cohen, *Ethics, Exegesis, and Philosophy*, 305.

57. Dominique Janicaud, "The Theological Turn of French Phenomenology," in Dominique Janicaud, Jean-François Courtine, Jean-Louis Chrétien, Michel Henry, and Jean-Luc Marion, *Phenomenology and the "Theological Turn": The French Debate*

[French original 1991], trans. Bernard G. Prusak (New York: Fordham University Press, 2000), 16–103.

58. Morny Joy, "Response to Kellner and Rappaport," in David Klemm and William Schweiker, eds., *Meanings in Texts and Actions: Questioning Paul Ricoeur* (Charlottesville: University Press of Virginia, 1993), 332.

59. Levinas, *Otherwise than Being*, 46.

60. Ibid., 6–7.

61. John Caputo, "*Adieu—sans Dieu*: Derrida and Levinas," in Jeffrey Bloechl, ed., *The Face of the Other and the Trace of God: Essays on the Philosophy of Emmanuel Levinas* (New York: Fordham University Press, 2000), 276–311.

62. Edith Wyschogrod, *Emmanuel Levinas: The Problem of Ethical Metaphysics* (New York: Fordham University Press, 2000), 234.

63. Indeed, on this score it is sometimes questioned whether Levinas can properly be called a "phenomenologist," given his replacement of appearances in the world with a Transcendence which is radically exterior to being. Husserl and Heidegger sought new ways to describe the appearance of "being" in the world, in contrast with what supposedly transcends it. See, for example, Edmund Husserl, *The Idea of Phenomenology*, trans. William P. Alston and George Nakhnikian (The Hague: Manrinus Nijhoff, 1971); and Martin Heidegger, *Being and Time* [German original 1927], trans. John Macquarrie and Edward Robinson (New York: Harper and Row, 1962). However, Levinas is claiming that Transcendence precisely *does* appear as a phenomenon in the "face" of the other person, and the term "being" is given the restricted meaning in Levinas of an opposed teleological interest. For an extensive and complex discussion of this question, see Jeffrey Dudiak, *The Intrigue of Ethics: A Reading of the Idea of Discourse in the Thought of Emmanuel Levinas* (New York: Fordham University Press, 2001), 317–94.

64. Ricoeur, "Naming God" [French original 1977], in Ricoeur, *Figuring the Sacred: Religion, Narrative, and Imagination*, ed. Mark I. Wallace (Minneapolis, MN: Fortress Press, 1995), 217–35, 224.

65. Mark Wallace, "From Phenomenology to Scripture: Paul Ricoeur's Hermeneutic Philosophy of Religion," *Modern Theology* 16.3 (2000): 301–13, 312.

66. Levinas, *Otherwise than Being*, 5 and 181, respectively.

67. Ibid., 180.

68. Emmanuel Levinas, *Totality and Infinity: An Essay on Exteriority* [French original 1961], trans. Alphonso Lingis (Pittsburgh, PA: Duquesne University Press, 1969), 39.

69. Ibid., 24.

70. Levinas, *Otherwise than Being*, 150.

71. Ibid., 145.

72. Levinas, *Totality and Infinity*, 67 and elsewhere.

73. Levinas, *Otherwise than Being*, 12.

74. Levinas, *Totality and Infinity*, 21.

75. Levinas, *Otherwise than Being*, 4.

76. Ibid.

77. Levinas, *Totality and Infinity*, 50.

78. Ibid., 304.

79. Levinas, *Otherwise than Being*, 11, 141, and 184.

80. Ibid., 11 and 184.

81. Ibid., 14–15.

82. Ibid., 15.

83. Ibid., 12.

84. Ibid., 14 and 185.

85. Ibid., 11 and 142.

86. Cohen, *Ethics, Exegesis, and Philosophy*, 290 and 344.

87. Richard Kearney, *The God Who May Be: A Hermeneutics of Religion* (Bloomington: Indiana University Press, 2001), 10.

88. Jeffrey Dudiak has claimed that Levinas's ethics suggests a "possible impossibility": We can see the necessity of responding to the face of the other, even though in the world of "being" such a relation ultimately "cannot *be*" (Dudiak, *The Intrigue of Ethics*, 249–51). I have pursued instead the reverse terminology of "impossible possibility" to emphasize that, however impossible it may seem, a response to otherness remains our primordial human *possibility*. In my view, impossibility can make sense finally only as a qualification on possibility, and not the other way around. In this I agree with Kearney's claim that God is a God "who may be," a God of *posse*, a God to be understood "neither as non-being nor as being but as the possibility-to-be" (Kearney, *The God Who May Be*, 8).

89. Levinas, *Totality and Infinity*, 51.

90. Jacques Derrida, *Circumfession* [French original 1991], trans. Geoffrey Bennington, in Geoffrey Bennington and Jacques Derrida, *Jacques Derrida* (Chicago: University of Chicago Press, 1993), 16–18.

91. Ricoeur, *Oneself as Another*, 339; see also Ricoeur, *Autrement: Lecture d'autrement qu'être ou au-delà de l'essence d'Emmanuel Levinas* (Paris: Presses Universitaires de France, 1997).

92. Ricoeur, *Oneself as Another*, 340.

93. Ibid., 355.

94. Kearney, *Strangers, Gods and Monsters*, 229.

95. Ibid., 12.

96. Ibid., 70.

97. Ibid., 230.

CHAPTER 4

1. Martin Luther King Jr., "Letter from Birmingham Jail—April 16, 1963," in Milton C. Sernett, ed., *Afro-American Religious History: A Documentary Witness* (Durham, NC: Duke University Press 1985), 438.

2. This dimension of moral creativity comes closer than the two above to human creating amidst the vast "creation" of the natural environment. As I note in the conclusion, interesting suggestions could be made along these lines in relation to Elizabeth A. Johnson's notion of "Creator Spirit," which she directly ties to feminism, and other perspectives on natural evolution (Johnson, *Women, Earth, and Creator Spirit* [New York: Paulist Press, 1993]). In this chapter, however, I am considering only human creativity in relation to human society.

3. Jürgen Habermas, *Moral Consciousness and Communicative Action* [German original 1983], trans. Christian Lenhardt and Shierry Weber Nicholsen (Cambridge, MA: MIT Press, 1990), 76.

4. Ibid., 104.

5. Ibid., 57.

6. Ibid., 66.

7. Jürgen Habermas, *The Theory of Communicative Action*. Vol. 1: *Reason and the Rationalization of Society* [German original 1981], trans. Thomas McCarthy (Boston: Beacon Press, 1984), 326–34.

8. Luce Irigaray, *An Ethics of Sexual Difference* [French original 1984], trans. Carolyn Burke and Gillian C. Gill (London: Athlone Press, 1993), 119.

9. Luce Irigaray, *Speculum of the Other Woman* [French original 1974], trans. Gillian C. Gill (Ithaca, NY: Cornell University Press, 1985), 225.

10. Pamela Anderson, *A Feminist Philosophy of Religion: The Rationality of Myths of Religious Belief* (Malden, MA: Blackwell, 1998), 190.

11. Judith Butler, *Antigone's Claim: Kinship Between Life and Death* (New York: Columbia University Press, 2000), 2.

12. Ibid., 58.

13. Ibid., 76.

14. Ibid., 82.

15. Ibid.

16. Ibid., 24.

17. Pamela Anderson, "Rereading Myth in Philosophy: Hegel, Ricoeur, and Irigaray Reading *Antigone*," in Morny Joy, ed., *Paul Ricoeur and Narrative: Context and Contestation* (Alberta, Calgary: University of Calgary Press, 1997), 51–68, 64.

18. Paul Ricoeur, *Oneself as Another* [French original 1990], trans. Kathleen Blamey (Chicago: University of Chicago Press, 1992), 249.

19. Ibid., 243–49.

20. Georg Wilhelm Hegel, *Hegel on Tragedy*, 2nd ed., ed. Anne and Henry Paolucci (Smyrna, DE: Griffon House Publications, 2001), 325.

21. Martha Nussbaum, *The Fragility of Goodness: Luck and Ethics in Greek Tragedy and Philosophy* [first published 1986], updated ed. (New York: Cambridge University Press, 2001), 63–67.

22. Ricoeur, *Oneself as Another*, 244.

23. Ibid., 243 and 247.

24. Henri Bergson, *Creative Evolution* [French original 1907], trans. Arthur Mitchell (Westport, CT: Greenwood Press, 1944).

25. Ricoeur, *Oneself as Another*, 288.

26. Ricoeur's criticism of Habermas is thus similar also to his above-mentioned criticism of Kant: "What I am criticizing in [Habermas's] ethics of argumentation is not the invitation to look for the best argument in all circumstances and in all discussions but the reconstruction under the title of a strategy of *purification*, taken from Kant, that makes impossible the contextual mediation without which the ethics of communication loses its actual hold on reality. Kant directed his strategy of purification against inclination, the search for pleasure or happiness. . . . Habermas directs his against everything that can be placed under the title of *convention*" (*Oneself as Another*, 286). Or, as Ricoeur says elsewhere: "[Habermas's] ethics of discussion . . . places itself in a perspective where convictions are reduced to conventions the protagonists in the discussion are assumed to have surpassed in assuming what is called a post-conventional posture. It is the task of any formalism, in eliminating all reference to the good life, to elude those situations of conflict linked to the evaluation of goods situated along the trajectory of the wish for a good life" (Ricoeur, "Conscience and the Law: The Philosophical Stakes" [French original 1994], in Ricoeur, *The Just* [French original 1995], trans. David Pellauer (Chicago: University of Chicago Press, 2000), 146–55, 154).

27. Anderson, "Rereading Myth in Philosophy," 54.

28. Ricoeur, *Oneself as Another*, 241.

29. Ibid., 242.

30. I am aware that in his early work *The Symbolism of Evil* [French original 1960], trans. Emerson Buchanan (Boston: Beacon Press, 1967), to which this concept of a "theology of divine blindness" in fact refers, Ricoeur attributes these "spiritual powers" to something larger than individuals, namely "the gods." Here, tragedy is defined as follows: "A non-dialectical contradiction; there we have the tragic. Thus Antigone and Creon destroy one another, and there is no third force that might mediate their opposition and embrace the good reasons of both. That a value cannot be realized without the destruction of another value, equally positive—there, again, is the tragic" (323). In this somewhat more Hegelian reading of tragedy, Ricoeur has not yet connected the tragic with free moral conviction. In fact, here he rejects tragedy as a fully adequate perspective on moral life because it highlights not human choice but "the *blind* character of necessity," the "wicked God" that reduces humanity to its victim (ibid., 323 and 326). His later use of tragedy at the heart of moral life demonstrates a more complex view of the relation of tragedy to freedom, although not of tragedy as historical distortion.

31. Ricoeur, *Oneself as Another*, 243.

32. Paul Ricoeur, "Guilt, Ethics, and Religion" [English original 1969], in Ricoeur, *The Conflict of Interpretations* [French original 1969], ed. Don Ihde (Evanston, IL: Northwestern University Press, 1974), 425–39, 439; see also "Freedom in the Light of Hope" [French original 1968], in Ricoeur, *The Conflict of Interpretations*, 402–24, 423.

33. Ricoeur, "Guilt, Ethics, and Religion," 439.

34. Reinhold Niebuhr, *The Nature and Destiny of Man*. Vol. I: *Human Nature* [original 1941] (New York: Charles Scribner's Sons, 1964), 178–79 and 199.

35. Paul Ricoeur, "Ideology and Utopia" [French original 1983], in Ricoeur, *From Text to Action: Essays in Hermeneutics II* [French original 1986], trans. Kathleen Blamey (Evanston, IL: Northwestern University Press, 1991), 308–24, 318.

36. Ibid., 320.

37. Ibid., 324.

38. Cornelius Castoriades, "Radical Imagination and the Social Instituting Imaginary" [English original 1994], in Castoriades, *The Castoriades Reader*, ed. David Ames Curtis (Malden, MA: Blackwell, 1997), 318–37, 333. I am sympathetic to Castoriades's efforts to describe social life as the constant creation of new social imagination, but I believe he lacks an adequate theory of human moral freedom and responsibility and hence of radical evil, as well, therefore, as a sufficiently primordial sense, expressible only in religious mythological terms, of the human capability for social creativity in the first place.

39. Despite not noting this parallel himself, Ricoeur's discussion of the *Antigone* does occasionally slip into language at least reminiscent of hope, as for example in the following: "Reconciliation rests on an actual renunciation by each party of his partiality and has the value of a pardon in which each is truly recognized by the other. Now it is precisely this reconciliation though renouncement, this pardon through recognition, that tragedy—at least the tragedy *Antigone*—is incapable of providing" (*Oneself as Another*, 248).

40. Although I do not pursue it here, it would be interesting in this connection to explore the creative dynamics in the traditional Christian image of the Trinity.

41. Immanuel Kant, *Critique of Practical Reason*, trans. Mary Gregor (New York: Cambridge University Press, 1997), 133–36.

42. Immanuel Kant, *Religion Within the Limits of Reason Alone*, trans. Theodore M. Greene and Hoyt H. Hudson (New York: Harper Torchbooks, 1960), 107–14; see my discussion in chapter 1.

43. Ricoeur, *Oneself as Another*, 290–91.

44. Paul Ricoeur, "À la gloire de la *phronèsis* (*Éthique a nicomaque*, livre VI)," in J. Y. Chateau, ed., *La verité pratique: Aristote. Éthique a` nicomaque, livre VI* (Paris: J. Vrin, 1997), 13; my translation.

45. Ricoeur, *Oneself as Another*, 269.

46. Ibid., 289.

47. Ibid., 296.

48. Paul Ricoeur, "The Act of Judging" [French original 1992], in Ricoeur, *The Just*, 127–32, 130–31.

49. Ibid., 132.

50. Ricoeur, *Oneself as Another*, 289.

51. Ibid., 288–89.

52. Without yet intending the word in its religious sense, Ricoeur tellingly suggests here that such convictions are implicit within "promises." For promising implies that in "giving one's word" to others, one is also establishing an independent social bond on which both self and other can rely over the vicissitudes of time. " 'From you,' says the other, 'I expect that you will keep your word'; to you, I reply: 'You can count on me'" (Ricoeur, *Oneself as Another*, 268). Mary Schaldenbrand has called Ricoeur's concept of promising an example of his larger hermeneutics of "kinship through conflict" (Schaldenbrand, "Metaphoric Imagination: Kinship through Conflict," in Charles Reagan, *Studies in the Philosophy of Paul Ricoeur* [Athens: Ohio University Press, 1979], 57–81). As Ricoeur himself puts it, promising is "finally a question of mutual recognition, of recognition whereby the other ceases to be alien and is treated like someone who is similar to me and in accord with fundamental human similarity" (Ricoeur, "Responsibility and Fragility: An Ethical Reflection," *Journal of the Faculty of Religious Studies* [McGill University] 21 [Spring 1993]: 7–10, 10). To make a promise to another or others—for example, a business contract or a marriage vow—is to express a phronetic conviction about how one's own and another's life remain different but also can now be "shared," shared in the sense of participated in by all concerned, representing a deeper common humanity.

53. Ricoeur, *Oneself as Another*, 272–73. At one point Ricoeur provides the example of the contemporary debate over abortion, which he describes as involving, in part, a social tension between an agential vision of humanity (tied "only to fully developed capacities, such as autonomy of willing, only adult, cultivated, 'enlightened' individuals") and a passive vision of humanity (tied only to "biologic" life or existence) (ibid., 270–71). Critical phronesis is charged with forming a new "intermediary domain" in this debate. Such a domain turns out, as it happens, to look not unlike that illustrated in the work of Carol Gilligan, in which the voluntary claims of the mother and the involuntary demands of the fetus yield to a deeper sense for humanity as related through practices of responsibility and care (Gilligan, *In a Different Voice: Psychological Theory and Women's Development* [Cambridge, MA: Harvard University Press, 1982], 105). For Ricoeur himself, the resulting transformed social imagination might produce what he calls "qualitatively different rights" accorded to the fetus at different thresholds of its "ontology of development." These would include, for example, "the right not to suffer, [followed by] the right to protection (this notion itself presenting several degrees of 'force' or 'emphasis'), [and finally] the right to respect, once something like an exchange, even asymmetrical, of preverbal signs is

begun between the fetus and its mother" (Ricoeur, *Oneself as Another*, 271–72). The purpose—whatever one may think of Ricoeur's actual proposal—is to develop new social practices around more profoundly shared visions of what it really means to be human.

54. Kathleen Sands, *Escape from Paradise: Evil and Tragedy in Feminist Theology* (Minneapolis, MN: Fortress Press, 1994), 11.

55. Erazim V. Kohák, "Translator's Introduction," in Ricoeur, *Freedom and Nature: The Voluntary and the Involuntary* [French original 1950], trans. Kohák (Evanston, IL: Northwestern University Press, 1966), ix–xxxviii, xvi.

56. Peter Joseph Albano, *Freedom, Truth, and Hope: The Relationship of Philosophy and Religion in the Thought of Paul Ricoeur* (Lanham, MD: University Press of America, 1987); Pamela Anderson, *Ricoeur and Kant: Philosophy of the Will* (Atlanta, GA: Scholars Press, 1993); Bernard P. Dauenhauer, *The Politics of Hope* (Boston: Routledge and Kegan Paul, 1986); David Klemm, *The Hermeneutical Theory of Paul Ricoeur* (East Brunswick, NJ: Associated University Presses, 1983); Theodore Marius Van Leeuwen, *The Surplus of Meaning: Ontology and Eschatology in the Philosophy of Paul Ricoeur* (Amsterdam: Rodopi, 1981); William Schweiker, "Imagination, Violence, and Hope: A Theological Response to Ricoeur's Moral Philosophy," in David Klemm and William Schweiker, eds., *Meanings in Texts and Actions: Questioning Paul Ricoeur* (Charlottesville: University Press of Virginia, 1993); and Kevin J. Vanhoozer, *Biblical Narrative in the Philosophy of Paul Ricoeur: A Study in Hermeneutics and Theology* (New York: Cambridge University Press, 1990).

57. Ricoeur "Freedom in the Light of Hope," 408; Ricoeur, "Guilt, Ethics, and Religion," 437; and Ricoeur, "Ethical and Theological Considerations on the Golden Rule" [French original 1989], in Ricoeur, *Figuring the Sacred: Religion, Narrative, and Imagination*, ed. Mark I. Wallace (Minneapolis, MN: Fortress Press, 1995), 293–302, 299.

58. Ricoeur, "Freedom in the Light of Hope," 406 and 409; Ricoeur, "Guilt, Ethics, and Religion," 438; and Ricoeur, "Hope and the Structure of Philosophical Systems" [English original 1970], in Ricoeur, *Figuring the Sacred*, 203–16, 206.

59. Ricoeur, "Love and Justice," 325.

60. Ricoeur, "Ethical and Theological Considerations on the Golden Rule," 299; see also Ricoeur, "Love and Justice," 325.

61. Ricoeur "Evil, a Challenge to Philosophy and Theology" [English original 1985], in Ricoeur, *Figuring the Sacred*, 249–61, 259.

62. Ricoeur, "Freedom in the Light of Hope," 424; and Ricoeur, "Naming God" [French original 1977] in Ricoeur, *Figuring the Sacred*, 217–35, 234.

63. Ricoeur, "Hope and the Structure of Philosophical Systems," 206; my emphasis.

64. Ricoeur, "Guilt, Ethics, and Religion," 436; see also Ricoeur, "Hope and the Structure of Philosophical Systems," 204.

65. Ricoeur, "Freedom in the Light of Hope," 411; my emphasis.

66. Ibid., 406.

67. Ricoeur, "Hope and the Structure of Philosophical Systems," 206.

68. Paul Ricoeur, *Critique and Conviction* [French original 1995], trans. Kathleen Blamey (New York: Columbia University Press, 1998), 154.

69. Ricoeur, "Naming God," 235.

70. Ibid., 231.

71. Ricoeur, "Hope and the Structure of Philosophical Systems," 206.

72. Ibid., 215.

73. Ricoeur, *Critique and Conviction*, 154.

74. Paul Ricoeur, *History and Truth* [French originals 1955 and revised 1964], trans. Charles Kelbley and others (Evanston, IL: Northwestern University Press, 1965), 12.

75. I discuss the relation of Ricoeur to liberationism in John Wall, "The Economy of the Gift: Paul Ricoeur's Significance for Theological Ethics," *Journal of Religious Ethics* 29.2 (Summer 2001): 235–60; and Wall, "The Creative Imperative: Ethics and the Formation of Life in Common," *Journal of Religious Ethics* 33.1 (Spring 2005): 45–64.

76. Gustavo Gutiérrez, *A Theology of Liberation: History, Politics, and Salvation* [Spanish original 1971], 15th anniversary rev. ed., trans. Sister Caridad Inda and John Eagleson (Maryknoll, NY: Orbis Books, 1988), 12.

77. Ibid., 139 and 174.

78. Jürgen Moltmann, *Theology of Hope: On the Ground and the Implications of a Christian Eschatology* [German original 1965], trans. James W. Leitch (New York: Harper and Row, 1967), 338.

79. Ibid., 224.

80. Ibid., 330. Ricoeur claims to have been "won over by" Moltmann's view of hope, which he interprets as one that "opens up a career for existence and history" ("Freedom in the Light of Hope," 404 and 411, respectively). However, he tends one-sidedly to interpret Moltmann to be suggesting that "the God who is witnessed to is not...the God who is but the God who is coming" (ibid., 406). It is fairer in my view to say that Moltmann, like most political and liberationist theologies, views the God who is coming precisely *as* the God who is whenever humanity acts in the here and now against injustice.

81. Sallie McFague, *Metaphorical Theology: Models of God in Religious Language* (Philadelphia: Fortress Press, 1982), 8.

82. Ibid., 9.

83. Ibid., 165.

84. Sallie McFague, *Models of God: Theology for an Ecological, Nuclear Age* (Philadelphia: Fortress Press, 1987).

85. McFague, *Metaphorical Theology*, 188.

86. King, "Letter from Birmingham Jail–April 16, 1963," 433.

87. Ibid., 440.

88. Hegel, *Hegel on Tragedy*, 51 and 237.

CONCLUSION

1. Reinhold Niebuhr, *The Nature and Destiny of Man*. Vol. I: *Human Nature* [original 1941] (New York: Charles Scribner's Sons, 1964), viii.

2. Philip Rieff, *The Triumph of the Therapeutic: Uses of Faith After Freud* [original 1966] (Chicago: University of Chicago Press, 1987).

3. Hans-Georg Gadamer, *Truth and Method* [German original 1960], 2nd rev. ed., trans. Joel Weinsheimer and Donald G. Marshall (New York: Crossroad, 1989), 9–30.

4. John Calvin, *Institutes of the Christian Religion*, ed. John T. McNeill, trans. Ford Lewis Battles (Philadelphia: Westminster Press, 1960), Book III, chap. iii, sec. 9, 601.

5. Niebuhr, *The Nature and Destiny of Man*. Vol. I: *Human Nature*, 293.

6. Stanley Hauerwas, *The Peaceable Kingdom: A Primer in Christian Ethics* (Notre Dame, IN: University of Notre Dame Press, 1983), 94.

7. Gustavo Gutiérrez, *A Theology of Liberation: History, Politics, and Salvation* [Spanish original 1971], 15th anniversary rev. ed., trans. Sister Caridad Inda and John Eagleson (Maryknoll, NY: Orbis Books, 1988), 168.

8. Emmanuel Levinas, *Otherwise than Being, or Beyond Essence* [French original 1974], trans. Alphonso Lingis (Boston: Kluwer, 1981), 149; my emphasis.

9. Arguably, the death camps also represent, although in a less complex way, a defeat of the teleological tension of the possible greater narrative unity of Germans within the German state, excluding vast dimensions of their own actually given historicity.

10. Elizabeth A. Johnson, *Women, Earth, and Creator Spirit* (New York: Paulist Press, 1993), 38.

11. Henri Bergson, *Creative Evolution* [French original 1907], trans. Arthur Mitchell (Westport, CT: Greenwood Press, 1944), 10, 27, 271, 274, 287–88, 292.

12. Immanuel Kant, "What Is Enlightenment?" trans. Lewis White Beck, in Kant, *Foundations of the Metaphysics of Morals* (Indianapolis, IN: Bobbs-Merrill, 1959), 85.

Selected Bibliography

Anderson, Pamela. *A Feminist Philosophy of Religion: The Rationality of Myths of Religious Belief*. Malden, MA: Blackwell, 1998.

Aristotle. *Nicomachean Ethics*. Trans. Martin Ostwald. Englewood Cliffs, NJ: Prentice Hall, 1962.

——. *Poetics*. Trans. I. Bywater, in *Introduction to Aristotle*, 2nd ed., rev. and enl. Ed. Richard McKeon. Chicago: University of Chicago Press, 1947.

Bergson, Henri. *Creative Evolution* [French original 1907]. Trans. Arthur Mitchell. Westport, CT: Greenwood Press, 1944.

Butler, Judith. *Antigone's Claim: Kinship Between Life and Death*. New York: Columbia University Press, 2000.

Caputo, John. *Against Ethics: Contributions to a Poetics of Obligation with Constant Reference to Deconstruction*. Indianapolis: Indiana University Press, 1993.

Ferry, Luc. *Man Made God: The Meaning of Life* [French original 1996]. Trans. David Pellauer. Chicago: University of Chicago Press, 2002.

Gadamer, Hans-Georg. *Truth and Method* [German original 1960], 2nd rev. ed. Trans. Joel Weinsheimer and Donald G. Marshall. New York: Crossroad, 1989.

Gutiérrez, Gustavo. *A Theology of Liberation: History, Politics, and Salvation* [Spanish original 1971]. 15th anniversary rev. ed. Trans. Sister Caridad Inda and John Eagleson. Maryknoll, NY: Orbis Books, 1988.

Habermas, Jürgen. *Moral Consciousness and Communicative Action* [German original 1983]. Trans. Christian Lenhardt and Shierry Weber Nicholsen. Cambridge, MA: MIT Press, 1990.

——. *The Theory of Communicative Action*. Vol. 1: *Reason and the Rationalization of Society* [German original 1981]. Trans. Thomas McCarthy. Boston: Beacon Press, 1984.

Hauerwas, Stanley. *A Community of Character: Toward a Constructive Christian Social Ethic*. Notre Dame, IN: University of Notre Dame Press, 1981.

Hefner, Philip. *The Human Factor: Evolution, Culture, and Religion*. Minneapolis, MN: Fortress Press, 1993.

Hegel, Georg Wilhelm Friedrich. *Hegel on Tragedy*, 2nd ed. Ed. Anne and Henry Paolucci. Smyrna, DE: Griffon House, 2001.

Irigaray, Luce. *Speculum of the Other Woman* [French original 1974]. Trans. Gillian C. Gill. Ithaca, NY: Cornell University Press, 1985.

Janicaud, Dominique, Jean-François Courtine, Jean-Louis Chrétien, Michel Henry, and Jean-Luc Marion. *Phenomenology and the "Theological Turn": The French Debate*. [French original 1991]. Trans. Bernard G. Prusak. New York: Fordham University Press, 2000.

Johnson, Elizabeth A. *Women, Earth, and Creator Spirit*. New York: Paulist Press, 1993.

Kant, Immanuel. *Critique of the Power of Judgment*. Trans. Paul Guyer and Eric Matthews. New York: Cambridge University Press, 2000.

———. *Critique of Practical Reason*. Trans. Mary Gregor. New York: Cambridge University Press, 1997.

———. *Groundwork of the Metaphysics of Morals*. Trans. J. J. Paton. New York: Harper and Row, 1964.

———. *Religion Within the Limits of Reason Alone*. Trans. Theodore M. Greene and Hoyt H. Hudson. New York: Harper Torchbooks, 1960.

Kearney, Richard. *The God Who May Be: A Hermeneutics of Religion*. Bloomington: Indiana University Press, 2001.

———. *Strangers, Gods and Monsters: Interpreting Otherness*. New York: Routledge, 2003.

Levinas, Emmanuel. *Otherwise than Being, or Beyond Essence* [French original 1974]. Trans. Alphonso Lingis. Boston: Kluwer, 1981.

———. *Totality and Infinity: An Essay on Exteriority* [French original 1961]. Trans. Alphonso Lingis. Pittsburgh, PA: Duquesne University Press, 1969.

Lingis, Alphonso. *The Community of Those Who Have Nothing in Common*. Bloomington: Indiana University Press, 1994.

MacIntyre, Alasdair. *After Virtue*, 2nd ed. Notre Dame, IN: University of Notre Dame Press, 1984.

———. *Whose Justice? Which Rationality?* Notre Dame, IN: University of Notre Dame Press, 1988.

Marion, Jean-Luc. *Being Given: Toward a Phenomenology of Givenness* [French original 1997]. Trans. Jeffrey L. Kosky. Stanford, CA: Stanford University Press, 2002.

———. *God Without Being* [French original 1982]. Trans. Thomas A. Carlson. Chicago: University of Chicago Press, 1991.

McFague, Sallie. *Metaphorical Theology: Models of God in Religious Language*. Philadelphia: Fortress Press, 1982.

———. *Models of God: Theology for an Ecological, Nuclear Age*. Philadelphia: Fortress Press, 1987.

Moltmann, Jürgen. *Theology of Hope: On the Ground and the Implications of a Christian Eschatology* [German original 1965]. Trans. James W. Leitch. New York: Harper and Row, 1967.

Nietzsche, Friedrich. *Ecce Homo* [German original 1898] in *The Geneology of Morals and Ecce Homo*. Trans. Walter Kauffmann. New York: Random House, 1967.

Nussbaum, Martha. *The Fragility of Goodness: Luck and Ethics in Greek Tragedy and Philosophy* [first published 1986], updated ed. New York: Cambridge University Press, 2001.

———. *Love's Knowledge: Essays on Philosophy and Literature.* New York: Oxford University Press, 1990.

Ricoeur, Paul. *The Conflict of Interpretations* [French original 1969]. Ed. Don Ihde. Evanston, IL: Northwestern University Press, 1974.

———. *Fallible Man* [French original 1960]. Trans. Charles A. Kelbley. New York: Fordham University Press, 1986.

———. *Figuring the Sacred: Religion, Narrative, and Imagination.* Ed. Mark I. Wallace. Minneapolis, MN: Fortress Press, 1995.

———. *Freedom and Nature: The Voluntary and the Involuntary* [French original 1950]. Trans. Erazim V. Kohák. Evanston, IL: Northwestern University Press 1966.

———. *From Text to Action: Essays in Hermeneutics II* [French original 1986]. Trans. Kathleen Blamey. Evanston, IL: Northwestern University Press, 1991.

———. *Hermeneutics and the Human Sciences: Essays on Language, Action, and Interpretation.* New York: Cambridge University Press, 1981.

———. *History and Truth* [French originals 1955 and rev. 1964]. Trans. Charles Kelbley and others. Evanston, IL: Northwestern University Press, 1965.

———. *The Just* [French original 1995]. Trans. David Pellauer. Chicago: University of Chicago Press, 2000.

———. *Memory, History, Forgetting* [French original 2000]. Trans. Kathleen Blamey and David Pellauer. Chicago: University of Chicago Press, 2004.

———. *Oneself as Another* [French original 1990]. Trans. Kathleen Blamey. Chicago: University of Chicago Press, 1992.

———. *The Rule of Metaphor: Multidisciplinary Studies of the Creation of Meaning in Language* [French original 1975]. Trans. Robert Czerny. Toronto: University of Toronto Press, 1977.

———. *The Symbolism of Evil* [French original 1960]. Trans. Emerson Buchanan. Boston: Beacon Press, 1967.

———. *Thinking Biblically: Exegetical and Hermeneutical Essays,* with André LaCocque [French original 1998]. Trans. David Pellauer. Chicago: University of Chicago Press, 1998.

———. *Time and Narrative,* Vol. 1 [French original 1983]. Trans. Kathleen McLaughlin and David Pellauer. Chicago: University of Chicago Press, 1984.

———. *Time and Narrative,* Vol. 3 [French original 1985]. Trans. Kathleen Blamey and David Pellauer. Chicago: University of Chicago Press, 1988.

Sands, Kathleen. *Escape from Paradise: Evil and Tragedy in Feminist Theology.* Minneapolis, MN: Fortress Press, 1994.

Schweiker, William. *Responsibility and Christian Ethics.* New York: Cambridge University Press, 1995.

Sophocles. *Antigone* in *Sophocles I,* 2nd ed. Trans. David Grene. Chicago: University of Chicago Press, 1991.

Tracy, David. *Blessed Rage for Order: The New Pluralism in Theology.* Minneapolis, MN: Winston Seabury Press, 1975.

Index